Labors from the Heart

Labors from the Heart

Mission and Ministry in a Catholic University

MARK L. POORMAN, C.S.C.
Editor

University of Notre Dame Press
Notre Dame, Indiana

Copyright 1996 by
University of Notre Dame Press
Notre Dame, IN 46556
All Rights Reserved
Manufactured in the United States of America

Library of Congress Cataloging-in-Publication Data

Labors from the heart : mission and ministry in a Catholic University
/ edited by Marc L. Poorman.
   p. cm.
   ISBN 0-268-01424-8 (alk. paper).
   1. University of Notre Dame—Biography. 2. Catholic universities
and colleges—Case studies. 3. Catholic Church—Education—Case
studies.   I. Poorman, Mark L.
LD4112.L33 1996   98-31823
378.772'89—dc20   CIP

*The paper used in this publication meets the minimun requirements of the American
National Standard for Information Sciences—Permanence of Paper for Printed
Library Materials, ANSI Z39.48-1984.*

To the Students of
the University of Notre Dame du lac

Contents

Introduction

After the promulgation of John Paul II's encyclical *Ex Corde Ecclesiae*, discussions on campuses and in print concerning the future of the Catholic university have yielded important questions, analyses, and conclusions. Critical conceptual groundwork has been laid regarding the spirit and substance of Catholic higher education in numerous articles and books such as Father Theodore Hesburgh's volume, *The Challenge and Promise of a Catholic University* and David J. O'Brien's study, *From the Heart of the American Church: Catholic Higher Education and American Culture.* There is a growing consensus among educators that the outlook is cautiously optimistic for the Catholic university in a post-conciliar Church and an increasingly post-Christian academy.

My own entrance into the conversation came when I served on the Mission Committee of the "Colloquy for the Year 2000," a fifteen-month internal study of the University of Notre Dame which began in the fall of 1992 and eventually set institutional priorities for the ensuing decade. Charged simply with considering the effectiveness of the mission of the University of Notre Dame, the committee quickly gravitated toward the "Catholic character question." In the course of the meetings of that committee as well as of a sub-committee responsible for writing a new mission statement for the University, I had the opportunity to explore the diverse ways in which people and their works embody and further the academic and religious mission of Notre Dame. Despite the sometimes tedious sessions of the committee—theoretical discussions of the nature of a mission, the close examination of mission statements of peer institutions, endless revisions of multiple drafts of our statement based on responses from students, faculty, staff, and alumni—I was edified by the task, mainly because it afforded me a broad view of the actual implementation of the Notre Dame's claim to be both Catholic and a university.

During the intervening time, I have often thought of the inspiring efforts of people who attempt to prove the Catholic university true to its mission. With confidence that their own testimony and reflections might similarly affect others connected to Catholic higher education, I asked colleagues at Notre Dame to write accounts of their own day-to-day work and involvement in the Catholic identity of the University. The result is this collection of essays by faculty, staff, administrators, and alumni which includes their personal perspectives on how that identity is realized in their own occupations, ministries, and vocations.

Some of the essays are written specifically about the individual Christian ministries offered at a place like Notre Dame—residence hall ministry, liturgical coordination, marriage preparation and enrichment, and adult Christian formation. Others are about faculty and administrative activities which find a distinctive home in a Catholic university—a law school's legal aid clinic for the poor and marginalized, an alumni association's continuing education program with a special focus on social justice and professional ethics, an innovative program for training a corps of young teachers for under-served Catholic schools. And some are narratives by people who have a professional or personal stake in the vitality of Catholic higher education—an alumna who provides a retrospective of the meaning of her education, a writer who "commits acts of public relations" on behalf of the University.

Many people assisted with editing and producing the book. I am especially thankful for support from Richard V. Warner, C.S.C., and Paul F. Doyle, C.S.C. Carole Coffin provided invaluable organizational and clerical assistance. Carole Roos edited the copy, made helpful suggestions about particular essays, and moved the project along in a timely fashion. I am deeply grateful to the authors for their stories and their labors from the heart.

MARK L. POORMAN, C.S.C.

A Catholic university pursues its objectives through its formation of an authentic human community animated by the spirit of Christ. The source of its unity springs from a common dedication to the truth, a common vision of the dignity of the human person and, ultimately, the person and message of Christ, which gives the institution its distinctive character.

As a result of this inspiration, the community is animated by a spirit of freedom and charity; it is characterized by mutual respect, sincere dialogue, and protection of the rights of individuals. It assists each of its members to achieve wholeness as human persons; in turn, everyone in the community helps in promoting unity, and each one, according to his or her role and capacity, contributes toward decisions which affect the community and also toward maintaining and strengthening the distinctive Catholic character of the institution.

From the Heart of the Church
(*Ex Corde Ecclesiae*), paragraph 21
John Paul II
August 15, 1990

The Challenge
of Adult Christianity

KATHARINE SULLIVAN BARRETT

Let the little children come to me. The reign of God belongs to
such as these . . . whoever does not accept the kingdom of
God as a child will not enter into it.

Luke 18:16–17

I have found new appreciation for these words from Luke's
gospel as I listen to my son, Kevin, pray at nearly two years of
age. He freely thanks God for everything from "Mama and
Daddy" to "raisins and Big Bird." His simple willingness to
say thank you for everything reminds my husband and me
how much more gratitude and trust we can always add to our
own lives of faith.

Although my primary experiences in ministry have been
with college-age students, I have discovered that my more
recently acquired identity as a mother gives me new insight
into my role as a member of the Campus Ministry staff at Notre
Dame. I work with students as they grow into adult believers.
At the same time my husband and I hope that, through our
lives, our prayer, and our instruction, our son will know and
trust in God's love even as he enters childhood. Through my
ongoing attempts to balance these two important parts of my
life, I find God's grace at work at each stage of a young person's
life as a child of God.

The challenge of adult Christianity means that we allow
our faith to become more and more childlike, so that faith

Kate Barrett is Director of Religious Education for the Office of Campus Ministry.

profoundly and fundamentally affects our lives as adults. We may long for the childlike faith that Jesus praises, yet we also value adult skills—self-reliance, independence, responsibility— which take us away from our willingness to depend on anyone, especially on a God who may not always seem present in our lives. In Campus Ministry, we talk often to students about developing their faith lives as adults. We encourage them to grow into their own relationship with God and with the Church, somewhat independently of their parents. Students find themselves tempted, however, to approach their faith with the same determination and desire for self-sufficiency and independence that they bring to their career planning. We even call one of our campus ministry programs "The Challenge of Adult Christianity," implying that our faith comes from our initiative, our willingness to accomplish a goal, rather than from our response to a God who loves us and asks our willingness to trust and love in return. When we attempt, then, to support students as they define their faith as adults, how can we help them find a childlike willingness to depend on God along with other important parts of their lives which call them to learn valuable adult skills?

Our challenge lies in helping students recognize and accept their deep need for God. Only then will they see value in developing trust in and reliance on God. My son, as a toddler, completely trusts my husband and me. He absolutely believes that, whether he needs his next meal or a ride down the stairways he cannot yet negotiate alone, we will respond with love. As he grows older, however, he will, as we all have, lose this automatic willingness to believe completely in anyone— even in us, his parents. And yet Jesus asks us to believe in him as completely as little children believe, to trust as fully as children trust in their own parents.

Our students, though exceptionally bright and gifted, naturally find adulthood itself challenging enough. In addition, they frequently do not feel equipped for the added challenge of defining and taking responsibility for their own faith. As campus ministers, we can offer students opportunities to learn that they will find no more important foundation than a willingness to depend on God and God's great love for them. At the same time we can help them to grow in self-reliance, responsibility, and independence.

In January 1993, Campus Ministry sponsored the first annual Rally Day for its new program entitled "Communities ND." We knew that small Christian communities had been flourishing in Latin America and Africa for some time and had started to thrive in parishes in the United States as well. We also had heard many Notre Dame students express a desire to reflect on and learn more about their faith. Recognizing these developments, Campus Ministry decided to create an opportunity for small Christian communities to grow on the Notre Dame campus. Reverend Thomas McDermott, C.S.C., and I, with much help from an advisory board of faculty, residence hall rectors, and students, began to map out what such communities might look like. We would bring together undergraduate men and women in groups of about eight to ten with an invitation to get to know each other, to pray, and to talk about the Gospel reading for the upcoming Sunday mass. We would provide them with resources and questions to spark discussion, but more importantly, *they* could lead themselves and each other in this process of discovery. These groups could meet every two weeks or so, following a simple format designed to help them share leadership and responsibility. We would stress a shared community of faith and encourage them to assume the challenge of defining and accepting responsibility for their spiritual lives as adults. As Tom McDermott often said, "nobody goes to heaven by themselves." Perhaps in small faith communities, students could learn leadership, self-reliance, and independence. At the same time they could learn to trust, to develop not only independence but a sense of *inter*dependence as well, and to love God as only small children can love.

As we continued to develop a framework for small Christian communities at Notre Dame, we tripped over a common stumbling block: marketing. What should we call this program? How can we make our idea attractive to students? We learned our first lesson when we tried to choose a name. Initially, we chose "Communities *du lac*." Beautiful, we thought.

Notre Dame's founder, Father Edward Sorin, C.S.C., chose the name *Notre Dame du Lac*; we would highlight a treasured bit of our University's history. Unfortunately, everyone else hated the name. The more contemporary usage of *du Lac* as the title for the University's handbook of rules and regulations for students had so taken over in people's minds that nobody, we were told, would join a group called Communities *du Lac*. Imagine trying to name your child after a relative with a beautiful name but a terrible reputation. In the end, our new program became "Communities ND: The Challenge of Adult Christianity."

Next we utilized every publicity tool we could dream up. We wrote personal letters to students; we asked *The Observer*, the student newspaper, to interview us and write a news story; we wrote to all the hall rectors; we hung signs everywhere; we spoke at meetings of the Hall Presidents' Council, the hall staffs and the hall liturgical commissioners. And we prayed that a few people would come together to pray and talk about the Gospels and about their faith as young adults. That first year, about 200 undergraduates signed up to join Communities ND. In the three years that have followed, about 200 more students have enrolled each year.

Our students both hunger to talk about their faith and fear that doing so, outside of certain "safe" settings, leaves them too vulnerable to take such a risk. Over and over again I have heard from participants in Communities ND how much they appreciate the chance to speak openly about their beliefs, their hopes, and their questions. Each conversation reminds me that we must not only provide these opportunities for them, but we must also begin to teach them that they soon will need to create such settings for themselves. Whether in a parish, in their own family, or in some other community, our students will bring valuable experiences and great gifts of faith. Part of our role as campus ministers, therefore, must include teaching our students how to minister to others. We can help them learn how to take their faith with them after commencement and to present it to the new community in which they live.

Communities ND probably can tell as many stories of disappointment and of joy as any of the communities in which we live, but one particular community consistently helps me to realize that we must have done something right. Seniors now in 1996, this group began their community as freshmen at the Rally Day in January 1993. We had an inkling throughout that first spring semester that this group possessed something special. The following September when Campus Ministry sponsored a "kick-off day" to help the groups reconnect after the summer, this community came, and definitely arrived a step ahead of us. "Last semester we always met beneath this tree outside Dillon Hall," they told us. "In the spring before we went home we picked a date in August to meet by our tree. We've already been meeting this semester."

As sophomores and juniors they continued regular community meetings, participated in volunteer service together, took a "road trip" to one community member's home in Ohio, and carefully and protectively checked out each other's dates. I visited with several members of their group after a campus ministry event in February 1995, their junior year. "Hey Kate, we just had the greatest weekend!" they told me. "We had a community meeting with our parents!"

Each February, the University and the junior class sponsor "Junior Parents' Weekend." Most parents attend this weekend, which gives the juniors a chance to serve as hosts, introducing their parents to their friends, professors, activities, residence halls, and worship communities. Parents learn about their children's lives as young adults. In the midst of the weekend, this particular Communities ND group planned a community meeting, similar to all their gatherings except that they all brought their parents and encouraged them to participate. The group loved it; they felt justifiably proud of the community of faith and friendship they had built, and their parents felt, also justifiably, overwhelmed and proud. I found myself somewhat amazed as I listened to them retell the experience. What better element of growing adulthood for parents to witness than their children taking on their own faith, assuming this challenge of adult Christianity? This community, now seniors, found in each other a place to trust in God, to rely on others without fear, and to recognize God's love through shared faith. In addition, they have already "practiced" bringing this experience to a wider community: the very people who first brought them into this world and raised them up in their faith.

In addition to Communities ND, I enjoy the great privilege of working with the Rite of Christian Initiation of Adults (RCIA) process. The RCIA, over the course of an academic year, prepares students to become Catholic Christians. These students come from a variety of backgrounds: some have never been baptized at all, others have been baptized into other Christian denominations. In addition, one or two participants each year come as baptized Catholics who have received little or no formation or education in the Catholic faith after their baptism as infants. The RCIA follows a regular format of stages and rites which serve both to *inform* and to *form* a participant in the process. In other words, a person seeking to become Catholic (a "catechumen," in the language of the RCIA) not only learns a body of facts about the Catholic faith, but also develops a relationship with God and with the Catholic community in which she will live out her new life of faith.

Perhaps, to be more precise, I should say not that the RCIA prepares, but only *begins* to prepare students to become Catholic Christians. I find our students somewhat demanding— they want encyclopedic knowledge of the Catholic faith before their initiation at the Easter Vigil. Over and over, I remind them that the RCIA begins a lifetime commitment, a lifetime of growing, learning, and deepening their faith. I tell them, "You would be so bored if you knew everything already!" They look skeptical. "I'm still learning about my faith, about the Church, and about my relationship with God—and anyone who takes their faith seriously would tell you the same," I say, boldly speaking on behalf of all the committed faithful. Their faces brighten somewhat. One of the most unsettling aspects of our faith, especially for these young, bright, and often quite driven men and women, is the realization that none of us ever finds all the answers. Our students discover in most of their classes that if they simply study hard enough they can excel. As their relationships with God and the Church grow, however, the "benchmarks for success" become much cloudier. When these same students realize that their lives of faith will never stop changing, much like a relationship with someone they care about, they experience a real leap in their growth. In the midst of struggling to "excel" in their relationship with God, they may, even if only briefly, take a deep breath, relax, and trust in God's desire and love for them.

"Elizabeth" (not her real name), one of the brightest students I have ever met at Notre Dame, came to the RCIA process as a sophomore having already read extensively about the Catholic Church. She could not seem to satisfy her appetite for knowledge about the faith. Throughout the year she read much more on her own than I ever asked of the RCIA participants through the program. Despite a very gifted mind and a real talent for writing, Elizabeth struggled with such shyness that she could not meet another's eyes in conversation. At the same time, largely because of her intellectual strengths, she made little effort to tolerate people different from her. She sought refuge in academics, and I found myself hard pressed to convince her that becoming Catholic meant not just learning facts about God and the Church but more importantly knowing and loving this God who called to us through other people. Throughout the year and through many difficult conversations with Elizabeth, I saw her ever so slowly begin to respond to and trust in God's call. Elizabeth did become Catholic, and began to challenge herself to interact with others and to overcome her shyness. She returned to the RCIA as a junior to help the new catechumens on their faith journey. During her junior and senior years, Elizabeth actively sought ways to develop relationships with others and to recognize God in diverse people and opinions. Although these tasks did not come as easily as her academic work, Elizabeth persevered, although she suffered several major rejections along the way. Now enrolled in a doctoral program at another university, Elizabeth still excels academically and works ever harder at personal growth. She hopes to teach in a university setting where she can combine her love for her faith with her love for academics.

Most often I find that our students grow in faith not because of anything we do, but simply because we provide resources and an opportunity to look at that challenge of adult Christianity in new ways. Campus Ministry also offers a program to prepare students for Confirmation, where I met "James" (also not his real name). James truly "caught the fire" of the Holy Spirit through his participation in the Confirmation process. When James began preparing for Confirmation as a sophomore in 1991 he most decidedly did not stand out as anyone special. He came from a very privileged background, and probably signed up for Confirmation because someone (his mother or father, I guessed) expected him to do so. At the beginning of the program, I met with each student individually. I could tell that James had had little religious education and even fewer opportunities to articulate his own beliefs. His weekly journal entries, required for the Confirmation program, usually consisted of some quick thoughts jotted down in pencil.

In November 1991, I assigned the Confirmation participants two chapters, entitled "The Discovery of Fire" and "In a Style to Which You Are Not Accustomed" from *Life After Birth* by Reverend William Toohey, C.S.C., the director of Campus Ministry at Notre Dame at the time of his death in 1981. The chapters focused on our commitment to social justice and to simplifying our lifestyles. James' journal entry for that week seemed to come from a different person. He wrestled with feeling—disturbed, intrigued, challenged, indignant, and perhaps most importantly, drawn to his faith in a whole new way. I wrote that famous phrase "SEE ME" in big letters on my response to his journal entry, and so we began—on his initiative—meeting once a week or more. Sometimes he would just show up at my office door with a piece of paper in his hand on which he had written a new list of ideas and concerns. James would fire questions at me as he tried to ascertain how these new insights into his faith affected how he would choose to live as a Catholic Christian. He asked me everything from "But what if I know I'll always *want* to have a great car, fancy vacations and nice things?" to "What can I do to follow Christ's example more closely?" Soon he began to ask how he could become involved in volunteer service in the community. Before

I knew it James had made a weekly commitment to the children's activities room at the Center for the Homeless, despite his concern over what might happen to his very nice car in the Center's parking lot. That led him to other volunteer experiences, including a week in Appalachia through a program at the Center for Social Concerns. He eventually chose theology as a second major along with his first degree in science, which required him to stay at Notre Dame for a fifth year to complete all his course requirements. During his year in Confirmation and throughout the following years, I watched James grow: in knowledge, in faith, in maturity, and in confidence and trust of God's abiding love for him. James still attends one of our weekly campus ministry programs, and nearly every week he waits around afterwards, ready with more questions. He will graduate with two degrees in May 1996 and is trying to develop a placement in which he can serve for a year in a third world country.

Friends and even colleagues have asked me, "How can you invite people into a Church which suffers from serious flaws; which sometimes seems so uninviting even to those of us who have grown up in it?" I hope my answers to this question have developed and grown more complete as I have learned more about myself and about the Church. My belief, however, that *we* are the Church, that we represent both its beauty and its imperfections, does not change. The Church cannot hide its human weaknesses and, lucky for us, at the same time God constantly, consistently, and lovingly guides it. We must learn to trust in the childlike way that Jesus asks of us, to believe fully enough to throw ourselves into building up the Kingdom of God. We seek to live as responsible, self-sufficient, and independent adults. At the same time we must also allow our faith to affect the way we treat others, not only on an intimate level, but within our communities and our world as well. If I can communicate something of these hopes to our students, whether through the RCIA, Communities ND, or one of our other programs, then I hope I can also encourage them to be a part of our Church, albeit quite human. I long to ask them to take on the "challenge of adult Christianity," for they too hear God's word. They too will feel a desire to respond; indeed, by choosing to participate in their own lives of faith, they have already begun to respond to God's call. I do not want them to resent an imperfect Church but rather to participate in it, sharing in hope for our potential as a Church if we dedicate our lives to Christ. Through this shared faith community, our students can face together the challenge of adult Christianity, open to a childlike trust in God as they enter adulthood.

A Journey of Faith
in Scholarship, Teaching, and Service

DAVID B. BURRELL, C.S.C.

I woke up the other day to realize that I had been on the faculty
at Notre Dame for thirty years. I did not quite know what to
do with that revelation, except to be grateful that I had not
spent all of them here! The reasons for that initial exclamation
will emerge, but it was immediately followed by an appreciation of how rich those years have been. For this university is
more than a university; it is a community of sojourners in faith,
animated for more than thirty years by the conviction so
consistently and elegantly articulated by one of our confreres,
John Dunne: that faith is ever a journey. Pilgrimage is as venerable a theme in Christian literature as it is a pillar of Muslim
practice. And the intellectual payoff of the metaphor is that one
need never get uptight about matters of faith: brothers and
sisters will be there to help us over the next hurdle, as they will
be present to help us celebrate each succeeding joy.

One of my early experiences of this occurred more than
twenty-five years ago on the day when *Humanae Vitae* appeared.
Like most Catholics of my generation I had been enlivened by
Vatican II's emphasis on Newman's call to "consult the faithful
in matters of doctrine," and heartened by the convocation of a
group of lay people to advise the pope on issues germane to
their married lives. Yet Paul VI had apparently felt compelled

Father David Burrell, C.S.C., is the Theodore M. Hesburgh Professor of
Philosophy and Theology. He also serves as Chaplain-in-Residence for the
married student residences.

to resist their advice on matters of artificial contraception, and I was deeply disappointed at that turn of events. It so happened that I had to deliver something to our seminary and in the entrance way met an older priest who had served many years in East Bengal. As we exchanged greetings he noticed my preoccupation and asked me what the trouble was, so I told him. His words of considered wisdom still ring clear: "Dave, never let a servant get between you and the Master, no matter how exalted the servant may be!" Subsequent reflections on the matters at issue have helped me to see that we were surely too sanguine about pharmacological solutions in those days, and that there may well be considerable wisdom in Pope Paul's decision, but the point remains: we can always count on the help we need to negotiate the sometimes labyrinthine ways of faith.

Part of what makes Notre Dame so propitious a place for the Church to do its reflecting on this shared journey of faith is the religious congregation in which I participate. Yet the wonderful irony is that Holy Cross, founded by a diocesan priest of Le Mans in France some one hundred and fifty years ago, can only be *part* of the reason. For we are not a group distinguished by history or a tableau of saints; we have no "Ratio Studiorum" or Thomas Aquinas in our midst to give us direction. As a result, we have had to find our way, and from very early on realized that we could not do it alone, but needed all the help we could get. So it was no accident that Notre Dame was the first Catholic institution of higher education in the United States to respond to Vatican II by re-incorporating under a lay board of trustees. Moreover, the very structure of our community was intended from the beginning to be a microcosm of Church: male and female, lay and clerical. The sisters were separately constituted at Rome's behest, and the brothers and priests separated at a local level in the forties to assure the integrity of the brothers' vocation, yet after Vatican II the prescience of the founder Basil Moreau's intuition emerged, as we saw more clearly how women and men, lay persons and clerics must work together to form the community we would call Church. Clericalism can always rear its head, and our history—early and later—is hardly bereft of it, yet the seeds of a pluriform community have been here from the beginning and have come increasingly to fruition over the past thirty years.

Pluralism is a taxing goal, yet crucial to a community of inquiry. I have detailed elsewhere how we worked to achieve something of that in our philosophy faculty at Notre Dame, under the astute leadership of an Irish priest and colleague, Ernan McMullin.[1] What we were seeking is all the more elusive in that 'pluralism' can easily become an academic euphemism for sheer diversity, or scant cover for absenting oneself from any shared endeavor to be left free to do one's own thing. That sort of libertarian freedom, however, turns out to be decidedly vulnerable to pressure groups, as is so evidently the case with the umbrella society which promotes it in the name of "liberalism." So the sixties' cry of "doing my thing" has been supplanted by an insistence on "political correctness" in the nineties, to the point where it is becoming increasingly clear that the exercise of human freedom requires an undergirding journey of faith to protect us from ourselves. That has certainly been my experience over the past thirty years teaching at this Catholic university while participating in a wider academic community here and abroad. And once again, the secret has been to remind oneself and others, in season and out, that we are on a *journey* of faith. That journey has taken me far from this campus—a singular advantage of participating in a worldwide religious congregation. After four years of theological studies in Rome, I began higher studies in philosophy in Québec, at Laval, only to complete them in New Haven at Yale. Yet the time outside the United States allowed me to master enough western languages for higher studies, and doubtless laid the groundwork for a later shift to Hebrew and Arabic, in an effort to respond to the Church's novel position vis-à-vis other religious faiths by discovering anew how interfaith and intercultural a world was that of Thomas Aquinas.

The witness of Father Ted Hesburgh had alerted all of us to the need to bring a global perspective to northern Indiana, lest Notre Dame continue in the orbit it had carved out for itself decades earlier when challenged by the maverick Holy Cross priest-scientist and veritable polymath, John Zahm, to become a university in fact as well as in name.[2] The call was too exigent a one for the dominant leadership in the Holy Cross in the early twenties, which settled for serving Catholics from Chicago who aspired to something more—but not very much more! Yet Zahm's impetus became a subterranean stream issuing in more and more Holy Cross religious urged on to further studies under the tutelage of James Burns, an ardent advocate of Zahm's vision, so that a modest yet formidable team was in place in the fifties to give that vision a second chance. And that team characteristically included visionary laymen as well, who were ready and anxious to respond to a call which they had been harboring in their minds and hearts, as well as transmitting to generations of students.[3] Yet the inverse centripetal pull would remain, perhaps endemic to a place calling itself 'Notre Dame' and so easily becoming a womb for so many, a shrine of idyllic beauty not to be disturbed by worldly concerns. That is the primary reason why those who live and work here, like myself, find it necessary to absent themselves periodically: to appropriate wider and liberating perspectives, only to return to inject them into a culture easily prone to parochial introversion.

Fortunately, and notably in the decades succeeding Vatican II, our Catholic perspectives were increasingly enlarged to embrace a world Church; one which in Latin America focused ineluctably on issues of justice, thereby challenging a myopic American foreign policy fixated on fighting world communism. We could feel proud to be Catholic, and sought different ways of giving those global realities flesh on our campus and in our curriculum, with students of an increasingly national cast yet still quite restricted in their aspirations. It is here that our pattern of living with students in residence halls has come to make a profound educational difference. It seems to have been part of Moreau's ethos, communicated and fostered by Edward Sorin, who made Holy Cross American in its outlook, to assure that its members always occupy themselves with some direct pastoral work, alongside their teaching or other ministry at the university. As a result, we have tended to create smaller communities with students where, by sharing their living situations, informal mentoring can supplant formal instruction to complete an education in faith. And the pattern has enriched us as well, for it has given us invaluable pastoral experience, if often limited to a specific age group, and until more recently, to but one gender. To inject within that mix a sense of faith as a journey, and of faith as an invitation to embrace the world, has become our call as Holy Cross religious—sisters, brothers, and priests—in this place. Yet, as I have insisted, that demands that we deliberately transcend the more centripetal pull of the place and challenge ourselves as well as our students to ever wider challenges of reason and of faith.

My own journey may offer an illuminating facet of our work and life here. Educated first in theology at the Gregorian in Rome under the tutelage of Bernard Lonergan, on what proved to be the eve of Vatican II, our theology was suffused with the French initiative called "la nouvelle théologie," which directed us to patristic and medieval sources. It represented an explicit effort to retrieve a Catholic tradition untrammeled by the polemics of the counter-Reformation, and proved to be the animating spirit of Vatican II, itself a conscious counter-point to Trent as well as a needed corrective to the restricted perspectives of Vatican I a century before. Our Holy Cross house was populated by seminarians from Canada, Haiti, Brazil, and (then) East Pakistan, offering us an international view of our own congregation, plus opportunities for linguistic diversity at home. Our summers were spent in the Südtirol, where we could practice German with the children. All this proved a singular preparation for the post–Vatican II church: intercultural in its texture and global in its aspirations. Subsequent study of philosophy, first at Laval and then at Yale, focused on the multiple uses of language, different approaches to logic, and abstruse issues of semantics. This all culminated in a dissertation on a peculiar subset of expressions which medievals called "analogous," terms especially apt for use in speaking of things that we cannot directly describe, notably God. It was that focus which gradually directed my work from issues in logic and philosophy of science to topics in philosophical theology. And that led, quite unexpectedly, to chairing the faculty of theology during the seventies.

But not before a great deal of time and energy had to be expended on questions of just war and conscientious objection, for my initial teaching years at Notre Dame corresponded with American involvement in Vietnam. It gradually became clear to us that the aura of craziness which appeared to dominate the sixties represented the release needed to put the so-called "just war theory" into action. That traditional set of reflections, designed to help one judge the propriety or impropriety of a given conflict, and so determine whether a Christian could morally take part in it, had been quietly but effectively put out of action by a little codicil which read: "the presumption lies with authority." And that little nullifying clause worked as well as it did because that is what every citizen prefers to do: leave the presumption with authority. After all, why else did we select those people? So presuming to pass judgment on the considered determinations of government requires a massive re-centering of the human psyche—something which traditionally bland discussions of "just war theory" never broached. We were meeting resistance daily, however, with students who were having to face impending action in a war that was increasingly questionable. Government responses invoked the codicil: how can mere citizens, uninformed as they are, presume to second-guess our considered judgments regarding the need to wage war in south-east Asia? After all, we have privileged sources of information. The rest is now history, but it wasn't for us at the time.

Impelled by the decisions facing our students, we were driven to consider moral issues which might otherwise have been left quite speculative. In preparation for marking the 15 October 1969 moratorium day, we made elaborate plans for an outdoor liturgy at which a selected group of students would present their shredded draft cards as their appropriate offering. All this would be quite public and was certain to be filmed by FBI agents, so we wanted to make sure that the students were themselves aware of the seriousness of their action. So we gathered for a series of meetings for the month preceding the action, requesting the expertise of some of our law colleagues to help these students clarify their motives by attaining the clearest possible view of the consequences of their intended actions. The decision on the part of a few not to take part in the action was a small indication that we had devised an adequate preparation. We were heartened by the presence of an itinerant Jesuit bishop from India, whom we drafted to preside, and edified by Father Hesburgh's presence among the congregation amassed on the quadrangle in front of the library. Afterwards, we processed down the main quadrangle, stopping at crosses to mark the victims of the war to date, arranged as a "way of the cross."

That evening, at supper in Corby Hall, Father John McKenzie, a Jesuit scripture scholar, living and teaching with us, sounded almost nostalgic as he remarked to my confrere John Gerber and me: "In the old days, you guys would be halfway to Portland by now!" (In times past, by Notre Dame community lore, Portland—our Holy Cross institution in Oregon—had sometimes been regarded as a penal assignment.) In fact, our actions were never publicly criticized by our local community, even though many doubtless disagreed with the steps we had found it necessary to take in the face of student conflict over Vietnam. We had deliberately arranged sessions to discuss the matter before we acted publicly, however, so that critics who had absented themselves from those sessions had been effectively disbarred from any criticism later. That experience proved to be invaluable in later situations where in our ministry we would find ourselves at odds with the powers that be—in this case, the United States government; in others, local governance. By openly stating the grounds of one's opposition, and the reasons for the differences in outlook or judgment, one could defuse in advance much latent criticism, and set the stage for constructive confrontation. Confrontation there needs to be when issues of principle arise, but principles can often admit of diverse interpretations which preliminary dialogue can smoke out. Here is where I have found a religious community to be particularly helpful in learning to live with mutual respect and to learn from each other. One more example of faith as a journey: no single person can have the answers; we are all finding our way together, even when we find ourselves at odds over the correct paths to take.

Chairing the theology department put me in line to assist Father Hesburgh in his effort to galvanize Catholic institutions of higher education around the world. I was first asked to travel to Leuven for a weekend in December 1971 to help constitute the Conference of Catholic Theological Institutions, an offshoot of the umbrella International Federation of Catholic Universities (IFCU). Less than two years later I accompanied him to Salamanca for a plenary session of IFCU itself. Building upon the formative experience in Rome, these gatherings convinced me of the need to understand Church and theology globally, so when our Holy Cross provincial superior, Bill Lewers, asked me if I would like to teach for a semester in Dhaka at the National Major Seminary, I jumped at the chance. Bill was experimenting with a mode of presence overseas which capitalized on Vatican II's opening to world-church, using our own congregation as the vehicle, where by short-term assignments overseas, local church at either end could be enriched through the changes wrought in the persons themselves. I can only say that the experiment worked wonders in my case, even if my initial enthusiasm may have been unduly influenced by escaping the duties of department chairman for a semester! I came to discover the richness of Holy Cross men and women in Bangladesh, most of whom had recently endured the vicious war of independence which the government of Pakistan had precipitated by refusing to seat the duly elected prime minister from East Pakistan. When their regulars wrought havoc in East Bengal, our sisters, bothers, and priests stood by their people, and one—Father Bill Evans—was cut down by soldiers on patrol. In that environment, I met intelligent young seminarians whom it was a pleasure to introduce to philosophy and came to appreciate the profound faith of Muslims, whom I had never before encountered.

There is a palpable sense of the presence of God among ordinary Muslims which cannot but astound a western Christian. I spent every spare moment in that fall of 1975

visiting our various mission outposts—by cycle, boat, or train—
where the selfless work of generations of men and women
won me instant acceptance. These were largely Christian
villages, immersed in a 92 percent Muslim environment, yet
that larger environment made its way into my psyche in ways
which I would only later discover. And I had discovered how
a mission opportunity could expand one's horizons; the
experiment of our provincial had borne its fruit: my life would
never be the same. I returned to Notre Dame to begin teaching
a course on issues in justice, animated by the experience in
Bangladesh: a course which has proved immensely formative
for me and especially useful to students who have been
similarly awakened by the "urban plunge" experience organized by our Center for Social Concerns. And alert as well to the
implications for theology of a world no longer centered on
Europe, but open, as was the Church in Bangladesh, to cultural
influences of a powerful new sort. A few decades earlier, a
French theologian, Jean Daniélou, had proposed a paradigm
shift for mission, which I had experienced in numerous ways
in East Bengal: missionaries do not so much *bring* Christ to
other lands and cultures as *find* him there. With some key
colleagues in theology, we revamped our graduate programs
to integrate a Judaica position into our curriculum of Hebrew
scriptures, New Testament, and early church. This initiative was
to prove invaluable to my own subsequent opening to Islam.

Another theologian, Karl Rahner, helped to precipitate that
move, building on the Bangladesh experience, plus a rare
opportunity in Jerusalem the summer before I had taught in
Dhaka. Sister Marie Goldstein, who had earned her doctorate
at Notre Dame in mathematics and education, had followed
her paternal roots to explore interfaith pathways in Jerusalem,
and organized six weeks of living and studying together on
the part of Jews, Christians, and Muslims, at the ecumenical
institute which Father Hesburgh had been instrumental in
founding at Pope Paul VI's behest on the road to Bethlehem,
atop a hill called Tantur. Through persons who were articulate
in their own faith-traditions, we learned how each other
thought and prayed, and so modeled what a new Middle East

would have to look like. So when I had completed three terms of chair of the theology department and agreed to serve for one year as rector at Tantur, my vision of ecumenism had already been expanded from the Catholic-Orthodox-Protestant mission of the Institute to an interfaith perspective. Yet it was Rahner's prescient lecture at Weston School of Theology in 1979 which gave me the language I needed to make a move personally. His retrospective interpretation of the underlying significance of Vatican II elevated the slim document *Nostra Aetate*, on the Church's relations to non-Christian religions, to preeminence among conciliar statements.[4]

Rahner's reasoning led him to re-periodize Christian history, with the symbolic dates 70/1970 marking the beginning and end of western European Christianity: as the destruction of the temple and the formation of post-biblical Judaism coincided with Paul's mission to Greeks and Romans, so developments after the end of the council had decentered the Church from its European axis and opened the way for an encounter of Christianity with other religions quite different from the agenda of the celebrated missionary movement of the previous four centuries. That encounter would place the newer (and in the case of India, older) Christian communities in a privileged position, for their daily interchange with individuals from other major religious bodies would help western Christians discover new faces of the Christ. My recent experience in Dhaka, where we had already adapted Rabindranath Tagore's poems as liturgical hymns, corroborated his analysis. So it became clear that I needed to enhance my own work on "naming God" by adopting an explicitly comparative perspective, but how? At the end of nine years of chairing theology at Notre Dame I flew to England and headed overland for the Holy Land, with a knapsack and a sense of adventure into a new life. On a Sunday morning in Leuven, Islam emerged as the religious culture which would claim my attention. I had just completed a book on Thomas Aquinas, and everything suggested that his synthesis of Hellenic philosophy and Christianity contained Jewish and Muslim elements which had never been adequately accentuated. If I could show how that classical synthesis was already an interfaith, intercultural achievement, Rahner's thesis would receive fresh impetus and legitimacy. The only rub was learning Arabic, which would prove to be the required asceticism.

The next two years were to alter my horizons appreciably, with the initial year as rector at Tantur followed by one of research in Isaiah House, where our common prayer and Eucharist were in Hebrew, enabling me to begin studying Arabic at Hebrew University while also leading a seminar in Aquinas and Maimonides. Approaching Islam through the philosophers, indeed the very ones on whom Thomas Aquinas had relied for his recasting of Aristotle, I became able to trace his path more surely and began the comparative study to which Rahner's vision had called me.

Bringing that perspective to Notre Dame was enhanced by a move to live at family student housing, where the 132 families (with 150 children) represented twenty-seven nationalities. My home encompassed in microcosm the global reach of which Rahner spoke, and with the help of a student spouse as peer minister I was able to learn a great deal about the world's religions and cultures in our efforts to bring the daily lives of student families in touch with one another, and so mine the riches that we knew were present in our modest University Village. My research took me each summer to live with the Dominicans in Cairo, where I was also able to come to know the families of some of our residents, all Muslims. One summer, my Egyptian friends asked me whether I had met the Saudi family who had moved in, remarking that they were the "richest family in the Village." Since everyone was trying to get by on graduate student stipends, that hardly represented affluence, but as I began to make the rounds of new residents, the Saudi student introduced himself as "a poor Bedouin from Saudi." That discrepancy in descriptions encapsulates the situation in the Arab world, where Egypt enjoys the respect of its cultural riches while the Saudis, conscious of their cultural poverty, buy their way with oil money.

In our interfaith and intercultural environment in University Village, we have learned how to discover how much we can gain from each other. Given our disparity of religions, the sole feast we can celebrate all together is one which features children: Halloween. Chinese children sport costumes as outlandish as any others, and our procession yields a harvest of photographs which adorn our Community Center for the ensuing year. Christmas finds most of our families home with grandparents, but for those who remain—mostly foreign—we announce a Eucharist at 9:30 a.m. followed by a brunch at 10:30, inviting everyone to one or both. The result is an intercultural feast, not unlike those parts of the world where people have long partaken of each other's celebrations—a sign of a world to come. Our ordinary Sunday Eucharist is marked by a preponderance of children, and a lesson in intercultural exchange, as someone brings something to eat, and we all linger afterwards for at least as long as the Eucharist itself to complete our celebration of the Lord's day.

For me, the greatest privilege has been to work closely with the young parents who are trying to create an environment for their children which does not lose the riches of their own culture. It is especially heartening to have a hand in the rites of passage of young women and men in becoming parents for the first time, noting how decisively this affects their appreciation of their own faith. When these families leave us, to move on to their first professional position, we must remind ourselves that our job is to get them out, for the bonds which have been forged are palpable. They are excited to be launched on their lives, yet realize ruefully that they will not be likely to find a community like this one again. By way of compensation, we come to appreciate that we will never have to stay in a hotel anywhere in the world again, for the friendships forged here span the globe. For me, working with student families has underscored once again the wisdom of Moreau's insistence that we all carry out some directly ministerial work in the midst of our teaching and administering at the University. I always tell people that it is the "best thing I do," not because I do not enjoy teaching and scholarship, which I clearly do, but because in this simple yet rich environment much of what I study and teach about understanding other cultures takes flesh for all of us to appreciate.

As I am engaged in translating a classical Muslim work by a twelfth-century religious thinker, al-Ghazali, on "faith in divine unity and trust in divine providence," I am able to discuss the nuances of the translation effort with a Muslim from Pakistan engaged in a research project on interest-free economics, or encounter a resident from Bulgaria who will tell me (in French) what it is like living in a multi-ethnic and multi-religious society. And these privileged occurrences form part of a daily tapestry of exchanges among children from diverse cultures, who are negotiating American schooling yet encouraged to speak their own language at home. As a person who has gained so much from intercultural exchange, I cannot help but appreciate the richness of our otherwise modest environment, and hope that my own enthusiasm can help a few over the inevitable transitions and extended winters of graduate study. We do our best to focus the life of the Village on the needs of our children, some of whom are already in high school, and like any other group of human beings, what community we manage to foster results from the efforts of a half a dozen residents—mostly women—who have learned how to attend to a context larger than their own domestic scene. I am happy to be a part of that.

I have especially come to appreciate the character of our largest plurality of students, who come from China. I was privileged to have as my campus minister for four years a young Chinese woman, who could attend to difficult situations with an unimaginable tact. Hard-working as Chinese are, they know how to have fun as well, all the while attending assiduously to the intellectual and cultural development of their children. It is heartening to watch a mother assisting her young child in daily piano practice. On my return from one of my visiting stints to teach Islam in the National Major Seminary in Dhaka, I had the opportunity to visit the homes of some of our Chinese students. It happened this way: before leaving in January I had invited all the Chinese students to a potluck supper, and put a large map on the wall to identify their places of origin. Those who had someone at home able to converse with me gave me their addresses and alerted their families that I would be visiting in July. When I arrived in town, I would show the address to my hosts (since visits to China in 1988 were still best orchestrated as academic junkets, and mine was arranged through the Academy of Social Sciences as a trip to study Islam in China) and they would tell me the number of the bus to take, and write on the back of my slip of paper the name of the bus stop. I would show that to the people on the bus, who would then usher me off at the proper place, and within a few moments I had found some guides to the residence itself. The only trouble I had was with addresses which some students had assiduously transliterated into English!

All this should give some idea of how my ministry as chaplain reinforces my intellectual work of comparative study of Jewish, Christian, Muslim philosophical theology. It is not that one is continually engaged in discussions of those very matters, especially in their medieval guise, which is my scholarly focus. It is rather that by living in an intercultural milieu one is constantly reminded of the fruitfulness of exchange and of comparative reflections, and so given an even greater impetus to keep working to forge a religious outlook which will keep nationalist politicians from playing the religious card to serve their deadly aims, as we have experienced in Bosnia. Such, to my mind, is the challenge to all religious groups in the twenty-first century, and we are engaged in a small-scale modeling of just that in our multinational Village.

NOTES

1. "A Catholic University," in *The Challenge and Promise of a Catholic University*, ed. Theodore M. Hesburgh, C.S.C. (Notre Dame, Ind.: University of Notre Dame Press, 1994), 35–44.

2. The Notre Dame library collection of John Zahm's work contains fifty-two book entries. By way of example, he wrote a book cataloguing the contributions of women in the history of science in 1913, under the pseudonym of H. J. Mozans: *Women in*

Science, which has been republished twice, the latest by the University of Notre Dame Press in 1991. The history of his contributions to scholarship remains to be written. His life was the subject of a doctoral dissertation published in 1956 by Ralph Weber, but the scope of that work is commensurately limited.

3. The history of these intervening years, a veritable seedbed for Zahm's ideas, remains to be written as well.

4. The lecture was published by *Theological Studies* (December 1979) as "Towards a Fundamental Interpretation of Vatican II."

Trailblazing: A Mission Enhanced by Faith and Commitment

CAROLYN M. CALLAHAN

Roman Catholic, African American, woman, Accountancy professor characterize the unique perspective that I bring to the University of Notre Dame. In addition, a social and family background of poverty also influences my world view. Viewing my attributes as a whole, I am in some sense always different. In an African-American community, I am a minority because I am a Roman Catholic. In a Roman Catholic community, I am a minority because I am an African-American woman. Among African-American scholars, I am a minority because I am a female in a male-dominated discipline. While these conflicting labels embodied in one human being have deepened my faith in God and increased my commitment to my academic work, they have also made me a more compassionate person. I can readily identify with the weak and the vulnerable and my heart is moved naturally to try to improve their plight. In an academic setting, I can readily identify with the difficulties of doctoral students as well as untenured assistant professors. I have developed a deep empathy for the vulnerable in the academy because I personally know the pain of being an "outsider" inside the university. While women have participated in American higher education for many years, academic women are still pioneers. Women of color in male-dominated disciplines are truly "trailblazers." We attempt to pursue research careers at major institutions against the odds. In 1991, I became the first African-American woman to be tenured in

Carolyn Callahan is Associate Professor of Accountancy, K.P.M.G. Peat Marwick Faculty Fellow.

my discipline at a doctoral-granting institution in the United States. Several had tried the path before me, only to decide the wiser course was to either retreat to their original doctoral institution or go forward at a historical black university. Without a strong commitment to my religious faith, my achievement would have been impossible. I tell my story now because it is my hope that in some way others might benefit from it. My story also speaks to the challenges before the professorate as well as the challenge before the University of Notre Dame. I feel that the overwhelming odds of a young black woman born in poverty becoming a faculty member at the University of Notre Dame is a testament to God's goodness and grace. This obvious fact enhances my ability to remain committed to my work.

My commitment to my academic career is deeply entangled with my religious faith. In pursuing an academic career, I feel I am merely following God's will for my life as I cannot remember a time in my life when I was not involved in scholarly pursuits. After long school days, I spent additional hours in the public library developing mathematical skills or reading great literature because I simply enjoyed solitary intellectual challenge. The privilege of being a college professor merely affirms who I am through God's grace. I love my work as my responsibilities as a university professor are aligned with my natural inclinations and abilities.

Although my formal responsibilities as a college professor are well defined, I view an academic career as a life of service to one's students, colleagues, and profession. My faculty responsibilities are encompassed within the formal mission statement of the University of Notre Dame as articulated by the president, Reverend Edward A. Malloy, C.S.C., in the final report of the *Colloquy for the Year 2000* in May 1993. However, I see my personal and unique mission at this university in a statement of instructions to the undergraduate students in the Notre Dame Undergraduate Program bulletin:

The University of Notre Dame is a community of students, faculty and administrators who come together to learn, work and grow in moral character. Central to the concept of community is belief in the importance of honorable behavior for oneself and for the community as a whole.

Although this statement is addressed to Notre Dame students, it is also an appropriate message for faculty, administrators, and staff. It appeals to me because it indicates that we are a community at Notre Dame. My personal responsibility to the community is clear. It is important for me to behave in an honorable way in all facets of my professional life. At Notre Dame, a religious educational institution, I believe professors should accomplish their professional tasks while adhering to the highest level of personal moral integrity. In short, for professors to learn and grow in moral character, we must do so within the context of our professional responsibilities of teaching, research, and service.

First there is teaching. When I go into the classroom, I feel a moral obligation to challenge my students on an intellectual level. Faculty popularity contests and grade inflation with its associated ills do not serve our students well. My greatest joy is when I am able to explain a complex concept so that my students can grasp it for themselves. I try to be respectful of individual learning styles and provide many opportunities for students to demonstrate mastery of difficult material. It is also my responsibility to be available to students. Consequently, I am generally on campus six days a week and students are allowed to come to my office on Sunday directly after 10:00 a.m. mass if they need additional help beyond that offered during the regular work week. Since Notre Dame's students also juggle multiple roles on campus, it is important to meet their needs. Most students feel that an undergraduate business degree is demanding and accounting is reputed to be extremely demanding. My goal is to help students have a good intellectual experience in my classes by providing a solid support base.

I am often told that the minority students need me as a role model (and they do), however, I feel that my majority students also benefit from my presence on Notre Dame's campus. Many of them have never interacted with a professional woman of color. I try to stress the importance of ignoring physical attributes in assessing competency as most Notre Dame students will work in multicultural business institutions. My goal is to create a supportive environment in the classroom where all can feel free to speak and learn. I really care about my students and try to express that by holding high expectations for them while providing a great deal of support inside and outside the classroom. Although the content and pedagogy of the accounting curriculum has changed in many ways in recent years, I have been, with rare exception, well received by the Notre Dame students. Even though I teach the technically demanding courses in the accounting curriculum, my students are very supportive of my efforts. They are generally polite, usually quite kind and respectful in the classroom.

Clearly, the content of my teaching has been influenced by being at Notre Dame. Specifically, at Notre Dame, a religious-based educational institution, it is important to discuss ethical issues. These discussions are important in an accounting curriculum. In business, concentration on short-term operating results has placed ethical pressures on accountants to compromise long-term productivity or human resources in order to "maximize the bottom line." Recognizing that my students are likely to be leaders in their chosen field, I would like them to be prepared to be effective on both a technical as well as moral level. Under the guidance of the department chair, I was charged with the responsibility of developing an ethics course for accounting students. Our course, Ethical Issues in Accounting, seeks to help Notre Dame students gain sound ethical reasoning skills. The purpose of the course is to increase our students' awareness of the ethical dimensions of complex business activities and decisions. We focus first on ethical reasoning models to examine the ethical dilemmas posed by real-world cases. Then we discuss how to respond institutionally to a known ethics violation. Students actually practice writing executive memos. They learn the skill of documenting inappropriate behavior in a professional manner. Although I wanted to develop an ethics course at other schools, I was unable to gain the support to do so. At Notre Dame, the course received full administrative and departmental support. I feel the course has fulfilled a need as most Notre Dame students have difficulty accepting the premise that ethical violations have become almost a norm in contemporary business interactions in American society. The initial reaction of Notre Dame students is always one of disbelief, although most of the cases are based on actual company history. Teaching a course on ethical issues is an accepted responsibility of being on the faculty of a Catholic university. Although there is emphasis on a stand-alone course, I try to raise ethical issues in every course I teach in the accounting curriculum. It is my hope that our students will leave Notre Dame with the awareness that strong personal ethical behavior is appropriate at all times, in all places, in every situation, in both personal and business settings.

While the content of my teaching has changed as a result of being at Notre Dame, I feel my methods have subtly changed also. Although our students are very intelligent and generally well prepared for the academic environment, many need to gain intellectual confidence in their innate abilities. Thus, assignments are structured so that students discover various analytical concepts on their own. In accordance with our newly developed accounting curriculum, small group interaction in class is encouraged. Utilizing computer technology and software is required. Our business students are generally placed in teams and are graded on both an individual and group basis. An emphasis is placed on both written and oral communications. Students gain confidence by simulating actual accounting practice techniques. Accounting curriculums have changed in response to the demands of the profession. The technology available in the new College of Business, as well as DeBartelo classroom building, has given the Notre Dame accounting faculty the opportunity to be leaders in accounting education in the United States.

In addition to my teaching responsibilities, I am also a scholar with research responsibilities. My research interest is focused on the analytical and mathematical development of empirical models that link information signals to equilibrium prices in the capital and product markets. I use mathematics as well as statistical analysis to support my work. I also integrate theoretical concepts from the fields of micro-economics and finance to enhance my research. Most of the empirical data I use is computer oriented and available on magnetic tape. A typical research day may involve a six-to-eight–hour stint at a computer terminal or an equal amount of time spent "pushing mathematical equations" in an effort to understand underlying static equilibrium economic models. There are very few women who choose to do capital markets research in accounting. However, I have always loved mathematics as well as statistics and selected the capital markets area of study out of keen interest. I'm excited about my research area and can easily become immersed in it. Sometimes, I actually lose track of time. My husband knows my habits and calls me promptly at 7:30 p.m. daily so that I will leave my office and start for home. As with most aca-demics, my days are quite full. I enjoy the quiet evening hours for doing research. I have always enjoyed analytical problem solving and remember learning basic algebra as a grade school student by studying the illustrations in math books in the public library. I cannot remember a time in my life when I was not studying and pushing myself intellectually.

As an African-American woman, it was not easy to gain acceptance in my research field. It took a concerted effort to build a network of colleagues that I could count on to review my work. Most academicians need critical feedback to improve their chances for top tier publications. In my first academic position, I felt very lonely and isolated on an intellectual basis. Although I did not know it at the time, my experience was not unique for an academic woman. Simeone (1987) indicates that although women have participated in American education for over 150 years, academic women are still pioneers, carving out a place for themselves in an unwelcoming, nonsupportive, and frequently hostile environment. As a woman of color, I experi-enced discouragement, neglect, hostility, and outright exclusion. It is difficult to describe my early years in academe without feeling emotional pain. I could not have survived this period of my life if it had not been for my faith. I found much comfort in a passage found in 1 Corinthians 1:13 directly related to surviving difficult times:

> *No testing has overtaken you that is not common to everyone. God is faithful and He will not let you be tested beyond your strength but with the testing He will also provide the way out so that you may be able to endure it.*

As an assistant professor, I really struggled to gain academic acceptance although my work had scholarly potential. A backward glance reveals that my early academic struggles really helped me, although it was the most difficult period in my academic life.

I came to academe with a strong corporate accounting background. On a management training track in corporate America, I never experienced overt racism or sexism. I was fortunate to be hired by a large accounting department of a major corporation where the chief accountant was interested in hiring and retaining skilled individuals. In his administrative role, he was intolerant of non-inclusive or racially intolerant behavior. Since this tone was established at the top and strictly enforced, I cannot recall any inequitable treatment. My supervisor's staff looked like the United Nations long before the word "multicultural" became popular. It is instructive to note that my former supervisor became a member of the vice-president's staff prior to his retirement. Perhaps it was because he focused on achievement and less on the physical attributes of his subordinate employees.

It saddens me to say that I learned about racism and sexism in academe, and I was truly demoralized by it. Like most academically inclined students, I truly admired professors as great intellects. It still is difficult for me to understand how many academicians can reconcile intellect with racism and sexism. Prior to entering graduate school, I had never experienced prejudice in my community, the Catholic Church, or as an undergraduate student. I was absolutely stunned by the accepted training of a doctoral student and totally unprepared for the emotional toll of the complex problems facing the few African-American women in academe. Central to my success was my religious faith.

During graduate school I stayed involved in the Catholic Church by teaching second-grade CCD classes. I also attended mass daily and joined a Bible study group. Although I met all intellectual challenges required by the rigors of my doctoral program, I found the accepted training of a doctoral student unduly intellectually restrictive and at times very demeaning. The isolation and loneliness was debilitating. After graduation, I decided to interact with my doctoral students in an entirely different manner, to treat them as my colleagues and to invite them to be full co-authors on my research projects. This approach not only benefited the doctoral students, it also benefited me.

In addition to my religious faith, the support of my immediate and extended family was extremely instrumental in my success. After two very difficult years as an assistant professor, I called my father and told him I was considering leaving the academic profession. I discussed the discouragement I felt in dealing with the constant hostility, loneliness, and isolation. My father quietly listened and then said, "Carolyn, you have always studied alone. You have always spent hours in the library alone. What is different about being at the university?" My reluctance to enter and remain in the academic world was much like Moses' reluctance in hearing God's call:

When God called Moses, Exodus notes:

The Lord said: *I have indeed seen the misery of my people in Egypt. I have heard them crying out because of their slave drivers and I am concerned for their suffering . . . I have seen the way the Egyptians are oppressing them. So now go. I am sending you to bring my people out of Egypt.*

Of course Moses objects and first he replies:
Who am I that I should go?

God replies: *I will be with you.*

Then Moses tries this one: *Oh Lord, I have never been eloquent, in fact I am slow of speech and tongue.*

Of course we know God replies: *I'll help you to speak and will teach you what to say.*

Moses replies: *Oh Lord, please send someone else to do it.*

I can identify with Moses. I wanted to be in an academic setting but I was hopeful God would send someone else to do the "trailblazing." I knew God was calling me to accept of my role. Although we usually do hear God's call, it is human to feel inadequate for a difficult life mission.

When I have moments of doubt, I try to remember my father's quiet conversation reminding me to be true to myself. In fact, the conversation with my father when I really wanted to give up proved to be a turning point in my career. My father had wisely reminded me of who I really was, a scholarly person. God had called me long ago to the academic profession and I had everything I needed to be successful. I reflected on the moment and decided I really wasn't lonely but I did need critical feedback on my work. In that instance, my attitude changed and I began to see the academic world differently. I knew I had to find intellectual support. It was at this point, I called MIT as well as several other universities to obtain the opportunity to participate in their research presentation series.

Since I did not have an in-house support group, I was forced to develop an academic network outside my university. I didn't know enough about the academic environment to be nervous at MIT. I simply wanted to know if my research ideas had validity. I am indebted to the MIT faculty who accepted me as young scholar and helped me to publish my first serious work after graduate school.

Another problem I faced was the lack of financial support to conduct research. Oftentimes, I could not obtain departmental research funds for my work. This forced me to consider other resources and I learned how to write research grants. In the third year of my academic career, I sought and obtained a competitive national research grant. The grant not only alleviated financial difficulties, it also helped me obtain national visibility for my work.

Although I managed to successfully negotiate various obstacles in those early years, it required great perseverance and a strong faith in God. Somehow, I never lost confidence in my work or my ability to carry out large-scale multi-year research projects. I caution, however, that the difficulty with focusing on my success story is that it may obscure the impact of oppression and exclusion while focusing on individual strengths. It is important that female faculty have the same institutional support as every other faculty member. Only then will academic institutions fully benefit from the research efforts of female scholars. As for myself, I survived those perilous first years and was tenured in early spring of 1991.

The achievement of tenured status at a research institution is a major accomplishment in the life of any young professor. For me, I felt it was one of God's small miracles. Indeed, achieving tenure had required publishing research in the top scholarly accounting journal, earning a university-wide teaching award, and participating on eight university or college committees. In addition, I was awarded a national competitive research grant in support of my scholarly work. Given the obstacles and barriers I faced, none of these achievements would have been possible in the short five-year pre-tenure period without God's unwavering grace and the devotion of my extended family.

With my professional life somewhat in order, I thought I would be able to focus on further development as a teacher and scholar. However, remaining at the university where I worked so diligently became impossible as I received word that my father was critically ill and needed me back home in Ohio. Although I was tenured in the early spring of 1991, shortly thereafter I left the East Coast to return home to be nearer to my father. Even though many of my friends and colleagues saw my decision to give up tenured status at a major research institution as astonishing, I never felt torn about the decision. In my life, it has always been God and family first, professional career second.

In the fall of 1991, I joined the Accountancy faculty at the University of Notre Dame and earned tenure for the second time in the spring of 1994. At Notre Dame, I did not have any difficulty becoming a member of a research group in my area of interest. I had managed to establish an academic track record. After reading some of my work, one of the most prominent scholars in the College of Business at Notre Dame wrote me a letter in which he expressed an interest in collaborating on joint research projects of mutual interest. I was finishing my last year at my university on the East Coast when I received his kind note. Although he urged me to accept the faculty appointment offer from Notre Dame, he indicated he would be interested in research collaboration irrespective of my final job selection decision. I was deeply touched by this offer. It was probably the first time that I truly felt the experience of one scholar relating to another scholar on the basis of a similar research interest. It is not surprising to me that this experience happened at Notre Dame. My Notre Dame research colleague didn't see my color or gender. He genuinely saw me as a scholar and intellect. I am still moved by the experience.

Most minorities, as well as most women, would like to be seen as serious scholars who happen to be a female or a person of color. Unfortunately, on many university campuses the gender and race issue are clearly present as an undercurrent. The gender issue is always "Is she serious about her work?" and the race issue is always "Is she really competent?" If these two screens are passed, it becomes possible to have an intellectual conversation about one's scholarly work. At Notre Dame, no one has ever challenged my competency or the intensity that I bring to my work. For the first time in my career, I feel I have matured as a scholar. My work seems to be much easier to accomplish as I no longer feel that I must first prove intellect or competency. I am intrinsically motivated and I continue to push myself as a teacher and scholar. A strong work ethic was instilled in me by my parents. It seems the success or failure of an individual to live up to his or her uniquely human potential depends to some extent on family background and support.

I am indebted to my parents for emphasizing the importance of a strong work ethic and self-reliance. In addition, they stressed the importance of relying on God and being a moral person. I was well blessed with loving supportive parents. Unfortunately, my mother was struck by a catastrophic illness at a young age. Our immediate care fell to my father and his eldest sister. My father assumed his increased parental responsibilities with enthusiasm and devotion. His children became the center of his life. Although he was challenged by poverty and an unexpected loss, he remained a caring, nurturing parent. He had great hopes that we would somehow live a better life than his own. In his mind, a good education was the first step in the right direction. Naturally, all of his life, my father was most supportive of my academic career. He never tired of telling anyone who would listen, "My daughter teaches at the university." His recent untimely death is still difficult for me. Within one year, I've lost both my parents. It would be easy to give in to the moments of despair surrounding so great a loss in such a short period of time.

However, as an African-American woman, I have been taught fortitude and self-reliance since birth. In addition, as indicated, my parents valued education and nurtured my talents. They were very proud of my academic abilities although neither had the opportunity to earn college degrees. My mother worked as a domestic and my father supplemented his wages as a factory worker by working a second job in construction. African-American women with extraordinary talents are generally valued for those talents in functional families. My parents pushed me much harder than my sisters. They both insisted that I work at my full potential. My mother always wanted me to have a college degree. She would always say "Go to college, Carolyn, and get a good job. [As a matter of survival women of the lower economic classes always work.] Even though you will probably marry, there is no money like your own money." My father's advice was a little different but had the same message. "Get an education. You may have to support yourself and your children

Another benefit of my racial heritage is that as an African-American woman, I have felt no necessary conflict between having a family and pursuing an academic career. African-American women have been working outside their homes and managing their families for generations. I had very strong role models to follow in my own family. I always knew I would probably work and also combine that work with married life. The only question was really the choice of occupation. It is important to note that I have a very supportive husband who has always encouraged me in my academic aspirations.

As I look back, I am very happy that I followed my parents' advice and somehow, through God's design, managed to survive those early difficult years of my career. I feel very privileged to be a faculty member at the University of Notre Dame. In fact, I know firsthand what it means to be a member of the Notre Dame family.

In my third year at Notre Dame, I became critically ill and faced very serious surgery with an uncertain outcome. Even though I knew in the middle of the 1993 fall semester that I was quite ill, I wanted to finish the term with my students and submit my current research to an academic journal. I had worked on the project for two years which is fairly typical in my discipline. Somehow, with God's help, I found the strength to finish the term. I completed my research paper and my application for tenure consideration. The night before I went to the hospital, I completed the grading of seventy-five final exams and finalized course grades for the semester. Even though I knew my health concerns were serious and possibly life threatening, I wanted to spend my last days, if God had so chosen, doing what I loved; being a part of a very special academic community. My husband offered to take me on an exciting trip abroad during this difficult time. The chairperson of my department offered many times to relieve me of my academic responsibilities during that uncertain ten weeks. I never wavered in my resolve to continue my life as an academic. I really wasn't interested in a world tour. All I wanted was to continue to work as long as possible and have my family near. The emotional trauma was much harder on my family than myself. I felt I was safe in God's hands no matter what the future held for me. It was difficult for my husband and children to imagine me sick since I had never been seriously ill. During this critical period, my husband insisted that a family member would accompany me to my office during the last few weeks before the impending surgery. The task fell to my youngest daughter, then a sophomore at Notre Dame. As I worked on my research in the late evenings in my office, my daughter often fell asleep from total exhaustion after attending her classes and following me around all day on Notre Dame's campus. She learned firsthand about the demands of an academic career and I learned to let her to care for me, not an easy role for a mother to play. A family's love is wondrous.

Although the outcome of the surgery was very positive, my brush with death confirmed in my mind that I am doing what God would have me to do. I don't seem to have the desire, opportunity, or talents for anything else. I also believe that facing one's mortality enhances the beauty and quality of life. The intangibles of love and faith become extremely important. It is difficult for me to understand conflict and hostility given the brevity of life. In a chaotic world, experiencing peace and love seems so much more important now. It's rewarding that love is a facet of the culture of Notre Dame.

I felt it personally during my illness. The outpouring of kindness, flowers, and letters from my students, colleagues, administrators, staff and members of the Holy Cross Order was overwhelming. It is difficult to articulate the special bond in the Notre Dame community; it's felt in the heart. Although the achievement of excellence is definitely stressed at Notre Dame, there is a ribbon of loving concern binding us together in our human frailties.

My perspective at Notre Dame is firmly based on my religious faith. In telling my story, it is my hope that all my students learn that perseverance and faith have their own reward. There are many benefits associated with overcoming life's challenges. My early academic struggles actually enhanced my intellectual development. Most important, I gained a strong commitment to my work as an academic scholar. Despite all the limitations and obstacles, I never considered giving up my chosen work, although there were many moments when I wondered if I could find an academic institution that would accept me as a scholar. Secondly, since I learned to manage the classroom and conduct research projects independently, I developed a level of intellectual confidence in my work that still motivates me today. In retrospect, I learned to handle the inevitable setbacks associated with an academic career and, perhaps what is most important, I learned in my heart how much I loved my chosen work. I was willing to endure much suffering to become an academic. After my father's encouragement at that critical moment of doubt early in my academic career, there was never a second time that I thought of giving up my life's work. I did come to accept that my advancement in the academic world would be slow and difficult if I continued to face unnecessary barriers and obstacles. Looking back, I am reminded of an African proverb: "That which does not break me, makes me strong."

And so I end where I began. I certainly had no idea how my life would unfold but I have always been very certain of God's love and profound presence in my life. It seems like a small miracle that an ordinary woman of color from a very common background is a faculty member at the University of Notre Dame. Indeed, I once again acknowledge that nothing I have accomplished would have been possible had I leaned to my own design. After all, I was quite happy studying in the library without benefit of any formal degree.

As an African-American woman at Notre Dame, I understand that to some extent the difficulties I faced as a young professor are the nature of the academic subculture. It is easy to neglect the intellectual needs of young scholars in the university. However, it is clear to me that my painful experiences were amplified by gender and race. Accordingly, this indicates the challenges facing the professors and the University of Notre Dame.

Notre Dame is a unique educational institution. Women and minorities are attracted to Notre Dame's emphasis on being a "community." It is one of our strengths. We should examine our institutional structure to be certain that our community is inclusive at all levels. As we continue our scholarly mission, it will be important to retain our religious and moral values in substance and form. As faculty are hired, it will be imperative to consider commitment to moral and ethical values as well as scholarly potential. In our deep love for Notre Dame, it is important that this university remain faithful to its mission statement as well as its unique position in higher education. As members of the faculty, we must accept the distinct religious and educational goals of Notre Dame as a condition of our tenure here.

My everyday prayer is always the same: Lord, please strengthen me so that I do not diminish Notre Dame by my presence. At the personal level, it is very important for me to make a contribution that enhances all that this University aspires to be. I embrace the responsibilities of the trailblazer and hope other women and minorities will follow my path.

REFERENCE

Simeone, Angela. 1987. *Academic Women: Working Towards Equality*. South Hadley, Mass.: Bergin and Garvey.

Becoming Catholic Together

KATHLEEN CANNON, O.P.

Issues pertaining to women are a gauge of how the Church and the University struggle to be Catholic. These issues raise in a particular way questions that go to the heart of Catholic identity—questions about the image of God and the full humanity of women, about what it means for a woman to be saved, and about communion among persons. Thus a consideration of such issues relative to the role of women offers particular evidence or nonevidence for the catholicity of the university. It goes without saying that the university must somehow give evidence as much as the church if the university claims to be Catholic.

My personal background has marked my interest in and concern for women's issues. I am a Dominican. The spirituality that undergirds my ministry is characterized by the Dominican spirit whose inspiration and vision is the quest for truth wherever it may be found and, in particular, the kind of truth that sets humanity free. The Dominican motto, *contemplare et contemplata aliis tradere* (to contemplate and to give to others the fruits of contemplation), requires a generosity of spirit and a willingness to share what is received with others. It also underscores that thought and action, reflection and commitment must be joined.

At its center, Dominican spirituality is Incarnational, concerned with embodying God's love, once incarnate in Jesus, now in Christ and in us. One of the profound implications of the Incarnation is that God has entrusted the ongoing co-creation of the world and of human history to human beings.

Sister Kathleen Cannon, O.P., is Associate Provost.

God's grace is active in the concrete and personal aspects of our lives. Because grace is at the heart of all things, I can affirm the goodness of the world, the goodness of life, my own goodness, and the goodness of others. And I can trust that God will give an unexpected future to the restricted scope of my own actions. It is not always easy to see how the Incarnation of God in Christ continually takes shape amid the nuts and bolts of institutional life at the University, but it is possible, upon reflection, to locate certain privileged moments where I would say unhesitatingly, yes, this is where the Incarnation continues to happen.

Like the lives of most administrators, my life is a very busy one, and in the press of the diverse tasks that fill my days, it is possible to lose sight of the single mission of the University. To help me to see all that I do as ways of calling the University to an authentic catholicity, I find it helpful to reflect on the biblical image of stewardship.

Stewards are persons who have been entrusted with some task or responsibility; they act as overseers or managers of another's household or property. They are aware that the goods they have been commissioned to manage are given not merely for their own interests, purposes, and uses, but are meant to benefit many. And they are glad to be able to do something for someone else. In the Gospel, stewards who see their role as preserving the *status quo* lose everything, while those who use their intelligence, talent, ingenuity, and skill to transform things are commended.

In light of the biblical perspective on stewardship, I understand my own ministry as having been entrusted with a variety of goods—with people and their lives, with information and resources. But whether I am dealing with sensitive personnel issues or working to enhance the status of women, I believe that all of the things I do in my ministry of university administration can be seen as ways of calling the University to an authentic catholicity.

One area of my work, one that I will only briefly note here, although it tends to claim the lion's share of my time, is helping people in sensitive situations: those facing the prospect of retirement; those dealing with the failure of a relationship; those suffering from serious illness or the death of someone close. I also have to deal with many difficult or conflictual situations: disputes among faculty; disagreements between professors and students; harassment problems of one sort or another. At times I have to assist someone to leave the University. But even this aspect of my work advances the catholicity of the University. Fundamentally a Catholic university is a community of learning to be sure, but it is also a community of care and concern, one in which *all* persons are encouraged to grow in every way—in mind, in spirit, in knowledge and wisdom and understanding. And even if the final ideal is only achieved imperfectly, sincere, honest, and constant effort deserves the highest appreciation.

Another area of my work has to do with issues that arise pertaining to women faculty and students. Since these issues will illustrate how both the church and the university struggle to be Catholic, they will be the principal focus of my comments. I will briefly recount the arrival of women at Notre Dame, then review the ambivalent relationship toward women reflected in the history of the Catholic tradition, which is the overriding context of Catholic higher education. Finally I will comment on three projects and draw out how each reflects an authentic catholicity.

History of Women at Notre Dame

Notre Dame is a relative newcomer to the world of coeducation. Although women were enrolled in the Graduate School from its beginning in 1932, and women religious studied in the summers at Notre Dame since 1918, the University, founded in 1842, remained essentially a male bastion for 130 years. That changed in the fall of 1972 when the first 325 female undergraduates began classes at Notre Dame. Initially there was a cap on female admissions; it took almost two decades for the University to become fully coed. The cap was removed by the Board of Trustees in May 1991 and now women are admitted almost but not quite at parity with men.

The advent of women on the faculty preceded by only a few years their arrival in the student body. Father Theodore Hesburgh, C.S.C., was behind the move to bring women onto the faculty. In 1965, the first two women were appointed to the full-time faculty. These first two women faculty did not come into a hospitable environment, not necessarily because people were being outright hostile but because in most cases, those already at Notre Dame simply didn't know how to be receptive. Even faculty women who arrived a decade later have suggested that women perceive themselves to be held to higher or at least different standards for promotion and tenure. Some of those first women won promotion and tenure only as a result of a class action suit in 1980, in which they argued that men with lesser qualifications were being promoted. In the 1970s, when women faculty were few, they were also not well represented in other aspects of the academic enterprise, for instance, in departmental, administration and university committees. Happily many of these factors have improved over the last two decades, though clearly more needs to be done.

Many of the obstacles to including women in the academic enterprise on fully equal terms are not peculiar to Notre Dame but are issues with which American higher education in general struggles. Still, since only a small fraction of the more than 150-year history of the University includes women, we do lag behind our peer institutions in significant ways—in the number of women on the full-time faculty, particularly in the tenured ranks, for example.

Images of Women in Catholic Tradition

At the same time, Notre Dame's struggles are unique insofar as the wider context of Catholic higher education is the Catholic tradition. The character and tasks of a Catholic university are shaped by the religious and intellectual traditions of Catholicism. Here we inevitably encounter problems that are still working themselves out historically in the long-standing Roman Catholic tradition. An examination of this tradition would do much to explain why, at present, we experience a glaring lack of models of women teachers (except as teachers of children) in our heritage. Theologians and saints with the normative weight of an Augustine or a Thomas Aquinas disclose to us through their writings the very deep struggle that Christian theology and the Church have had in accepting women as the full Image of God, or as equal partners with men, or as necessary to men in any activity other than procreation. The *intellectual* and spiritual history of women in Christianity, which is directly related to teaching (and also to preaching), has yet to be written.

Allow me to take just a brief look at this tradition to which all Catholics, men and women alike, are heirs, a tradition that is living and unfinished and a tradition in which we still stand. The church and the academy have inherited Christian theology's love-hate relationship with women. There are, of course, biological misunderstandings in the tradition: the gross physiological errors of the theologians who thought, for example, that females are misbegotten males; the supposed ritual uncleanness of women that prevented women from even entering the sanctuary; the mythologies surrounding women's association with the original sin, with evil, with temptation. But here I am concerned mainly with the way in which women's abilities of mind and speech, both so closely related to teaching, were evaluated by significant theologians.

Women were believed to be inferior to men, not only physically but also intellectually. Augustine attributed Eve's fall to her weak mind which was foolish enough to believe the serpent. "As a child is to an adult," he said, "so is woman to man." More profoundly disturbing was Augustine's idea that woman lack the full image of God. Drawing on the writings of Paul, Augustine held that man is the image of God, woman the image of man. Woman was identified with the irrational side of the human psyche, with passions and lower reason. Thomas Aquinas, who did grant spiritual equality to the sexes, nonetheless was led astray by faulty biology. With Aristotle he agreed that, "women are lacking in firm rational judgment despite instances to the contrary. Their conduct is not based on solid reasons but is easily swayed by feelings. If a rare woman happens to be more learned or holy than a man, let her teach privately but not publicly." And St. Bernard once quipped of Eve, "She spoke once and threw the world into disorder." Clearly this is a dismal and ultimately non-Christian estimation of woman's intellectual capacities and her capacity to image God. Not surprisingly, this appraisal of women's intellectual endowment was carried over into the early institutional structures of the Church and beyond, and has been systematically reexamined only in the past twenty-five years.

Well, isn't this all changed now? Have not two great women saints been named doctors of the Universal Catholic Church? Most gratefully, yes. The title "Doctor of the Church" applies to those known for personal holiness, exceptional theological insights, and knowledge of the spiritual life. In 1970 the title was bestowed by Pope Paul VI on Teresa of Avila and Catherine of Siena; it signifies, among other things, women's capacity for true wisdom and learning, the appropriateness of women teachers, not to mention the tremendous holiness of the saints. Teresa and Catherine have been named permanently fruitful symbols of wisdom, teaching, writing, holiness, preaching, and contemplating the Word for all Christians.

Despite the significance of this declaration, ecclesiastical documents on women over the past twenty-five years still bear the vestiges of the concept of woman as lacking the eminence or the full power of reason that men possess. Papal documents convey a certain ambivalence toward women; the current pope simultaneously affirms women's social contribution, but highlights and romanticizes motherhood. In his "Letter to Women" issued July 10, 1995, in anticipation of the Fourth World Conference on Women in Beijing, Pope John Paul II refers to the historical and cultural conditioning that has created "an obstacle to the progress of women." He acknowledges that women have not been given credit for their intellectual contributions or their achievements in history and he apologizes for whatever part the Church has played in the marginalization of women.

The pope's letter is a strong and stirring affirmation of the dignity, equality, and giftedness of women. At the same time, however, the pope restates that women and men are complementary to each other, that certain gifts or qualities are divinely determined to belong to one sex only (e.g., public leadership to man; domestic work and motherhood to women). This stereotyping of characteristics as feminine (e.g., compassion, passivity, etc.) or masculine (e.g., power, authority, etc.) is problematic. It leads to assigning roles on the basis of gender rather than on the basis of gift or ability. This reinforcement of stereotypical gender expectations limits the potential of both men and women. The day for these incongruities is drawing to a close, I am certain of that; still my own experience tells me it is not over yet.

Opportunities for Change at Notre Dame

Some of the Church's main attitudes toward women have had a profound impact on a Catholic university struggling to maintain both catholicity and academic integrity. Notre Dame has worked hard to enhance the climate for women students, faculty, and staff. I will describe three recent efforts to enhance the status of women. It is worth repeating here, however, that I do not see these as only women's issues but as wider University issues. To speak of what benefits women is to speak of what benefits all in the University community. The examples described below are not unique to Notre Dame, but the issues well illustrate how the Church and the University struggle to be Catholic. They help us to see how a Catholic university is continually reshaped by its tradition and how, in advancing these efforts, the university is advancing its right to call itself Catholic.

Child care. An important addition to the campus in the fall of 1994 was the Early Childhood Development Center, an on-campus child-care facility. Not only did it have an over-full enrollment of 172 children in its first year of operation, there is a long and growing waiting list for admission. For twenty years the University had cooperated with and supported a child care program based at St. Mary's College (which is still the case today), but that program had reached its limits. I was convinced that the issue needed immediate and careful attention and so I formed a committee to study the matter and make appropriate recommendations.

Most of the literature we reviewed suggested the case for establishing child care should be made on the basis of the university's self-interest (e.g., hiring and retaining faculty). We were convinced, however, that the reasoning of a Catholic university had to go beyond the university's interests narrowly construed, and ought, in fact, to be considered as an expression of the university's mission. Consistent Catholic emphasis on the family and its centrality, as well as Church teaching on the need for institutional support for families, could certainly be used to encourage university support. The language used by the American bishops in their document on children and families, *Putting Children and Families First*, is that of a "creative partnership" between families and the supporting institutions. The bishops understand child care as a significant way to foster that partnership. In their earlier document, *Equal Justice for All*, the bishops stated that lack of day care can have a detrimental effect on women. This may be evidence of a growing awareness by the American bishops of women's changing role in society.

The on-campus child-care facility is one way that Notre Dame can support families in their care of children. Parental leave is another. Because parents can easily and regularly visit their children on campus, there is more interaction between parent and child than with other child-care options. I also know that it has helped to alleviate some of the stress felt by faculty with young children, who often feel torn between family and professional responsibilities.

Not long ago I was poignantly reminded of this experience of competing loyalties when I was reading a personal statement of a faculty member who said he almost lost his family in a frantic effort to finish his dissertation. This frightening possibility caused him to reevaluate and to realign his priorities; he put his family first. Given the increasing pressure on faculty to establish a research record as well as to participate in university and departmental activities outside of the normal work week, a Catholic university cannot view child care as a merely peripheral institutional concern.

Child care raises some other important issues that merit reflection, namely issues of family, of public and private roles for women and men, and of work. Although women still bear an inordinate responsibility for early child care, it is the case, at least on our campus, that more men are willing to share child and home care. I agree with Lisa Cahill of Boston College who observed that the very presence of child-caring fathers on campus helps to erode stereotypes of women (as maternal, relational nurturers) and as essentially "different from" men. Moreover, this more balanced sharing of both domestic and private roles by women and men is a move toward greater cooperation in the family. Rather than viewing this movement as a challenge to traditional Catholic values or as an accommodation to changing career expectations, we might see it as offering some possibilities for a new theology of family life, in which parenthood would be seen as the full responsibility of both partners. In her essay entitled "The Mystery of Being Human Together," Mary Aquin O'Neill, R.S.M., speculates on this possibility and suggests that,

> There is great promise for discovering, not only possibilities for the humanity of women to embrace ways of being and works traditionally reserved for men, but also the reverse. The humanity of men is equally capable of giving life and love; Catholic pedagogy must reveal that to them. The talk should be as much about fatherhood as about motherhood ... as much about fathers bringing up the child as mothers bringing the fetus to term. Most of all, Catholics should be led to discover in the ecclesiola [*the church in miniature*], as the Second Vatican Council called the family, a life as sacramentally real as that in the parish church. To do that, the church will require fathers as well as mothers in the home, mothers as well as fathers at the altar.

Finally, the child-care issue raises questions about work. The Catholic tradition sees human work as a critical part of human existence, as something that can either sustain or enslave us. At a recent symposium, two women graduates of Notre Dame, both university professors, indicated that the questions they ask about work have changed. They suggested there is a myth of productivity that implies that if one is not willing to spend sixty or seventy hours a week working, one is not really dedicated to, not really serious about scholarship. They questioned the self-absorption this encourages and asked whether it can produce healthy, balanced members of society, good parents, or even good science. They wondered if it is necessary to build an artificial wall between one's work life and one's personal life. As women have entered the public workplace, has it become a better place for everyone to be?

Inclusive Language. My first year as Associate Provost (1990) and Chair of the Faculty/Student Committee on Women coincided with the University's celebration of the Year of Women. It seemed an appropriate moment to formulate a gender-inclusive language policy. While some individual departments had already adopted a policy of using gender-inclusive language, the University as a whole had no such policy. I drafted a policy statement, a very modified version of which was accepted by the Faculty Senate and Academic Council, that calls upon members of the Notre Dame community to use respectful and gender-inclusive language in its official proclamations and documents and to adopt such usage in the conduct of their work. However small it may seem in retrospect, it was an important first step for the University to insist on such a policy, for it indicated a willingness to take concrete action.

Language is important; it shapes worlds of meaning and creates social systems. Male-centered language, because it renders women invisible and implies inferiority, works to the personal, political, and social disadvantage of women. While the University policy focuses on gender-inclusive language, it was written in the awareness that exclusive language can be based on other factors, such as race, or class, or physical ability. Moreover, carelessness about one group of persons can replicate itself as a patronizing attitude toward other groups with lesser status.

Scott Boehnen, a recent graduate of Notre Dame, reminded us in his valedictory of groups who intentionally create a destructive language because they realize the power language possesses. He challenged the graduates to start changing the world by changing the language the world uses, thus changing the way we think about a new world order, about the environment, and about half the human species. At the same time, he noted the appropriateness of looking to that universal community that takes the name Catholic to create a new language, a "Catholic" language, one that frames the very terms of debate on the most vexed problems of today's world.

While the issue of language remains controversial for some, in my view it goes right to the heart of our catholicity insofar as it tests our conversion to a community that welcomes everybody. Indeed, as my colleague Catherine LaCugna of the theology department has often noted, "becoming a community of inclusiveness ultimately has as much to do with language as with how we see ourselves and relate to one another."

Gender Quotas. Finally, another important step for the University was the gradual removal of gender quotas in undergraduate admissions. While the 1972 class of 325 female undergraduates accounted for 8 percent of the class, women now comprise 47 percent of current incoming classes. Father Hesburgh has often suggested that the admission of women was more than symbolic, for it raised the quality of the students and improved student life. As the University prepares to celebrate the twenty-fifth anniversary of co-education, however, it is essential to realize that to be truly co-educational means not just that women are present but that women's questions can be asked, and women's special issues will be taken seriously. At times those questions may be the same as men's, at other times different. Dr. Nancy Haegel, a 1981 graduate of the University, expressed this caution when she was recently presented by the Alumni Association with a Women's Award of Achievement. She suggested that a Catholic university should be "a place where a wider variety of questions could be asked. Questions from the mind, heart and soul." Also she noted that the task of true education might be that much harder at a Catholic university since, in fact, Catholic women's voices are seldom heard in the Church.

My principal point has been that issues pertaining to women are a good illustration of how the Church and the University struggle to be Catholic. Such issues help us to confront elements in the Catholic tradition that are non-Catholic, indeed ultimately even non-Christian, and they raise fundamental questions about what a fuller or more authentic catholicity would look like. They offer, therefore, particular evidence or non-evidence of the catholicity of the institution. Among other things, this discussion allows us to observe that we are evolving both as a university and as a church in our understanding of what the term "catholic" means.

Since the University communicates its Catholic religious identity both through what it says and what it does, through its official mission statement and also in the way it embodies justice, care, and respect in its practices and policies, then we cannot be indifferent about issues like child care, inclusive language, and the full incorporation of women in the academic enterprise. Indeed, in advancing these efforts Notre Dame is advancing its right to call itself catholic.

The Food of Truth

JOHN C. CAVADINI

What will the eternal life of the saints be like? This was the subject of a famous conversation, reported in Augustine's *Confessions*, between Augustine the newly baptized and his mother Monica. Its setting in the text is poignant, for it occurs as mother and son are waiting to take ship for a voyage back to their native Africa, a voyage which Monica will not live to make. Standing at a window overlooking a garden in the courtyard of their temporary lodging at Ostia on the Tiber, they are both anticipating their journey home, although the reader knows that Monica is to complete her journey in a sense other than the one expected. The exact words of the conversation are not preserved, but Augustine reports that their joint venture in imagination also had results beyond their expectations:

> There we talked together, she and I alone, in deep joy . . . discussing what the eternal life of the saints could be like. . . . And our conversation had brought us to this point, that any pleasure whatsoever of the bodily senses, in any brightness whatsoever of physical light, seemed to us not worthy of comparison with the pleasure of that eternal Light, not worthy even of mention. Rising as our love flamed upward towards that Selfsame, we passed in review the various levels of bodily things, up to the heavens themselves, whence sun and moon and stars shine upon this earth. And higher still we soared, thinking in our minds and speaking and marveling at Your works: and so we came to our own souls, and went beyond them to come at last to that region of richness unending, where

John Cavadini is Associate Professor of Theology.

You feed Israel with the food of truth: and there life is that Wisdom by which all things are made. . . . And while we were thus talking of His Wisdom and panting for it, with all the effort of our heart we did for one instant touch it; then sighing, we left the first fruits of our spirits bound to it. . . . (*Confessions* 9.10, translation by F. J. Sheed, adjusted)

The passage is arresting in its beauty and it prompts us to look closer. We notice that in fact Augustine and Monica are talking all the way through the passage. The so-called "vision" at Ostia could equally well be called the "conversation" at Ostia, for Augustine and Monica's dramatic vision of truth is wholly coincident with their conversation. The vision does not come after it as its fruit, but in the course of it. The text is very clear— there is no interruption of the conversation, not the slightest instant of separation between the conversation and the moment of vision, but rather the "vision" occurs "while we were talking." Further, the vision is shared. It is not the Neoplatonic escape of each "alone into the alone," but the sudden deepening of a conversation to the point of shared insight, arising from and experienced through talk.

What will the eternal life of the saints be like? Judging from this passage, the nearest experience we have of it now is in conversation, not so much with God, but with each other, at leisure, the pleasure of "just sitting around talking," as Dorothy Day says in another context regarding the start of the first Catholic Worker house of hospitality. And despite the fantasies which teachers may furtively indulge on occasion, the most important conversations at college, at seminary, or at graduate school are probably the ones that go on outside of the classroom, where hopes and dreams, visions and ideals, strategies and projects, disappointments and disillusionments are shared, and the moment of deepening insight is also a moment of deepening affection or admiration or respect. This is the touching of Wisdom with the effort of the heart, the momentary attainment to the place where "God feeds Israel with the food of truth," not yet the whole truth, but a glimpse, a moment with a legacy of longing and empowerment that extends beyond the years at school, to a life, in society at large, bent on and hungering for truth.

Therefore, when at Commencement and Convocations, along with the University Mace and many overstated (if irresistible) bathrobes, the Pursuit of Truth is extracted from camphor and exhibited in spectacles of rhetoric as the most precious of all the exotic specimens in the possession of the University, we ought to take it with a grain of salt. In a way, of course, the pursuit of truth is a precious possession of the University. But, if it belonged only or even especially to the University, there would be little reason to engage in it at all. The University cannot credibly aspire to being the only or even the primary locus of the pursuit of truth. As enamored as I am of the classroom, or even of graduation ceremonies (in proper dosage), I am hoping that the life of the saints in Heaven will not have too much resemblance to an eternal commencement ceremony, however gala the heavenly robes, or to the universe's largest classroom, even if it is the very Logos who is perpetual lecturer. If the conversation, not the speech, is the ultimate locus of the pursuit of truth, then my role as a teacher must be to further the aims and aspirations of conversations which will not occur primarily in my classroom or even, ultimately, at school. I regard it as the primary task of school studies in the liberal arts to contribute to this pursuit by imparting to the student's conversation a share of sophistication and attentiveness which makes it possible for a student to own his or her own voice ever more fully, and to listen ever more capably to the nuances and moment of someone else's most deeply held convictions, hopes, and dreams. It is my job to elevate and enlarge the capacity for the sincere and mutually illuminating conversation that binds people in affection or respect. It is in this way that I regard myself as contributing towards "clarification of thought," to take another phrase from Catholic Worker lore which I sometimes adopt as a synonym for "pursuit of truth."

This "conversational paradigm" affects the mechanics of my teaching in very specific ways, evident (I hope) from my comments on a typical first day of class. On the first day of class I talk to students about paper writing. I explain that one thing we will be making a very big deal about in here is "precision," explaining further that I distinguish "precision" from "accuracy" ("Talk about splitting hairs. . ." one student seems to sigh). "Accuracy" is a prerequisite for precision but can never be an adequate substitute. "For example, friends," I continue, "it is accurate to say that both ants and antelopes are animals, but it does not give you a very precise notion of either. It is accurate to say that both St. Benedict and Billy Graham teach love of God and neighbor, but that does not give a very precise sense of either one. It is accurate to say that for St. Thomas "charity" and "art" are virtues, but that is not enough to help someone understand why from Thomas's view charity will bring you to the life of the saints but art on its own will not."

Continuing, I try to explain how "precision" is also distinguished from cliché, as its exact opposite. Clichés are comforting, since almost everyone will nod their heads in agreement when they read or hear them, but they are not very precise and sometimes not even accurate. For example, "St. Benedict is very anti-materialistic" is a sentence which relies for what negligible impact it has on a cliché that people with spiritual aspirations of some sort are opposed to "materialism." That does not give us a very robust or precise picture of Benedict, who was not in any way against matter or material goods, but hoped that by sharing all possessions in common monks would learn to form communities which did not pay deference to the status private wealth confers. Far from finding your own voice, reliance on cliché is a way of renouncing your own voice, and with it the pursuit of truth. To rely on cliché is to rely on the comfortable voice of the culture at large, to become its uncritical channel, transmitting all its truism, its dull and sometimes hurtful commonplaces. "A cliché is like a placeholder for meaning," I hear myself saying. "It enables the reader to keep reading with no lapse in grammar or sense, but with only a minimal level of commitment to a position from the writer. A cliché is like a black hole in the middle of a paper, sucking all the hapless precision in its immediate environs out of sentences and paragraphs, swirling it all into a dark meaning-void . . ." ("a meaning *what*?" someone seems to think, as I notice a face settle into that grim look of resolve, "Remind me to drop this class!").

Continuing, I explain that the quest for precision is the quest for one's own voice, for the ability to represent oneself ever more deeply and fully in a conversation, and to be able to listen ever more carefully and attentively to what the other voices in the conversation are saying. "In this way," I explain, "the preparation of papers and the research that goes into them are preludes to and the bases for conversation. In a paper, you offer a reading of a text, as accurate and precise and imaginative as you can make it, and that then becomes the basis for entering into conversation with others, some of whom have done the same. Your preparation enables you both to speak and to hear better, both about the texts themselves and about issues which they raise (or fail to raise)." I try to explain, too, that the primary locus of this "pursuit of truth" which the quest for precision represents will ultimately not be in this classroom (no surprise registering on any faces on that score), and will not even be at school, but beyond in the life of the student when he or she has left the University, in the shared give and take of common life.

Seeing hints of incredulity around the room, I try to emphasize that the usefulness of the virtues that go into success at school exercises is not limited to school ("That's right," the faces of those shifting in their seats seem to say, "we all want to spend the rest of our lives cramming for finals"). Tempted beyond my resistance, I hear my voice launching into an anecdote. "I myself learned one particular virtue of communication—the virtue of being concise—completely apart from an academic context, when I worked in a previous life as a municipal Sanitation Collector." ("Now *that* sounds *really* useful," someone seems to think.) "For some of my five years as a garbage collector I was Union Representative for our Local, and in that capacity I came one day to write up my first grievance against the Town on behalf of a fellow employee. I was thrilled with the two-page (single-spaced) result over which I had labored long hours and in which I had employed many lovely rhetorical flourishes not only about our contract but about justice in general and the rights of workers in particular, the dignity of humanity and of labor, the doctrines of popes and even the Theodosian Code (omitted from the final draft), and other compelling extras like the timeliness of response expected, etc. When I received my written reply the next day I ripped it open with confidence. No one could possibly have rebutted my arguments in such a short time, even if they could have recovered from being dazzled by them. I was greeted with a response that took up all of one line. The letter, rather dryly, noted, 'Grievance denied.' Translation: 'Could you please get to the point, John?'"

Thankfully, one person in the room manages to laugh (presumably having already learnt the meaning of charity or at least art). Someone else remarks, "What you really learned was that you needed a new job, right?" (More laughs . . .)

But what *will* the eternal life of the saints be like? Can miracles occur? What is the road to God? As a teacher of the history of theology, it is my job after the first day of class to consider the ways in which the tradition has answered these and questions like these. I aim to provide students with a sense of the richness and breadth of the theological tradition, and thus to make it possible for students to draw upon that tradition, and in increasingly sophisticated ways, in their own conversation.

It is here most of all, however, that we encounter the struggle against Public Enemy No. 1, cliché, and this applies not only to answers to the questions we bring to the texts, but above all to the questions themselves. When we ask, "Can miracles occur?" we assume a) that we know what a miracle is, and b) that theologians and persons of faith in the past have had the same understanding that we have. Is it sufficient, or even necessary, to talk about miracle as a "violation of natural law?" Students tend to assume that ancient thought is more naive, less sophisticated than modern up-to-date thinking, especially since ancient thought was not "scientific" in our sense. And in one sense this is true. We certainly have the right to ask *our* questions, questions which do take into account world-views which the ancients and medievals did not have, the lack of which makes them seem "naive." But this means only that we have to go more carefully—more precisely—in search of *their* sophistication, to acquire a sense of their questions and the thoroughness of their approach to the answers. Origen, for instance, considers the question of miracles as closely tied to the question of "magic" and provides a sustained discussion of the difference. We no longer worry so much about "magic" or "sorcery" *per se*, but it is interesting to think about whether some of what *we* would include under "miracle" *he* would worry about under the category of "magic." Does acquiring a sense for his question as well as his answers help us in any way to have perspective on our own questions and thus help us with our own answers? Can we get a better sense of the limitations of the way in which *we* ask questions, even as we see that we in fact do need to ask them?

The same is true for certain questions of biblical interpretation. Students come to class assuming that, owing to modern scientific theory, our own period is unique in having difficulty with the literal interpretation of (e.g.) the Adam and Eve story. They imagine that the tradition is uniformly more credulous regarding this story, and it is interesting for them to find that in fact the literal interpretation of Genesis 2 has been difficult for many Jews and Christians since at least the first century, although for reasons different from our own. For example, on philosophical grounds both Philo and Origen (Jew and Christian, respectively) wondered whether the story, if taken literally, were worthy of God. What kind of a God is it who wanders about in a garden having lost track of the very beings he just created, and must resort to asking them where they are? Sophisticated allegorical interpretations of the passage were developed to deal with just these difficulties. We of course will not want to repeat the allegories to answer our own questions, but a lesson in the degree to which these difficulties were felt and the degree of care and sophistication taken to answer them—with checks and balances all their own meant to preclude allegorical interpretations which were simply arbitrary—can help us as we consider the parameters we might use in our own struggles to articulate the non-literal levels of meaning in this text and others.

A final example might be the category of "vision." What does it mean to have a vision? Students often assume that this is a relatively straightforward thing. Visions are hallucinations and modern people recognize them as such and have learned to dismiss texts based on reports of visions as simply naive. How odd to regard these as in any sense revelations from God!—as the twelfth-century theologian Hildegard of Bingen clearly does in her work the *Scivias*, wholly structured as it is around a series of visions she received. Students are therefore often surprised to find that Hildegard herself not only struggled to clarify what she meant by a "vision," but that she used her special, visionary experience as a resource for problematizing the broader category of vision itself, that is, of the "normal" vision we use when we see the world with our eyes. Perhaps, she suggests, our view of the world is not as objective as we think; perhaps it is so deeply formatted by self-centeredness that it is in fact distorted; and that were we to begin to be healed from such "pride" (as Augustine would call it) the very way in which we see the world would change. Perhaps, she suggests, it is time for a revisioning of the world from a new perspective, one based on the love revealed in the Passion of Christ and available to us in the Eucharist. Hildegard invites all her readers, in the twentieth as well as the twelfth century, to rethink our reflexive acceptance of what we in fact do see as the same as what we ought to see.

As I hope to have made clear by now, it is my aim to encourage students on all levels to see the tradition as a resource for the "clarification of thought." I try to encourage what I think of as "critical appropriation" of the tradition, which I distinguish both from a) simply repeating past positions as though their contemporary application were completely unproblematic (hence "critical"), and from b) regarding the tradition as mostly irrelevant, or even pernicious (hence "appropriation"). I want students to come to be able to reflect too, on the idea of tradition itself—on how a tradition grows, on its moments of continuity and discontinuity, on the streams of reading and rereading, interpretation and reinterpretation, triumphs and achievements, as well, too, as on the obsession and blindspots and distortions. Wouldn't we want to rethink the Crusades? If Bernard of Clairvaux approved them, Francis of Assisi was disgusted by them, and perhaps his reaction deserves a second look. Why haven't the women's voices in our tradition been heard loudly enough? It is time to listen more carefully. And, as John Paul II has made clearer than any of his predecessors, it is time too to disown the anti-Jewish rhetoric that has come to be so deeply ingrained in parts of our tradition. Perhaps the Augustinian rhetoric of critique of all cultural forms in the light of God's self-emptying love in Christ may serve as our resource for renewal on this score (and others).

Students sometimes complain about the difficulty of the texts we read in class. And it is true, as I am regularly forced to concede, that (e.g.) copies of Thomas's *Summa Theologica* are not among the top ten items most frequently accompanying family trips to the beach ("Just what I always take when I go to the beach," one student laconically mused, "'Honey, I packed the *prima pars* next to the beachball and sun lotion, OK?' NOT"). I point out that this is exactly why we read them here, in class, where we are able to think carefully about them and learn to talk precisely amongst ourselves about what they mean and about the issues they raise. Nonplussed, many students in a required theology course find to their dismay their preliminary expectations fully vindicated—that Thomas is an acquired taste—and yet, as I try to warn them, many tastes, once acquired, are addictive (like coffee), and reading Thomas once is at least to take the risk, however slight from their point of view, of someday finding oneself sneaking a miniature-sized copy of *Question* 1, disguised as a deck of playing cards, to the Outer Banks, or the Virgin Islands, or wherever one goes to get away.

Apart from my teaching, my work in the department also involves research and writing, and I find myself very often forced by circumstances to reflect on the connection between these two sets of activities. On the one hand, I worry about the effects that the high profile rhetoric of "national research institution" has had on undergraduates. Students in general tend to learn of their own importance and of the importance of their education partly through the eyes of others. If they are taken seriously, they learn to take themselves seriously. If they sense that they are not an institution's first priority, they *learn* not to take their own education seriously. To headline the rhetoric of "a national research institution" is to risk a university culture in which the prestige associated with being an undergraduate, and with teaching them, is threatened. On the other hand, if one imagines research to be a kind of specialized learning, then it is easy to see how both teaching and research can be common elements in the larger enterprise of learning, and must then at least partly coincide. For example, if it is true that in preparing and giving the lectures for my medieval survey "Roads to God" I am primarily "teaching," it is no less true that in attempting to construct and refine a coherent survey of medieval theology I have developed a reading of a set of texts from Gregory's *Dialogues* and Bernard's *Homilies on the Song of Songs* to Teresa's *Interior Castle* and Pascal's *Pensées* which I hope at some point to turn into a book. Even the act of delivering a lecture or of responding to student comment and question is as much learning as it is teaching, because the attempt to articulate an insight or clarify a point to someone having difficulties understanding is a constructive moment which begets further insight and new agendas—"clarification of thought" (and as a bonus is also very entertaining to students, who like to see you try to think on your feet—translate, "sweat").

Teachers who continue to identify themselves as learners are much more likely to find themselves open to learning from their students' insights and conversation. Teachers who themselves are active writers are much more likely to understand students' problems in writing and to come up with creative ways to help them. Further, teachers who themselves are active readers can speak with conviction and pleasure to students about the skills of critical and careful reading. Teachers who identify themselves as continuing students in their discipline pay their own students the immense compliment of taking students' learning seriously and of growing with them. In this way, students learn to value their own selves as learners, and so to acquire the characteristics we associate with an educated person—the ability to ask useful or interesting questions, to make articulate and graduated judgments of assent or dissent, to respect other people's judgments and ways of being while at the same time submitting all claims (including one's own) to a continuing critical scrutiny.

We all know that the detailed results of one's research do not always or even often enter the classroom. But one's own research is a kind of reservoir of insight and energy, a kind of spiritual resource which enables one to teach with poise and confidence. Unmitigated teaching is draining, to the point where one feels one has nothing left to give. It is difficult to share the joys of search and insight, the aesthetics of learning and of disciplined self-expression and dialogue, if the exigencies of teaching are so pervasive that one has no time to attend to the formation of one's own voice. Finally, however, research cannot stand on its own as an absolute good in a university setting. At least in arts and letters, the more distant research gets from teaching and from the day-to-day exigencies of explanation and critique, the less one has to explain oneself in basic terms on the beginning level, the more infrequently one must return to the fundamental texts and assumptions of one's discipline—then the more dislocated and disconnected one's research gets from a human context, and it becomes progressively less humane, less liberal, and ultimately irrelevant. In a sense it comes down to a kind of uneasy balance or tension which can't be entirely resolved because each is necessary to the flourishing of the other, and sometimes precisely in forms and under conditions which for a given space of time precludes the other. Balance here is a question of the mutual perspective each activity provides on the other, with the bottom-line first priority necessarily reserved for teaching.

What will the eternal life of the saints be like? Even on the long, daily walks I take across the quad to and from the Rock I have yet to overhear a student conversation on precisely that topic. Yet on this very walk I have (accidentally of course) overheard more than my share of conversations bordering (for me) on the poignancy of the one shared overlooking the garden at Ostia. Recently I overheard a discussion between three hefty boys coming from, I imagined, their workout at the Rock. One had seen the movie "Dead Men Walking" and the other two, apparently death penalty advocates, had not and were in fact determined not to see it. The first spent his walk from the Rock arguing down the arguments advanced by the other two on behalf of the death penalty, resisting not only the arguments, but also the subtle insinuation that to be against the death penalty was somehow not appropriately masculine enough. The whole second half of the walk was occupied with the soliloquy-like reply of the first student, who first worried that mistakes were bound to be made and innocent people killed, but then rested his case on a point about the admittedly guilty— that they too were human, that vengeance is a never-ending circle, that with our limited, finite knowledge we did not have the prerequisite perspectives to make decisions about which person's actions warranted death, and that refusing to enact the death penalty meant leaving the most ultimate questions of justice for God alone to judge. The earnestness in his voice left its mark in the other students' silence, and all, including the surreptitious fourth party to the conversation, seemed to share a long moment of deepening insight to match the deepening shadows of the afternoon. I spent the rest of my own walk homeward careful to savor a moment of vicarious joy on behalf of this student's teachers, but mostly feeling that somewhere back there on the path through the quad we had stumbled, however evanescently, upon that region of abundance where "God feeds Israel" unfailingly "with the food of truth."

Women at Our Lady's University

Often, when I introduce myself to people at meetings or conferences and tell them that I teach at the University of Notre Dame, the first question is, "How does a woman manage in that macho atmosphere?" The fame of the football team combined with the less than a twenty-five–year history of women on campus manage to give Notre Dame a reputation as a men's school that allows women to attend. While it surprises me more now than it did a dozen years ago, the question is valid and one about which I have had many conversations with other women on campus. The question always strikes me as somewhat ironic, though, given that the symbol of Notre Dame, recognized worldwide, is the statue of Mary standing on top of the Golden Dome.

The question is also not unique to Notre Dame but one that women at every Catholic college face. "Our nation's Catholic colleges are not sanctuaries for everyone, but are instead diverse and daring environments where women struggle every day with issues of justice, experience of marginality, and clashes with discrimination."[1] Many of the women I spoke to at Notre Dame echoed those sentiments.

The response of women at Notre Dame to so-called women's issues is similar to that of women at other universities, in business, and in society at large. There are some women who delight in being at Notre Dame and who do not perceive any difficulties. There are others who focus only on the problems that women have had and continue to have. But, like most

Sister Regina Coll, C.S.J., is Professional Specialist and Director of Field Education in the Theology Department.

of the women I associate with, I find myself somewhere in the middle, enjoying, relishing even, my years at Notre Dame while at the same time experiencing anger and discouragement at what I perceive to be decisions or behaviors that are insensitive to women. Notre Dame has been a welcoming and supportive place; it has also been a source of disappointments and frustrations. One of my friends maintains that that is because so much more is expected of Notre Dame. Be that as it may, in this essay, I will share both the joys and delights and the pain and frustration of being a Notre Dame Woman.

Last year, a special issue of *Initiatives*, the Journal of the National Association for Women in Higher Education, focused on "Feminism on a Catholic Campus." Their choice of language may be more to the point: the question is not just women on Catholic campuses but feminists on Catholic campuses (that, of course, includes some of our male colleagues).

The women and men at Notre Dame who people my days and the extraordinary moments known as "Notre Dame moments" have become precious parts of my life. My dozen years here have put me in touch with some of the most interesting and involved people I know. I was more at home in my first month here than I was after two years at another Catholic university. That is saying a great deal for someone who has all the chutzpah of New Yorkers who really do think that the world is composed of New York and everywhere else.

The students whom I meet are bright, interested in learning, and fun to be with. Their enthusiasm for life and their conviction that they can contribute to a better future inspires me. My work with the women and men who are preparing for ministry in the Master of Divinity Program moderates my skepticism, revives my lost idealism, and gives me great hope for the Church in the next millennium. To see young people so committed to Christ and to the Church convinces me of the value of the teaching ministry I am involved in.

I do not mean to suggest by these remarks that the M.Div. students are starry-eyed or naive and uncritical about our society or our Church. They are Christians who struggle with the great questions and issues that confront today's Church and who are committing their lives to service in and with and for that Church. Our M.Div. graduates hold significant ministerial positions in dioceses, parishes, hospitals, campuses, and service organizations dedicated to alleviating suffering in society. While I could say so much more about the M.Div program and the talented women and men who are involved in the program, I will leave that to Mark Poorman, C.S.C., who is focusing on our program in his essay.

Each year I teach an undergraduate course in feminist theology and find that as the years have passed, the students are better prepared and able to think more critically about the issues that are being raised by feminist scholars. The women and men in that course, for the most part, have theology as a first or second major. Since it is an elective for juniors and seniors, the students come with some maturity, a great interest in the topic, and an eagerness to put their faith in conversation with feminist theologians. It is exciting to see them struggle with the ongoing conversation between Feminism and Christianity. Each year the course gets more interesting; the questions and issues raised by the students more significant and the discussions more challenging. Each year I learn something new about the Church from the students who have no live memory of the pre–Vatican II Church. Their interests, ideas, and questions seem so much more significant than mine were at their age.

In the fall semester 1995, I team-taught the course with Catherine Mowry LaCugna for the first time. As with most who attempt team-teaching, we were discovering and inventing the process as we went along. Usually, one of us made the initial presentation and the other followed by addressing the material in a different way. The students were unusually verbal; at first the small number of men (7) more so than the women. But as the term progressed, the women responded to our expectations that they find their voices. Discussions were lively and students learned from each other as well as from us. Catherine and I learned to present our prepared material in the midst of questions, challenges, and alternative opinions.

No matter the topic—and we surveyed theological topics

from the Trinity, Christology, anthropology, ecclesiology to ethics, social justice, and spirituality—the students kept returning to the thread that we hoped tied the course together: relationality. Speaking of God as relational in Godself; of human beings as related to God, to self, to others, and to the universe led to the idea of human responsibility—to God, to self, and to all creation.

In planning the semester, we decided that the students would benefit from hearing the women theologians whom we are fortunate to have on the theology faculty. We asked each of our colleagues to speak about her ongoing research so that the students would have the opportunity to see how theology develops and how theologians struggle with questions. The bright side of that decision is that the students heard scholars of the caliber of Mary Rose D'Angelo, Josephine Ford, Blake Leyerle, Jean Porter, Maura Ryan, visitor Elizabeth Johnson, C.S.J., and doctoral student Susie Babka. Our guest lecturers added a richness that Catherine and I alone would not have been able to share. They explained their methodology, spoke of insights they had garnered in their research, and of the questions that still remained to be pursued. Sharing our podium with so many others reinforced the message that we announced at the beginning of the semester. We did not want to press our agenda, to create clones who thought as we did; rather we tried to expose the students to the broad and sophisticated literature that is feminist theology.

The down side of our decision to invite our colleagues to class is that both Catherine and I felt that we did not have enough time with the class. There were so many ideas we wanted to discuss, so many issues that needed further study, so many questions that still need pursuing. I feel as if I have half the course still bottled up inside me.

Like other academics, I serve on a variety of committees. Many of these committees—both official and unofficial—focus on the role and participation of women at Notre Dame. One committee of which I am most proud is one which worked for four years to inaugurate the Gender Studies Program. Sonia Gernes and Joanne Aldous and I formed a troika of sorts and with the help of many other women entered into a process that was at times frustrating, at times energizing, and always surprising. We met with deans, faculty, students, and development persons; we wrote grant proposals, criteria for course inclusion, and a vision statement. What we tried to do was to develop a vision, produce a structure, and introduce a new program into the curriculum that focused on issues of gender. In 1988 the Gender Studies concentration was finally a part of the Notre Dame curriculum. It started with seven cross-listed courses, nineteen faculty, and fifteen students. The Gender Studies Program is now a thriving concentration (Notre Dame's identification of a minor), involving eighty faculty, offering more than forty-three courses to approximately seventy-nine concentrators and other interested students.

The influence of the Gender Studies Program extends far beyond the course curriculum. The directors have been creative in focusing attention on gender issues. Kathleen Biddick currently serves as the director and graduate student Marie Kramb as coordinator. Among their many initiatives are the newsletter *Gender Matters*, a Faculty Forum on Gender, an annual award for Outstanding Scholarship on Gender Issues, another for undergraduate students in Excellence in the Creative Arts, and the recent creation of a Gender Studies Web page. The Gender Studies Critical Issues Roundtable addresses current issues on campus and often takes action on these issues. At this writing, the final stages of preparation for the first annual conference on Graduate Research in Gender Studies at Notre Dame are just about finalized. This concentration is one of the most active on campus and has contributed greatly to the changing atmosphere for women.

A second committee—informal and unofficial—is composed of a group of women and men who have claimed for themselves the title, "The Committee on Notre Dame's Position on the Ordination of Women." We were careful in the wording of our title to note that we are not a committee sponsored by Notre Dame but rather are a committee committed to keeping the question alive on campus. We are a group of faculty who are concerned for the Church, its mission, ministry, and ministers. Interestingly enough, this committee came into being not because of theologians but because a graduate of the Business School wrote to her former professor, John Houck, of the pain she experienced because of the Church's present stand on the ordination of women to the priesthood. She expressed her disappointment that her cherished Notre Dame was not taking a leadership role in helping to redefine women's role in the Church. John had never even thought about the question before but her letter forced him to attend to the issue. What we have here is another case, so common among teachers, where professors learn from their students. CNDPOW, as we are affectionately called, has invited bishops, theologians, ministers, faculty, and students to speak, debate, conduct workshops and prayer services on the many facets of ministry in the Roman Catholic Church.

Since his awakening to feminist concerns, John regularly takes his classes to the famous Word of Life Mural on the Hesburgh Library wall facing the football stadium, generally referred to as "Touchdown Jesus." He asks them to study the mural and to discuss what they see. It takes a while but eventually some students recognize that there are no women in the mural. John delights in proposing that we need another mural on the Hesburgh Library wall.

A student group that was fostered by the CNDPOW is called SAIM, Student Advocates for Inclusive Ministry. They have been recognized by the University, receive the same privileges as other clubs, and have a small budget with which to pursue their vision. One of their first projects undertaken by these students was to interview their bishops and pastors about the role of women in the Church. For the most part, that experience was a positive one. One bishop encouraged and challenged his student visitor to continue the work of SAIM with the reminder that Ginger Rogers did everything Fred Astaire did, but in high heels and backwards. Another bishop told his visitors to hold on to their ideals. "Young people get things done," he said.

Under the tutelage of Kathleen Beatty, S.S.J., SAIM has also conducted retreats and prayer days and sponsored lectures and panels, many of which are co-sponsored by CNDPOW. The programs sponsored by SAIM have helped me to understand these young post–Vatican II people better. They have lived their whole lives in a Church that is redefining itself and cannot fathom some of the ongoing ecclesial difficulties. In one of the panels, a young woman spoke of her desire to be ordained since she was twelve. She said, "Now I am twenty and I am tired of the struggle!" Tired, indeed! But for young Catholics, who have not lived through the changes in the Church, it seems as if nothing has ever changed—a situation that they do not easily understand, given the pace of change in society today. No matter, they are the hope for the future—Catholics who love their Church and who want to help it to be all it can be.

While there have been many exciting advances for women on campus, it would be a mistake to suggest that we have approached anything like utopia at Notre Dame. As a feminist, I am only too aware of the shortcomings of the University and the difficulties experienced by many women.

It is a *sine qua non* of feminism that the personal is political, and conversely, the political is personal. Therefore, in order to discuss my experience at Notre Dame, it is advisable to place Notre Dame within the larger context of university life in these United States and within the culture of the Roman Catholic Church. Individual women's experiences at ND may best be understood in the light of today's culture, especially the culture of Catholic universities.

In preparing this article, I spoke with women faculty and administrators, with groups of women students, and with women at other Catholic universities. For the most part, Catholic women who teach at Catholic universities appreciate their Catholicism and identify themselves as Catholic. That definition, of course, covers a broad spectrum of Christians who claim the name Catholic. Judith Wilt, Chair of the Department of English at Boston College, identifies three sources of identity for these women. Having been nourished by a Church that teaches the dignity of each human being, having learned from feminist theory to celebrate womanhood, and having been recognized by the academy as an intellectual, they are able to identify themselves as Catholic, Feminist Academics. But the source of their strength is often the source of their problem as they attempt to bridge the divide between those three roots of their identity. They are variously identified as "the administration's tame feminist, feminism's tame Catholic and Catholicism's lame apologist for the institution's devotion to . . . 'mere secular academic freedom.'"[2] Trying to live all three with integrity often invites the response Wilt describes.

Women at the University

Studies and surveys indicate that universities are dangerous places for women. I am not speaking about the dangers to women's bodies, even though college-age women, eighteen to twenty-two years olds, are most at risk for rape, especially date rape and other forms of sexual harassment. I am not speaking about insulting and disturbing messages women might receive in e-mail or by phone or the graffiti scratched into the carrels in the library. These forms of harassment, typical in so many university settings, are well documented and help us to understand the intimidation that is inflicted on women every day. I do not even refer to 'sexist humor' that is sometimes used by professors to spice up an otherwise dull lecture. The danger to women to which I refer does not have to do with those kinds of demeaning treatment. I speak of faculty—both women and men who *inadvertently* communicate negative attitudes toward women concerning their abilities, career choices, and personal goals. The Project on the Status and Education of Women conducted by the Association of American Colleges is one among the many surveys that indicate that female students are less likely to be called on than male students, they are interrupted more often than men, encouraged less, receive less eye contact, and get less informal feedback.

Recent articles on the topic speak of women "losing their voice" as a result of this unconscious prejudice abound. Bright women who until their teens showed self-assurance and assertiveness learn that the consequences of such behavior may be more than they are willing to accept. Women who find their voice and who do speak up or challenge are called strident for the very same behavior for which their male colleagues are rewarded. Many of the women I meet in class still have to learn the lesson of poet Adrienne Rich—they must unlearn not to speak.

We end the undergraduate course on feminist theology with a short prayer service. Last year, the student-liturgists took as their theme, "Find Your Voice." They prayed to have the courage to speak even when their remarks may not be taken as seriously as their male counterparts or when their contributions are not accepted, or even when they are just beginning to think through an issue. Of course, one of the results of losing one's voice is that one's ideas and thoughts do not have the benefit of feedback, they are not challenged or affirmed, and therefore do not develop as easily as they might.

An experiment conducted by members of the Modern Language Association indicated that papers assigned a male name received higher grades than the exact same paper assigned a female name. This, from both male and female professors. I would like to repeat that much of this behavior is inadvertent and that male and female professors are equally guilty. The unconscious biases inherent in the greater society have a unique way of manifesting themselves on campus.

While we have done no studies at Notre Dame, there is nothing that convinces me that faculty here are any different from elsewhere. My discussions with faculty, graduate, and undergraduate women provided sufficient evidence to enable me to make that judgment.

I regret what individual women, the university, the church, and the world are missing because of the "lost voice" phenomenon. In recent years, Notre Dame has admitted students who average in the top 6 or 7 percent of their high school graduating class. Women of this caliber need to be encouraged and supported in their development. It seems to me that Notre Dame has a double responsibility in this area. First as a university, but more importantly, as a Catholic institution. The foundational Christian doctrine that every human being is made in the image of God demands no less.

We, women and men who teach at Notre Dame, have not yet been able to discover how to address this phenomenon.

Morale among academics is influenced by recognition of their work, acceptance of peers, and also by salary and status considerations. According to statistics compiled by the American Association of University Professors, women full professors at the top twenty-five universities earn considerably less than their male counterparts. Notre Dame ranks fifteenth on this list, which sets it on the better side of the negative curve for women. Happily, it is not included in the list of Roman Catholic Colleges (Boston College, Fordham, and Catholic University) identified as *notable* because of large gender gaps in salary. We might say, bad as things are, they are not so bad.[3]

The situation is not quite so rosy regarding the number of women who are administrators, full professors, or hold chairs at Notre Dame. In his annual report to the faculty, Provost Timothy O'Meara reported that in 1985, thirty-five men and two women were chair holders; ten years later, seventy-eight men and two women were chair holders. He writes that "[w]ithout awareness of these subtle inequalities in treatment, it is unlikely that things will change."[4]

Catholic Notre Dame

Catholic colleges and universities are reflecting on what it means to be Catholic in response to the 1990 mandate of the Apostolic Constitution on Catholic Universities. At Notre Dame, faculty and administrators who addressed the topic generally agree that the Catholic character of a university is not just determined by the number of Catholic faculty; nor in the number of priests, sisters, and brothers who serve the university; nor even in the number of masses celebrated each week. The institution itself must be recognizably Catholic in its life and operation. Mary Boys (in writing about Boston College) contends that "A university also teaches about its religious identity by the way it is itself Church, i.e., by the way its structures, policies, personnel, and curriculum embody and develop justice, mercy and care."[5] Issues of social justice, so

significant in ecclesial documents of this century, demand
attention to injustice wherever it is found. We might look at
salaries of staff, or consider if our investments are in line with
the pastoral letter of the United States Bishops, "Economic
Justice for All." Or we might attend more to racism and sexism
on campus, the American bishops having labeled both as sin.
All of these issues have been raised in the lectures and panels
presented by faculty and administrators on the question of
Notre Dame's Catholic character.

Less has been done on the effect on women of some
Catholic ideas. In their attempts to be faithful to Catholic
tradition, Catholic colleges need to be aware of the consequences of the Catholic predilection to identify women by
their physiology (mother, virgin, whore). This and the emphasis
in some recent official documents on an anthropology that is
based on complementarity between women and men militates
against acceptance of women's intellectual and leadership gifts.
If women 'complete' men and that complementarity is
determined by God, then women's roles, talents, abilities, and
even virtues are different from men.

Virginity and motherhood are identified by Pope John Paul
II as "two particular dimensions of the fulfillment of the female
personality." Virginity and motherhood are called "the two
different vocations of women." Women in religious vows are
referred to as "spiritual mothers."[6] Defining women by what
they do or do not do with their bodies ignores the whole female
person—mind, soul, spirit—as well as body. In an atmosphere
where the focus on women is primarily as mother or virgin, it
is difficult for women to be taken seriously as scholars and
as students. I believe that the religious definition of women by
their bodies and the playboy mentality are flip sides of the
same coin. If the institutional church began to define women
in more fully human terms, more boys and men may begin to
see women as more than bodies. This restricted definition also
works against the growing number of male colleagues who
share more fully the responsibility and experience of parenting.

Notre Dame, Our Lady, the woman honored in such a
unique way at the University has been revered as Mother and

Virgin. Her virtues have been extolled in the school song as
"tender, loyal and true." I would suggest that it is time to focus
on Mary the first disciple who heard the word of God and kept
it rather than on her motherhood or virginity, both of which
restrict our vision of Mary to physical attributes. As Pope
Paul VI noted, "[The Virgin Mary] is held up as an example to
the faithful for the way in which in her own particular life she
fully and responsibly accepted the will of God, because she
heard the word of God and acted on it, and because charity
and a spirit of service were the driving force of her actions.
She is worthy of imitation because she was the first and most
perfect of Christ's disciples."[7]

Notre Dame need look no further for its model of "Catholic
Character."

NOTES

1. "Making Connections for Women in Catholic Higher
Education," *On Campus With Women*, Association of American
Colleges and Universities 24, no. 2 (Fall 1994): 1.

2. Judith Wilt, "Ubiquitous, Lost and Found: A Study of
Catholic Identities," *Initiatives: Journal of the National Association
for Women in Education* 54, no. 4 (1992).

3. Reported by R. B. Slater in "The Gender Pay Gap," *The
Monthly Forum on Women in Higher Education* 1, no. 3 (December
1995): 23–27.

4. "Annual Report of the Provost to the Faculty concerning
the Provost's Advisory Committee," Timothy O'Meara, August
22, 1995, p. 13.

5. "Life on the Margins: Feminism and Religious Education,"
Initiatives: Journal of the National Association for Women in Education
54, no. 4 (1992).

6. *Mulieris Dignitatem*, pars. 17, 21, 22.

7. *Marialis Cultis*, February 1974, #35.

Living as Catholic "Family"

JOHN AND SYLVIA DILLON

During the summer of 1994, we moved to South Bend from a small rural town located on the Vermont border in up-state New York. For our twelve years there, we raised our two sons in a hundred-year-old restored farmhouse. We never locked our doors, kept the car keys in the ignition, and elected as mayor each year the same person who was also our barber and postman. Really! For part of our time there, we directed the religious education program in the one Catholic church in this predominantly Catholic town, and for part of the time we taught in the theology department of a Catholic high school in a city thirty miles south of us. Most everyone in town knew us by name, which had its plusses and minuses, and relatives and in-laws lived nearby in Vermont. We were never without family or friends to celebrate holidays or special occasions, like birthdays, first communions, and the opening game of Little League season.

One may ask why we would uproot ourselves from all that was comfortable and familiar, and leave this stable and nurturing environment. We have also posed this question to ourselves, especially during some of the long, grey days that hover over South Bend during the cold winter months. The answer may lie somewhere in this essay, as we share with you how and why we came to Notre Dame and how we think our work might contribute to the Catholic character of this institution.

It seems true in life that we don't always appreciate the things that we have until we have lost them. It is easy to take for granted the simple necessities of life that bring us fulfillment

John and Sylvia Dillon are Directors of the Marriage Preparation and Enrichment Program in the Office of Campus Ministry.

and comfort in the day-to-day business of living. We may have been experiencing some of this loss as we drove to South Bend. We looked out over the expansive farms and corn fields of the Midwest and noticed how the sky seemed to spread forever without a mountain peak or hill to interrupt its flow. The seeming emptiness of the land, void of the familiar evergreens and maple trees that cover the New England landscape, somewhat paralleled the emptiness that we each felt as we disconnected ourselves from all that we once considered home.

But we also remember the comfort we felt when we first spotted the Golden Dome, like a beacon welcoming us to South Bend and guiding us to our new home at Notre Dame. Our unspoken thoughts were about the hope that we would find again, "under the Dome," what we feel is most important in our lives: faith, family, and community. We hoped to begin a new chapter in our lives that would continue our story of growth and openness to wherever God leads us.

And thus, we came to Notre Dame to work in the Office of Campus Ministry. We were hired as a team, a married couple, to co-direct the marriage preparation and enrichment programs, to work in areas of religious education, and to coordinate outreach to the married graduate students and their families at University Village. The first question we are often asked is: "How can you work with your spouse all day and still remain married?" For us, it seems very natural. Initially, our co-workers tiptoed outside our office door whenever they noticed it closed, thinking we might be having an argument, but now they know that we are usually just counseling a couple. We suspect that we are somewhat of a novelty, and in fact, honestly believe that part of our vocational/career success has been that our work somehow makes a more powerful statement when we do it together. We have worked together for most of our careers, sharing both professional and domestic responsibilities. Two months after our own college graduations, we found ourselves on the same connecting flight out of Chicago bound for Portland, Oregon. Coming from different parts of the country and from different Catholic colleges, we had each made the decision to volunteer some time in service before starting "real life" in the working world. We were both headed for a week of orientation at the University of Portland before beginning our service in the Jesuit Volunteer Corps. We would later discover that we had both been assigned to the same inner-city parish, St. Leo's, in Tacoma, Washington, along with twenty other volunteers who formed the largest JVC community sent to any one placement that year and most likely for any year since. We learned about the challenges of living in Christian community as we engaged in a wide variety of ministries: teaching in the elementary and high schools, directing the parish religious education program, and staffing the food bank, advocacy center, and emergency shelters. Our own relationship grew out of a strong friendship that began in the evening hours spent writing and editing the parish newspaper after a long day of teaching. We had many opportunities to practice conflict resolution and good communication skills as we blended different temperaments and styles into writing one coherent newspaper. Four years later we were married at St. Leo's Parish, celebrating with the community that had taught us much about the way Christians should live. We asked our family and friends to make donations to Catholic Relief Services in lieu of wedding gifts, and our decision generated some controversy, especially from our parents, who knew that we were painting book shelves in between classes at Seattle University to pay for our graduate studies in religious education. Our volunteer experience had taught us to appreciate the true gifts in life and this was pivotal in shaping our future lifestyle and vocational choices.

The other question we often hear regards our job description. People wonder how we can attend to so many different things at once. First of all, there are two of us, so that certainly helps! Secondly, the work we do is an extension of what we already consider to be the most important things in our own lives, namely, faith, family, and community. These values have become the cornerstone of how we measure the meaning of our lives and the quality of our work.

In preparing couples for marriage, we hope to strengthen their knowledge and understanding of the sacramental commitment they are planning to make. We can offer only a glimpse into the marvelous mystery of love and faithfulness that God calls us to in marriage, knowing that full understanding of the promises made comes with a lifetime of living the vows. Early one morning, a timid, nervous voice on our answering machine asked if we might have some time to talk. Later that day, we felt privileged to hear the story of a young woman who was obviously in a healthy and loving relationship. Though she was positive of both her commitment and that of her partner, she could not help but be haunted by the painful memories of the deceptions that led to her own parents' divorce. Feeling that she could not live through that again, especially in her own marriage, she was looking for some assurance that the love and commitment they both felt would always be there, no matter what happened in their lives. Because it had happened to her parents, she worried that it could happen to her. She wondered how anyone could be absolutely sure of making the right choice. Hopefully our advice and counsel were helpful to her, but in the end, there was no assurance that we could give that would take away all her doubts and fears. The very nature of sacrament makes God's grace tangible in the witness of the gathered Christian community and helps give concrete assurance to what we cannot know for sure. We felt that her concern was a sign of someone who understood the awesome responsibility that is involved in the Sacrament of Marriage, as well as an expression that such a commitment does need to be grounded in faith. We endeavor to live that same commitment in our marriage, and as we reflect upon the characteristics of healthy relationships with other couples, we recognize and work on the strengths and weaknesses in our own.

Sometimes we work with couples who are reluctant to engage in the sacramental preparation process because they see no real connection between their faith and their marriage. We remember several particularly tense sessions with a couple who had absolutely no agreement on or interest in issues dealing with religious orientation. Their primary reason for choosing to be married in the Church had much more to do with his family's wishes than with personal beliefs. As they attempted to dismiss this aspect of their relationship with flip comments and philosophical arguments, we found ourselves in the position of having to tell them that a valid marriage in the Catholic Church requires a certain predisposition of faith. Trying not to alienate the couple, we discussed what the Catholic Church means by a sacramental marriage and asked them to be open minded to the reading materials we gave them, our future counseling sessions, and the Pre-Cana Retreat experience. We were surprised when they came back after the retreat to thank us for the positive experience and to say that the presentations and personal sharing of the team members had helped them to understand how faith and the support of a Christian community would nurture the marriage commitment. They admitted that the area of their own religious development was one that they needed to work on together. We felt satisfied that we had not backed down from asking the "tough questions" and that we had helped them to view their lives from a different perspective. Couples like this challenge us and the Catholic community at Notre Dame to give more than lip service to the powerful impact that our tradition and beliefs can give to sacramental marriage, especially in a society that so trivializes relationships and commitments.

As parents, we are continually challenged to teach and model the convictions and beliefs of our faith in hopes that our own children will cultivate habits of virtue, the voice of conscience, and the ability to make moral judgments that will bring them the happiness God intends for their lives. It is an incredible joy and challenge to watch them grow, celebrating their achievements and gifts, challenging them to use those gifts in the service of others, and offering forgiveness and comfort when they fail. Our work in Campus Ministry allows us the unique privilege to experience this same opportunity with our students as they struggle with important life choices during a critical time of growth and development. The college years are a time when decisions and actions can have a lasting effect on the path a person will walk. It is somewhat like a safari that is filled with wonder and beauty, but also holds the possibility of great danger at every turn. As adults, we hope that young people will embrace all that life has to offer, while at the same time encouraging careful, reflective decisions and choices.

Our efforts in religious education spring from a conviction that it is important to be able to articulate what you believe and why you believe it, so that faith becomes a way of life. We desire this for ourselves and for our children as well, and therefore, our teaching becomes a natural vehicle for our own growth in faith and practice.

During a visit, we listened to a young man tell about feeling somewhat overwhelmed in his theology classes when he had been a student here. While he considered himself to be a religious person, he had felt intimidated on the academic level and had found that he had large gaps in his knowledge and understanding of the practice of the Catholic faith. He had felt that many of his questions were so basic that he was embarrassed to ask them, assuming that everyone else knew these things already. We have discovered that this experience is not unique; there are many students who know they love their faith, but realize that they know little about it. One such student who worked with us on a project in campus ministry had enjoyed four years at Notre Dame and had obviously been touched by its spiritual dimension, since he was considering entrance into a religious community. He happened to notice a poster in our office announcing the dates and times of the Triduum celebration, and rather sheepishly asked what the Triduum meant, admitting that he had never experienced these three days of worship. Our previous teaching and work in parish ministry support the fact that such incidents are not unique, and that for a variety of reasons, students do not always possess the fundamental basics of the faith that we might expect. As campus ministers, we share in the responsibility of providing opportunities for students to learn the content of their faith as well as to explore the issues and questions that affect the integration of faith into their daily lives. With this in mind, we have designed "Power Lunches," forty-five–minute gatherings over lunch that include a brief presentation on a topic of

Catholic faith or practice, questions and discussion, and handouts for further reading on the day's theme. Our initial sessions have proven rewarding, with students frequently staying beyond the allotted time to ask further questions, with requests for copies of our materials to share with friends and family, and with students asking for more information on specific topics that they are hearing explained for the first time. Though we always hope for a larger audience, our regular participants are an enthusiastic group and new faces appear each week. We are confident that Power Lunches, as well as other creative approaches to religious education, meet a need of today's students.

Our Catechist Formation Program, first organized in the fall of 1994, provides another rich opportunity for religious education. The goal of this ministry is to place Notre Dame students into local parish religious education programs (with supervision, support, and resources), where they teach or act as teacher assistants on various levels ranging from kindergarten through high school/youth ministry. Our intent is not only to provide a valuable resource and service to local parishes, but to enable our students to articulate their beliefs while participating in a growth-filled experience of teaching and sharing faith. At a recent staff meeting, Father Richard Warner, C.S.C., apologizing for such short notice, asked us to gather some students from various programs to say a few words about their involvement with campus ministry at a luncheon for an important benefactor. After a few hurried phone calls and a sketchy explanation, we held our breath as several catechists stood to share their experiences. In humorous and poignant stories, they proceeded to describe the needs they were discovering as well as the value of learning while teaching. One student summarized the prevailing sentiment by saying, "This is the best thing I do all week and I intend to continue teaching after graduation." We currently have over fifty student catechists working in twelve local parishes and are hopeful that this Catechist Formation Program may promote a future desire to be part of an essential ministry in our church.

In ministering to married graduate students and their

families, our goal is to help build a supportive and nurturing community at University Village. We help to facilitate friendships that will offer support and companionship to families who journey here, far from their own families, cultures, and beliefs. In this process, we are enriched by new friends and ideas and become part of this unique community that represents over thirty countries. Once again, our work becomes a natural outgrowth of our belief in the importance of Christian community lived out.

The Catholic character of Notre Dame is visibly displayed in the prominent places of the University, such as the Basilica, the Grotto, the theology classrooms, and the chapels in every residence hall. On a campus tour it is easy to see and hear the sights and sounds of Catholic faith and worship. But as with most tours, you do not necessarily see the less spectacular sights unless you stray off the beaten path. If you are tempted to wander to one distant corner of the campus, you would find evidence of this same Catholic character thriving on East Cripe Street in a small ranch-style house located behind the local Bob Evans restaurant. This nondescript house serves as the community center for University Village, and if you were to enter it on any given Sunday, you would find the room crowded with families celebrating liturgy. You might also be fortunate enough to witness a baptism, such as one recent celebration where an African family raised their child high in outstretched arms to ask for God's grace and blessing. On any other day, you would be certain to find something of interest happening in the community center: Bible study groups, prayer groups, a child care co-op, English classes, pot-luck dinners, educational workshops, or any of a multitude of activities designed to support and enrich the lives of students and their families. Though our ministry to the Village does not always have a directly spiritual tone and often involves rather humble efforts to meet very basic human needs, we are convinced that our care and concern leaves a lasting impression upon these families. Hopefully, they will bring back to their homes a firsthand experience of the Catholic identity and character of Notre Dame as an institution that strives to live the Gospel values.

We are reminded of a near tragedy that occurred this past summer when the five-year-old daughter of a family from Mozambique was stricken with encephalitis and lapsed into a deep coma. She was rushed to Riley Children's Medical Center in Indianapolis where a team of rare disease specialists cared for her in the intensive care unit for three weeks. As word spread through the Village, families responded with prepared meals, transportation back and forth to Indianapolis, and child care for a three-year-old sibling. Friends made frequent visits to the hospital to keep vigil with the family and to offer comfort and support during the long recovery process. Miraculously, this child suffered no permanent health problems and a joyful community welcomed her back after a three-month hospital stay. From the academic advisor who re-arranged exams and research deadlines for a worried father to the Office of Student Affairs who waived rental fees for the family during these difficult summer months, the University community demonstrated personal care and concern for a member of the Notre Dame family. This "reaching out" has much to say about the Catholic character of Notre Dame and the mission of the University as a whole.

One final thought about how we have experienced the Catholic character and identity of Notre Dame involves our work on a book of prayers being compiled through Campus Ministry. It is our plan to collect, edit, and publish these prayers in a book that might become a daily source of inspiration and comfort, as well as a keepsake to mark one's years at Notre Dame. We have been impressed by the number of people who have responded with both contributions and enthusiastic support for a project they see as worthwhile. Reading the hundreds of original and traditional prayers submitted by students, faculty, staff, and alumni has given us insight into the rich and diverse spirituality that imbues this campus.

After twenty years of teaching in Catholic schools and working in parish ministry, we see Notre Dame as a unique environment in the sense that it possesses resources, talent, and the ability for theological reflection and religious practice that go well beyond the capabilities of the average school or parish. We also know that there is much to be learned about ministry from the people and places beyond these confines. Perhaps one of the best things we can do is to ensure that those who have joined us here for a while, possibly searching for something more than the usual academic environment, will move on equipped with the tools and vision to integrate their Notre Dame experience with the incredible potential that lies beyond to the very real benefit of the wider church and world community. There is no utopia; in this human world there is likely no institution that perfectly embodies all of the ideals it espouses. However, in the short time that we have worked here, we have seen concrete evidence of a strong Catholic tradition and heritage and the desire to share the knowledge and experience of this way of life. Our contribution is very much on the grassroots level, helping students to make connections between faith and life. We are grateful for what our ministry gives back to us and to our children, thankful that we accepted the invitation to embrace new opportunities to serve, and blessed to be a part of a community that values what we cherish most.

Being Catholic at Notre Dame

MICHAEL O. GARVEY

An apology is in order at the outset. A personal perspective on Notre Dame's Catholic mission and ministry requires an autobiographical, rambling, and uncomfortably confessional mode, so kindly permit me to be excessive in my use of the first person singular and, it goes without saying, to risk sentimentality. When I was a very little boy, the sound of the anglicized phrase "Notre Dame" was able to stir my imagination and increase my pulse rate, but what it evoked in my mind and excited in my heart had little to do with the Mother of God, less to do with any sort of education, and nothing whatsoever to do with football. It may have been possible to explain to me in those days that Notre Dame was a university serving the Catholic Church and conspicuously sponsoring a famous collegiate football team, but such explanation could never have held my attention very long. I knew that Notre Dame was a place, and a most amazing place at that. It was a magical oasis, a mysterious garden in which we children were allowed an hour or two of play whenever my parents undertook what seemed to us the endless drive through fields of corn and soybean from Springfield, Illinois, where we lived, to Sharon, Pennsylvania, where my grandparents lived. When, years later, a particularly exacting secondary school English teacher required me to memorize Coleridge's "Kubla Kahn," I had not the least trouble with the lines

> So twice five miles of fertile ground
> With walls and towers were girdled round:

Michael Garvey is Assistant Director of Public Relations and Information.

89

And there were gardens bright with sinous rills,
Where blossomed many an incense-bearing tree;
And here were forests ancient as the hills,
Enfolding sunny spots of greenery.

From earliest childhood, I had known a nearly identical
site. I had visited there, loitered there, and, thanks to a
Byzantine network of familial and tribal and marvelously
sectarian associations, even belonged there. What Coleridge
allegedly glimpsed during an opium-induced stupor was
something my family and I took for granted. And during the
sporadically opiated counter-cultural years of the late sixties
and early seventies, when I was a student here, the magic of
the place was able to startle me all over again.

The magic was partially physical, of course, having to do
with a child's perception of lush lawns, candles aglow in the
grotto darkness, ducks in waddling procession along a clay
lakeshore, sunlight glinting off a golden dome above the
sycamore treetops, an omnipresent aroma of something fine
cooking in a nearby dining hall kitchen, the suggestive quiet
and darkness of Sacred Heart Church, congenial faces, bel-
lowed greetings, and the hearty laughter of well-cared-for
young people. But it was partly associative, too, I suppose.
Older people, usually alumni related to me, had gradually
brought me to appreciate that this was beloved ground; that
it straddled two major continental river systems, and that
the Potawatami, and even more ancient people, had lived and
suffered and prayed and died here; that freebooting voyageurs
had carried their canoes and weapons from the Saint Joseph
River through these very woods to the headwaters of the
Kankakee, a ghostly place they called Parc Au Vaches because
it was there that the skeletons of buffalo, mired, starved, and
picked clean by vultures used to protrude from the mud flats;
that among those voyageurs perhaps even Pere Marquette
had come through here to set the Eucharistic table at which
the Lord would be waiting for my Irish ancestors when they,
a couple of centuries later, would arrive, paradoxically bearing
Him in their midst already; that many great men (and women,

like my mother's friend the venerable Sister Madeleva, whom we'd visit at her alma mater across the road and who once gave me a medieval pilgrim's staff with a bell appended) had done great things and thought and argued, learned and worshipped, and befriended one another here; that my father had lived inside that particular arch, and that my uncle had walked with my aunt along this particular lake path, too shy just then to propose, and that it had been before that particular building that my grandpa snapped a photograph of my dad, a much younger version of my dad looking like a much older version of me. All of these early experiences suggested to the child I was then the truth of the Richard Wilbur line I would read as the English major I was later: "What love sees is true: The world's fullness is not made but found." Enough. There are thousands of students, alumni, faculty, staff, and friends of the University with enthusiasms and handicaps similar to mine. We all may share a tendency to "fetishize the local," but that tendency isn't necessarily a reprehensible one. The manner in which most of us have been introduced to the University is not unlike the manner in which most of us have been introduced to the Catholic Church. What begins as a sensual matter of light, warmth, and comforting sights, tastes, sounds, and smells eventually gives way to an adventure of the spirit involving memory, imagination, wonder, and love. What begins as a pleasant encounter reveals itself as a mystery worth staking one's life on. We could be accused of being maudlin, I guess, but so could the wedding guests at Cana. Such emotion is redolent and even nauseating to some sensibilities, but I think it is to genuine religious belief what manure is to healthy soil.

In any event, I offer my susceptibility to the allure of this magic only to defend a decision I made some years ago to accept a job at Notre Dame, even when I knew that the decision would force me to commit acts of public relations. I am no longer the child whose parents liked to break long car trips on a fascinating and beloved section of ground, nor am I any longer the English major who followed parents and uncles and cousins and brothers and sisters through the intense intellectual, moral, and spiritual experiences which uniquely composed (and I hope still compose) Notre Dame's undergraduate student life. But because I have been both of those people, I hope I have become and will always remain a son of the Church. To the extent that the University of Notre Dame is able to inspire, encourage, develop, celebrate, and sustain among its students, faculty, and administrators a filial love of the Catholic Church, it will always seem to me an institution worth dying for. Even filial love (perhaps especially filial love) is vulnerable to scandal, of course, and there have been times when the administration of the University, no less than that of the Catholic Church, has strayed dismayingly from its mission to "redeem the time," in the late Frank O'Malley's wonderful phrase. But, as I remember Norman Mailer telling a bunch of us earnest sophomores during the early 1970s, Notre Dame is one of the only universities where you can use the word "soul" without necessarily hearing snickers from your audience. It is still not completely unrealistic to dream here of making Christ visible to a deliriously secular culture.

As far as I'm concerned, public relations is an intrinsically dubious profession, and people who regard it as a *portable* profession—like, say, teaching, plumbing, or medicine—strike me as intrinsically untrustworthy. When the Devil appears in Walker Percy's novel, *Love in the Ruins*, he identifies himself as "a liaison between the public and the private sector." Public relations is, in this very specific sense, the Devil's work, and it neither surprises nor disconcerts me to hear the phrase uttered as a pejorative, given that PR professionals have assisted such institutions as Calvin Klein, Inc., the Coca-Cola Company, and the Department of Defense. A teacher can teach well or badly in any school, and a plumber need not fret very much about the source of his or her paycheck. But decent PR people (and there are more of them than you might imagine) need to be a bit more self-conscious. I would argue that Notre Dame is one of those exceptional institutions in which it is possible simultaneously to practice public relations and to maintain one's integrity. I would not make such an argument, for example, about Planned Parenthood.

All of us in our office are assigned a variety of tasks, but each of us has a sort of specialty, or "beat." My own beat is, roughly, religion at Notre Dame, which is much like football at Notre Dame, come to think of it, in that controversy seems inevitable. Sometimes the controversy results from Notre Dame's being simultaneously an American and a Catholic myth, because America and Catholicism are not always compatible. There are, for instance, students, alumni, faculty and administrators who regard as quite nearly blasphemous the manner in which the American flag is venerated at the baccalaureate Mass. There are many who regard the University's participation in the nation's military adventures under the auspices of its R.O.T.C. programs as irreconcilable with its Catholic mission. In Catholic history, such arguments are at least as old as Saint Martin of Tours, the pacifist martyr and patron saint of conscientious objectors, whose relic is enshrined in the main altar of the Basilica of the Sacred Heart.

But there are more recent instances of religious neuralgia as well. An excitable faculty member not long ago equated the mild suggestion that committed Catholics ought to predominate on our faculty with a justification of ethnic cleansing. It was a moment of unintentionally comic relief in the crucially important discussion of how the University might maintain and enrich the Catholic identity which is its most precious and distinctive resource. Last year a furious South Bostonian Irish-American called up to say that during a football weekend visit with his daughter, he'd uncovered the ominous fact that a residence hall on our Fighting Irish campus was named in honor of Saint Edward, "an English king, no less!" He was serious. I've received phone calls and occasionally answered letters from Catholics who want the University to take a stand on the veracity of the apparitions of Mary in Medjugorje, and from people outraged that a Martin Scorcese film based on the Nikos Katsanzakis novel, *The Last Temptation of Christ*, was shown on campus. (Most of those callers, incidentally, were as outraged by the doctrine of the Incarnation as by the Scorcese movie, and they seemed to espouse a denial of Jesus' humanity that was condemned as a heresy 1600 years ago during the

Council of Constantinople. I have had slight pangs of conscience for not mentioning this at the time.)

Some public controversies cause as much personal pain as institutional stress. The University's refusal to "recognize" a specific organization of gay and lesbian students has recently been read as simple contempt for gay people instead of a sincere, if awkward, attempt to honor Catholic Church teaching on sexuality. To be accused of cowardice and bigotry is no less unpleasant for me, I suppose, than to be stereotyped as a loathsome sexual predator is for a gay person. But perhaps such insults are instances of grace, and opportunities for me to share in some small way a far more difficult cross born in excruciating loneliness by so many homosexual men and women here.

And then there are the less public, internal controversies that afflict any large institution. There are a few serious and several petty gaffes, blunders, quarrels, grudges, vanities, and turf battles which charity and discretion, almost as much as survival instinct, forbid my describing here. The inevitable local gossip about such matters is usually good natured, but all too frequently it is not. Even while we staff, faculty, and students seethe on all sides of such controversies, many of us manage to surround the Eucharist together. I pray that we aren't standing in vain within that burning mystery, and I'm grateful to work (and argue) with men and women whose prayer is, in this respect, the same as mine.

Not only because of what my wife and children assure me is a curmudgeonly disposition, but also because I work neither in classrooms nor in residence halls, I have little formal contact with students. Aside from occasionally snarling at what strikes me as avoidably adolescent behavior on the quad or in the Huddle, I have few "ministerial" relationships with them. There are student interns in our office, of course, and members of the student media, most of them very likeable young men and women whose friendships I have often come to treasure. And as I get older, I'm increasingly delighted and bewildered by how many students know me as an uncle, a cousin, a godfather, or a close friend of the family. I hope I live up to my responsibility to stand "in loco parentis" for all Notre Dame students. When people complain that the phrase "in loco parentis" describes an inappropriately condescending or stifling relationship, I immediately conclude that they are, or would be, lousy parents. I think all of us who work here are obligated to offer our students an unabashedly parental love, welcoming them into a community of religious belief, intellectual inquiry, and devotion to the weak. It is a family in which we elders who are here longer than four years are, for a time and whether we or they like it or not, their parents. The most important thing parents teach their children is what to love, and the only way to teach children what to love is by loving what is worthy of one's love.

I guess I'm as sectarian as the day is long, because I believe that what is most worthy of my love is Christ, made visible in my wife, my children, my family, my friends, those with whom I work and play and pray and contend. What is most worthy of my love is Christ crucified and risen and present in the Church. I try to remember these things when I'm at home with my family. On my best days, I manage to remember them at work, too, reassuring myself that such love can enliven and transfigure even this job, even this place.

The Door

MARY JANE GRIFFIN, O.S.F.

The door opens.

Every profession has basic tools. For some the tool might be a ruler, a pencil, a computer, an easel. The rector's basic tool is the door of the rector's room. The door is the locus of the beginning and the ending as well as the growing of the relationship between the resident and the rector.

People come to the rector for a myriad of reasons. No one's reason is ever exactly the same as another person's, but many are similar. When a resident approaches the rector's door, how does she do it? With a knock, a bang, a tap, a brush?

The door frames different pictures of people. They come from and go to a variety of places, peoples, and possibilities. Changes within us produce different experiences and outcomes. Some stories I remember in a special way because their lives made marks upon mine.

She saw them do it. What should she do? Yes, she should go and report it to the professor. Would anything happen? She didn't know. She reported it. Nothing happened.

Another came home with a black eye. Her friend saw her and had to help her get help for herself. A long time for healing was needed.

One woman had to be in chemistry because her father was. She struggled for two years. At the end of her sophomore year she walked in and said "I switched." "To what?" "Communication. I have to overload and go to two summer sessions, but I am so happy!"

Sister M. J. Griffin, O.S.F., is Rector of Howard Hall.

And there was the one who volunteered with a service organization for a year. She volunteered for a second year, creating her own service and reflection. She studied for ministry in the Church.

Two weeks into the semester, the phone rang. A father called, worried about his freshman daughter. She was his oldest child. He was not sure she was happy at Notre Dame. She was quiet and a bit shy in the beginning. He just didn't know if she liked it and didn't know if she felt she could do the work. He wasn't sure if she was getting along with her roommate. There was one more thing he said that he hesitated to add. He didn't know if she liked football. Having fully outlined the problem, as an alumnus himself, he felt better.

He did not want his daughter to know he called. But he was very worried about her. I told him I had not heard anything unusual. His daughter sounded normal to me with the adjustment of freshman year. I said I would ask the Resident Assistant to speak to her and her roommate to see what was going on and we would go from there.

The R.A. had conversations with both women, one was more quiet and reserved, the other very friendly and outgoing. The R.A. encouraged both to become more involved with each other. Two weeks later I was sitting at my desk, looking out the window. The two roommates were out on the grass, tossing a football.

By graduation the shy woman had changed. Both she and her father cried joyfully together about her university experience. The following fall in the dining hall on a football weekend, the father told me the new story: daughter number two wanted to enter Notre Dame the following year!

To be a rector is to continuously experience beginnings and endings of different moments in people's lives. To be a rector is to participate in an expression of love which is beyond any one of us as individuals. To me this expression of love among those who live in the residence halls is very similar to the energy of love revealed in the Trinity. The love of the creator empowers the servant to share the spirit. This love is continuously recreated and renewed. What happens in the residence hall is that the service and energy, as they are shared and freely given, become an expression of mutuality among all in the community and beyond.

For a rector this expression of the energy of life may take radically different forms. I might be with a student, telling her that her mother died, while a second student in another room may be leaving the university for continued violation of university policy, and yet a third woman in yet another room rejoices over the news of a fellowship for post-graduate work for the next year.

For rectors our lives are constantly framed by the door; the door to the hall, our room, the resident's room. Who is coming in the door? How are they? What is happening to them? When I meet someone at my door, I usually recall where I was with the person in our last exchange. It may have been a freshmen introductory small group meeting, a sophomore mid-point meeting, a hall officers' meeting, a disciplinary meeting, a resident assistant interview, or a senior exit interview.

The tasks of each year follow a rhythm of energy. They begin with the welcome of the freshmen. Each freshman is invited to write a letter to herself describing who she is today and who she wishes to become. These letters are returned to them as seniors and serve as memory markers of their growth and development to themselves.

After the first day of orientation the parents gather with the hall staff to learn about Notre Dame from the hall perspective. Immediately following, the freshmen gather in the chapel for two enormously important reasons: to see each other and to meet the hall staff. In both meetings, with the parents and the freshmen, the staff promise to share all that is life at Notre Dame with the women in the hall and especially those in their own section.

Much is ahead of each person in the chapel, be they student, parent, or staff person. What anyone will learn in the next four years cannot be identified and neatly described. What can be promised is change as well as an opportunity to grow into that change. For the next four years the program of development, consciously and unconsciously, to effect and to enhance change is the P.I.E.S model. Each person is invited in the community setting of the residence hall to grow and contribute Physically, Intellectually, Emotionally and Spiritually. P.I.E.S. is the framework of our life in common.

As the staff begins the meeting with the freshmen, three questions are posed to the group. These questions remain in different versions for all four years, marking the relationship of individuals to their community. The staff invites the freshmen to these questions:

Who are you?

Where are you going?

How can we help you?

Those three questions will occupy much time among all the people in this room. These questions chase people, student and staff, in many ways during the time of each year.

This life in common, the sharing of life in community, can be a ministry of wasted time. To waste time is to stand with someone in life as God works around, among, and within that person. I "do nothing" with someone, observe, talk about small life areas as weather coming and work finished. I wait for someone to maybe trust me or someone else enough to open up for more substantive conversation. What is being accomplished is not our way as rectors, but rather God's way, as expressed and lived out in this time, in a student's life.

To be patient and open to the growth which occurs in students is a challenging opportunity for growth for the rector. What they and sometimes "we" forget is that the person in charge of one's life is oneself. Therefore, the person who makes the choices and enacts the decisions is the one whom one sees in the mirror. That person is the leader of one's life. As may be expected, this reality is difficult to accept . . . always.

The activity of being a rector is to wait with people as they search to make sense of their cycle of life experience, encouraging them in their enthusiasm, pain, and wonder. My journey with them is to help them learn what they are facing in their own lives. The energy is to encourage them, enable them and empower them to be themselves in their own way. The gift in community is to give room for such growth. As individuals gain trust of themselves and others in a community, they become full members. In receiving from and contributing to others, opportunities for growth occur. As students feel a connection and desire to make contributions, they are enabled to be their truest selves.

As 80 percent of communication is nonverbal, all life in the hall is very open to public view. The rector and the resident have the constant challenge to work at knowing and being known by oneself and the other. The rector may miss something. But given all the residents in a hall, they rarely, if ever, do. The residents, especially the seniors, know me better through their observation than I may know myself at times. The reality is that by living with others in the hall community, we all see everything in each others' lives. Can we respect that, allow it, nurture it, challenge it, and live with it? In a certain sense no boundaries exist in this relationship of life in common and together.

At the door people present themselves dressed in different questions. The quest for home and what place *is* home are central ones. As students make Notre Dame their home, they begin, usually for the first time, to make a home. In close and cramped quarters with people one does not know, "to make a home" presents a challenge. The challenge to make a home is different as seniors live, work, play, and pray with very close friends in intentional relationships. Both steps are necessary for the homes each person will make upon graduation from Notre Dame.

Raising questions in people's lives is a major activity of the hall staff. Perhaps raising questions is too brazen an image to convey the reality of the process. The process could more carefully be called identifying opportunities for growth. Construing questions as opportunities reminds the person asked that each one makes her own choice as to whom she wishes to become. This choice is essential and one to which we all are continually called.

Contact with residents is distinctly different from that of a family or a classroom or a job. To frame opportunities for growth with irregular or sporadic contact with residents is always challenging. Life changes as does its schedule. The best ideas and plans for programming and possibility in a hall are in constant competition with a hundred other choices every hour. Our work as staff is to provide opportunities to gather.

The opportunity to integrate in a conscious way what one's life and direction might become is a critical aspect of one's experience at the University. That integration is a life-long process which receives enormous infusion of insight and movements during these four years. One's faith and values are examined in every experience according to P.I.E.S. Why do you exercise; what did Francis of Assisi teach; how do you feel about what your friend said; what is God doing in your life these days? These questions fit the usual scope of life in the hall.

The integration of education begins to take hold in a resident's life in a conscious way. To become a whole person means one must learn how to reflect about one's life and values. The activity of reflection as a methodology of life must be practiced consciously and continuously in small and significant ways for each of us to understand how important it is in our lives.

The subject matter of one's education as a member in the hall is one's own life. Each one comes to face that life and the story of it as they enmesh themselves in their majors, their relationships, and thoughts of their futures. The content varies with each individual but the broad issues are the same as in any human community: wanting to be loved and to love; wanting to know oneself well enough to accomplish the task of being oneself; and wanting to understand where one might contribute who one is.

The nature of our relationships in community can be revealed in the frequency of conversation, the length of such conversation, and the substance shared. What we all come to know among ourselves in this life in common is that we all are growing. Change and life are happening to and with all of us, but we may not be growing in ways we want to be or in ways we want others to be.

Another question which people ask themselves at different times concerns the quality of their relationships with their friends. Do they take each other for granted? Are one's friends helping one to become who one is supposed to be? Who can help me find people like myself? Some of these questions can be talked about directly and some must be approached much more subtly. Some questions the resident raises and sometimes the staff or friends raise them.

As rectors we participate in a process of teaching and enabling students to be empowered and to actively search their faith and their expectations of the Church. Our collaboration in community is meant to inspirit their response so that their involvement in the future will make a difference. The Church is changing. What will their lives look like in the Church in ten years, in twenty, in thirty? How will they lead the Church?

All of us today are in a very difficult time within the Church. It is a challenging experience. Today, we are creating Church in which we do not know exactly who, what, where, and how it will be in the future. How do we prepare these young women and men to embrace, continue in, and lead such a Church in their lives? Conversation must be constant. New models and images must be offered. Dialogue among all of us is not optional.

Our life in common produces changes within all of us.

The seniors gather in the chapel on Mother's Day, the Sunday before graduation. During the homily they offer reflection and dialogue with each other about what they have learned from each other in their life in common. They continue their celebration at their dinner and throughout senior week. They leave with expectations and questions about life, self, others and God.

The door opens.

Word, Sacrament, and Blessing: The Ministry of the Rector of the Basilica

DANIEL JENKY, C.S.C.

The great gothic cathedrals of Europe have sometimes been called "Bibles in stone," because their architecture, sculpture, and stained glass were all designed to tell both the stories of the scriptures and the foundational stories of the Christian Church. This narrative function is actually embodied in the very structure and material of these churches, and so these places have been revered down through the centuries as effective images of our faith. Their religious significance certainly has everything to do with what happens there, but what happens there has also been formed by the very "story-telling" of the place. These buildings testify to the profound sacramental story of Catholic Christianity. Christ is the image or the "icon" of God, and the community of his disciples is called to be his image in this world. That material world has itself been sanctified and changed, because in Jesus Christ, the Creator has entered into creation. Through that Incarnation, the image and likeness of God has been restored to our humanity. The sacred spaces of our tradition are intentionally designed and designated to celebrate this greatest of all stories.

I have the privilege and great personal joy of serving as the rector of Notre Dame's main church, the Basilica of the Sacred Heart. This campus church located in the American Midwest also has its own story to tell. The architecture is not the "pure

Father Daniel Jenky, C.S.C., is Rector of the Basilica of the Sacred Heart.

gothic" of Europe but rather is often called "gothic revival" or sometimes even "prairie gothic." Like all the oldest buildings at Notre Dame, Sacred Heart is built of yellow clay bricks, formed from the very mud of Saint Mary's Lake. The central pillars encase the trunks of enormous hardwood trees that also came from the University's grounds. Using these local materials, Father Sorin and his religious confreres deliberately set about the task of recreating the ancient gothic traditions of Catholic Europe in the new circumstances of nineteenth-century America. Once again, the architectural plan has something very deliberate to say. The University of Notre Dame is self-consciously Roman Catholic in its identity and design. The Main Church stands directly next to the Main Building with its famous Golden Dome. At Notre Dame, faith and learning therefore stand side by side, at the very heart of the campus. From this central axis, the University extends down Notre Dame Avenue and out toward the wider world it was founded to serve and educate.

Like many other "Domers," my very first experience of this Notre Dame story took place when I was still very young. I was with my sister and some cousins visiting another relative, a Sister of Loretto working on her master's degree at summer school. Right after we visited the bookstore, she took us all around Sacred Heart, pointing out its many splendors and retelling its story of faith and devotion. As I recall, what most impressed me was the Reliquary Chapel, filled with the bones of countless saints and its vivid wax replica of the young martyr Severa, with a gory sword slash across her throat. Apparently the character of religious interest among nine-year-olds hasn't changed all that much over the years. Now that I work here, hardly a day passes that I don't encounter some other Notre Dame family with children in tow, asking for directions to Saint Severa. I usually catch bits and pieces of their retelling of the stories of the martyrs, the stories of the Stations of the Cross, the stories of Our Lady, the saints, and all the angels in glory, smiling down from their shining images on the walls, the windows, and the ceilings. Every day I see parents pointing to the cross, to the altar, to the tabernacle, telling the story of God and Jesus Christ to their children and teaching them how to pray. Sacred Heart is like a rich and vividly illustrated book. Even without a word being spoken, this beautiful building tells Notre Dame's Catholic story to everyone who walks through the doors and has eyes to see.

The University of Notre Dame has sometimes been called America's largest "Catholic theme park." Besides all the many crosses, statues, and religious shrines sprinkled across the campus, at last count there are also forty-two functioning and quite visible chapels. Most students usually attend Sunday or daily masses in their dormitory chapels. The Basilica, for its part, functions rather like a central shrine among these many other places dedicated to public worship and private prayer. Liturgies at Sacred Heart are nearly always crowded, but those crowds change nearly every day. Students might come to mass at the Basilica when their parents are on campus, or when they simply want a change from their dorm. Sacred Heart is also filled up by Notre Dame faculty, staff, hoards of visiting alumni, local Catholics from town, and tourists from almost everywhere. At any mass, there might be people from all over the country and even from all over the world. Planning a liturgy at Sacred Heart must always take cognisance of the fact that on any given occasion, most of the congregation, the lay ministers, and even the priests are at least a bit unfamiliar with the way things are normally done. The Basilica staff itself is only a small component of a much larger campus ministry team, and there are also hundreds of other priests, religious, and lay ministers at Notre Dame whose service brings them in regular contact with the main church. An essential part of my job as rector is to function as host, master of ceremonies, and sometimes even as referee, so that all can participate and hopefully feel welcome.

Sacred Heart's pastoral program normally includes many occasions where the Notre Dame faithful can be "hatched, matched, or dispatched." Alumni from all over the country love to bring their children back to campus for Baptism. There is also a waiting list of almost two years to get married at Sacred Heart, and that is despite the fact that we usually have four weddings each and every Saturday, except of course on football weekends. Many "Domers," some of whom were baptized and married at Sacred Heart, also make careful and precise provision to have their funerals celebrated here. This is the place where Holy Cross religious profess their final vows, are ordained to the priesthood, celebrate jubilees, and also have their own funerals. This is the place where Notre Dame students can make adult decisions about faith and service, where perhaps for the first time they may experience the immense spiritual richness of Holy Week, or where they gather as a multitude to grieve at the untimely death of a friend and classmate. This is the place where the University always celebrates its most solemn occasions and anniversaries. There are so many collective Notre Dame memories associated with all these people, their prayers, and their stories told and re-told within the walls and under the roof of this sacred old building. School stories become family traditions, and family traditions become part of the texture and reality of this church's own particular story.

I would like to share a few personal stories about my own ministry at Sacred Heart. The first has to do with confessions or what is now more properly called the Sacrament of Reconciliation. One hears all the time these days that this sacrament is not as popular among Catholics as it once was. I can only report that at Notre Dame, large numbers of people come to confession, Monday through Saturday, week after week, year after year. Besides many opportunities in the residence halls and campus religious houses, priests hear confessions in the Basilica before the two weekday masses and every evening after supper. At most University gatherings, during Advent, at Christmas, during Lent, and especially in Holy Week, phalanxes of confessors and seemingly endless lines of penitents regularly come together to celebrate the Lord's gift of grace and forgiveness. Of course, we have the great blessing of a large number of priests who make themselves available for this ministry. Somehow as well, the intensely Catholic atmosphere at Notre Dame seems to "give permission" to all sorts and ages of ordinary believers to come to confession. The Holy Cross pastoral tradition has always tried to make the sacraments easily accessible for our students as well as for visitors to campus. Notre Dame still has many of the traditional characteristics of an old French Catholic boarding school. Most of the Holy Cross community live with the students in their residence halls, and no one makes any apologies whatsoever for the University's Catholic character. This living tradition greatly encourages religious practice, very much including Reconciliation.

It is not that unusual to have someone begin their confession in Sacred Heart by saying they just flew in from Los Angeles or from New York because they wanted to come to the sacrament here at Notre Dame. At other times it might be a busy parent dropping off a young boy or girl for a summer sports camp. They are already on campus. They stop into Sacred Heart to say a quick prayer, and seeing so many other people in line moves them to come to confession. Often they have already undergone a profound personal conversion or some deeper religious experience. The sacrament often only formalizes and reassures with the Church's prayer what has already taken place in their hearts and in their lives. At many other occasions, the penitents are mostly students, some of whom are experiencing the first serious moral crises of their adult lives. Some are very familiar with the sacrament, while others haven't gone since before their First Communion.

Perhaps the most demanding confessions for myself and for most confessors are those of the living saints who often frequent the sacrament. Many devout people come to Notre Dame for prayer and retreat. A surprising number of Catholics from many different places consider the Basilica their spiritual home. Among these are some men and women of profound religious experience and extraordinary holiness. It is a very humbling challenge to try to say a word of insight or comfort to someone who is already so very close to God. One rather senior and very wise priest has more than once said to me after hearing confessions: "I know I'm not that smart. It really must be the Holy Spirit who tells us what to say." After hearing confessions for only a few minutes or even for hours, I know that I always feel the almost tangible power and goodness of God in the very experience of ministering this sacrament. I'm the one who keeps getting converted. I'm the one who is helped to grow in my own faith because of the faith and sincerity of others. I have had to personally learn all over again that I cannot be a "good confessor" unless I too am a sincere penitent. Renewing the grace of Baptism through the Sacrament of Reconciliation is certainly one of the perennial and life-giving Gospel stories of Sacred Heart.

Preaching this story, that extraordinary Good News of Jesus Christ, is another essential aspect of ministry at any church and certainly at Sacred Heart as well. The Basilica, however, serves a school community made up primarily of very bright students and many distinguished scholars. Academics tend to listen to homilies and sometimes even rate them rather in the manner of theater or restaurant critics. Priests and religious have occasionally also been known to pay attention to a sermon, and at times they can be even less tolerant than their lay colleagues. It can be quite an intimidating task to homilize before an assembly often so replete with advanced degrees and a full complement of Holy Orders. At Sacred Heart, the congregation really expects good preaching, and in a certain sense, they are rather spoiled. They have the unusual luxury of tremendous variety among their preachers, simply because there are so many priests at Notre Dame. All of these clerics are university trained, and many are teachers with considerable experience in communication. One of the more onerous tasks of being the rector is that I normally schedule the celebrants and assign the homilists. Pity the poor priest who climbs into Sacred Heart's venerable pulpit without sufficient preparation or attention. If he "crashes and burns," I will certainly hear about it. When things don't go well, it is certainly to some degree my fault. Part of the Basilica's story and an important aspect of the University's tradition is to keep striving for excellence, especially when it comes to preaching the Gospel.

Sacred Heart is also a place where the art of "chancel prancing" is practiced and hopefully perfected in all its many diverse forms and varieties. We have, for example, hosted the entire conference of American bishops. We have welcomed the International Federation of Catholic Universities, and organized countless liturgies in several languages and a wide variety of styles. We are always receiving a cardinal from somewhere and a group or a conference from somewhere else. Our own regular liturgical schedule ranges from the elegant pieties of a "smells and bells" mass to the carefully orchestrated impromtus of a folk mass. The Liturgy of the Hours, Penance Services, Lessons and Carols, Halleluia Night, Hymn Fests, Stations of the Cross, Benediction, Rosary, and just about everything else that might bring Catholics together under the general heading of "prayer" all have a home in Sacred Heart. We have the Liturgical Choir, the Folk Choir, the Woman's Choir, the Schola, a Community Choir, a Spanish Choir, and a Bell Choir. Our Sacristy and its many services are almost as complicated and perhaps even better organized than IBM. Rehearsals for just about everything in the Basilica take place morning, noon, and night. The secretary who schedules all of this often needs the steady nerves and fearless courage of an experienced air traffic controller on a Thanksgiving weekend. My colleagues and I on the Basilica staff are normally the ones who hold the book and point to the prayer when all these liturgies finally take place.

An important component of this liturgical story at Sacred Heart involves all the special arrangements for the annual football season. Our planning committee sometimes jokes about what liturgical scholars may one day make of any records of our meetings that might somehow survive into future ages. What arcane and totally inaccurate academic interpretations may be proposed for all our extraordinary plans, unusual arrangements, expanded schedules, and elaborate posters for the liturgies of such exotic events as "the Michigan" or "the USC" weekend. Anyone now alive at Notre Dame surely must recognize and accept the fact that football exercises an enormous impact upon the pastoral life of the University. Starting at least by Thursday before most home games, large crowds of fans start showing up at Sacred Heart. By Friday, the Basilica masses are jammed with people, and by Saturday, literally thousands of visitors pass through the church every single hour. The Grotto is always ablaze with newly lit candles, and all the regularly scheduled Sunday masses and all the specially scheduled additional masses are filled to capacity.

I usually spend a good part of these weekends walking around Sacred Heart or standing outside before or after mass, just saying hello to people. Former students sometimes recognize me, while I tend to still remember them the way they looked when they were only nineteen or twenty. Everybody likes to be remembered, and reaching for names is one of the persistent and important challenges of ministry at a school. Even complete strangers will often pause just to say hello. Many people ask to have medals or rosaries blessed. Parents ask if you know their children. Old alumni often inquire about the even older and sometimes long deceased priests. Some people will request prayers, and still others want to stop if only for a moment to simply talk about God. Right or wrong, like it or not, football is somehow connected with Notre Dame's religious character.

Certainly many people feel so intensely loyal to our school and to its team precisely because of Notre Dame's Catholic tradition. After a defeat, a Saturday Vigil mass in the Basilica can be more grim than any Good Friday. After a victory, the mood is almost as exultant as at a joyous Easter. Win or lose, the Notre Dame crowd will still show up in impressive and sometimes even intimidating numbers. They are on campus for the game, but they also enthusiastically take advantage of the many opportunities offered for worship and for prayer. I really believe that God sometimes deliberately uses even football as an opportunity to tell the Christian story.

Certainly the most important aspect of ministry at Sacred Heart has to do with the fact that it is offered mostly for and with young people of college age. Men and woman in their late teens and early twenties usually begin to make some real adult personal decisions about their faith. This is certainly an appropriate time to ask questions and to use their minds to learn more about God and Christianity. At this age they also possess almost limitless stores of energy and zeal to put their growing convictions into practice for the service of God and neighbor. Certainly not every Notre Dame student is a believer, and not every Notre Dame Catholic is always faithful. Serving at Sacred Heart, however, affords me almost a daily experience of being with very many young Catholics who so obviously love God and are very enthusiastic about their faith.

The problem here is usually not how to get people to show up, but rather how to match their interest with challenging programs and opportunities for involvement. If you ask for volunteers, an army may appear. Notre Dame has more Eucharistic ministers than some good-sized dioceses. At the Basilica we have student readers, student servers, student ushers, and student choirs. When the University is in session, students are involved in all our programs, and their presence gives a special character to worship in the Basilica. Serving young people, ministering together with young people, and being mostly in the company of young people also adds spirit and enthusiasm to someone like me, whose age is now much closer to fifty than to forty. Being a priest in this setting makes it very easy to be optimistic about the Church and its future. Being a priest at Sacred Heart is clearly a privilege that I deeply appreciate. My own story about ministry has been significantly formed by the continuing story of this much revered and magnificent old church. Being a Holy Cross priest at the University of Notre Dame and serving at the Basilica of the Sacred Heart of Jesus are certainly great personal blessings for which I daily give thanks to God.

Both Catholic and Scholarly

JAMES R. LANGFORD

Looking back, it is clear to me that everything that happened in my life prior to my coming back to Notre Dame in 1974 as Director of the University Press, pointed in some providential way toward that happy event. Notre Dame is truly my home. My father, Walter Langford, taught Spanish and Portuguese here from 1931 until right before I came back. There has been a Langford at Notre Dame for some sixty-five years and counting. I grew up here; delivered newspapers and campus mail here as a boy and served as a campus guide for two summers. I studied at Notre Dame on a journalism scholarship and then left on a journey that took me first to the Dominicans for ten years and then to a career in book publishing that started at Doubleday, continued at the University of Michigan Press, and finally brought me home to head the Notre Dame Press.

University press publishing began at Oxford University more than 400 years ago. Even then, the publishing system looked to saleability over substance with the result that very important manuscripts, many that expanded the frontiers of knowledge, often went unpublished because they did not promise a profit. Oxford, and subsequently all great universities, regarded it as part of its mission of research, teaching, and service to see to it that such manuscripts were published and made available to scholars, libraries, and students around the world. More succinctly, as one press director put it, "University presses exist to publish the best books possible short of bankruptcy."

Jim Langford is Director of University of Notre Dame Press and Concurrent Assistant Professor in the Arts and Letters Core Course.

Notre Dame formally launched its press in 1949 largely to publish books under the aegis of the Committee on International Relations at Notre Dame. It went on to build a large, diverse, and reputable list in the 1960s under the directorship of Emily Schossberger, the first woman administrator at Notre Dame. But the Second Vatican Council outdated many theology and liturgy titles and, by the early 1970s, the Press had fallen on some hard times in terms of both finances and self-definition. The Press I inherited had been placed on probation for five years; either there would be a strong press or no press.

I accepted that challenge because of a deep conviction that there needs to be at least one very strong Catholic university press in the world and that Notre Dame is the place where that press should be. There are presses at Fordham, Georgetown, Catholic University, Duquesne, and Scranton, but Notre Dame seems to me closest to the kind of quality that would be able to rank with the best secular university presses such as Chicago, Yale, Princeton, California, Columbia, and so on.

Over the past two decades our program has grown and stands, I think, as living proof that George Bernard Shaw was wrong when he professed that a Catholic university is an oxymoron. Our Press has mined the Catholic tradition by publishing or republishing classic works by St. Thomas Aquinas, St. Anselm, William of Ockham, John Henry Newman; it has developed an important series of volumes in American Catholic history; it is a leading publisher of philosophy, political theory, ethics, medieval studies, and Mexican-American studies. Notre Dame Press books are used in undergraduate and graduate courses at more than 200 colleges and universities in the United States and receive enough reviews in intellectual media around the world to fill a 300-page book each year.

Without ever diluting our Catholicity we have been able to publish thought-provoking works that address issues of national, international, and secular concern. There is at Notre Dame a deep respect for free speech responsibly used and there is also a tolerance for responsible dialogue within the Church.

We have, on occasion, received both laudatory and angry letters from those on the right and on the left regarding books we have published. I see that as a sign of success.

What is Catholic about our work is that we solicit and develop books that explain and explore the tradition and bring it to bear on matters of importance to scholars and to all with a stake in the intellectual, cultural, and pragmatic concerns of our time. If the University is the place where the Catholic Church does its thinking, the Press is one of the places where that thinking is brought to the world. That is what gives me and my colleagues at the Press our sense of mission. We derive genuine satisfaction from knowing that what we do matters and echoes in the world. One example: several years ago, in conjunction with the Center for Civil and Human Rights at Notre Dame, we published the English language translation of the two-volume report of the Truth and Reconciliation Commission, which documented and dealt with the crimes of the Pinochet regime in Chile. Last year, the office of Prime Minister Nelson Mandela of South Africa called to let us know that the Chile volumes would be the model for South Africa's own judicial resolution of abuses under apartheid. We have helped truth and justice reach around the world.

Being at a Catholic university does not shield one from the full range of human types, fancies, and foibles. There are no guarantees that some in the community will not miss the point of its being Catholic on the one hand or a university on the other. What I find in the Catholic context is a worldview that is openly based on faith while at the same time is ready to embrace any truth that can illuminate that faith or help bring it through the mind to the heart. St. Thomas Aquinas, challenged for his use of the pagan Aristotle's philosophy, replied "Take the truth no matter where you find it." I cherish working at Notre Dame in part because here we do not need to be afraid of the truth or of where it leads us.

Working at a Catholic university as a book publisher and part-time teacher has provided membership in a community that, in the final measure, adds rather than subtracts from the well-being of the mystical body of Christ. Though the Press, the community, the people here may all fall short of our goals and ideals, the calls to goodness and excellence are never silenced here. The people I have met here, administrators, faculty, staff, and students, have in subtle but real ways deepened my faith and fueled my hope. I like to think that the books we publish do the same for others.

Leaning on an Inheritance

JEAN LENZ, O.S.F.

I thought I was the only one sweating it out in Farley Hall on one of the hottest June nights in South Bend history. Close to midnight there was a knock at my door by a young scholar, flushed with the heat. "Will you come outside and run through the sprinklers with me?" she asked. "They just turned on, but I don't want to go out alone." For the moment I stood still with a stare and an open mouth. Then I simply closed the door behind me and we left the building laughing.

There was a great full moon in a hazy southeastern sky. I felt a touch of mysticism in the air. We ran south taking the long way around the Peace Memorial through great sprays of water that arched every which way over the sidewalks into our faces and over our bodies. Then we ran north along Cavanaugh and Zahm catching a glimpse of the Dome drenched in midnight lights. In all, we "did" the north quad as we say, finally arriving back at Farley's south entrance—drenched, laughing, out of breath, a bit exhausted, so refreshed.

Curiously, that precious midnight moment has settled in me more and more as a fitting image of my twenty-three years of ministry at Notre Dame. I came to campus with a bit of reluctance in my heart in the fall of 1973, a year after the first undergraduate women arrived on campus. I knew I was headed for unchartered waters when I learned during an early interview that there was no written job description for the rector position. At the time, a priest-administrator offered an intriguing response: "Just come and share life. Then at the end of the year we'll write up what happened and hand it on to

Sister Jean Lenz, O.S.F., is Assistant Vice President for Student Affairs.

those who follow after." And so, for twenty-three years I've been sharing life and adjusting job descriptions.

From my earliest campus days, I courted a deep hunch in my heart that someone had laid a great inheritance of ministry at my feet which got "handed on" in great part by much story-telling from one generation of graduates to the next: from fathers to sons and grandsons and great grandsons. Now daughters would begin to add their heritage.

I was also intrigued by the fact that over the years graduates had entered the Congregation of Holy Cross and found themselves in a variety of academic, administrative, and staff positions also "handing on" the University. The same with lay faculty members who, I discovered, had done their undergraduate work at Notre Dame only to go on to graduate studies at some other university with an eye to returning to their Alma Mater as a professor.

Yet, in the midst of all this generational intrigue, some families arrived with sons and daughters who had never laid eyes on Notre Dame. New bloodlines were always welcomed.

I learned quickly that I should lean hard on this "inheritance" and let myself feel the strong support as well as the incredible expectations of many around me to bring Farley Hall into a unique moment in Notre Dame's history. Since its construction in 1947, Farley had been an all-male residence; now it was destined to become a hallowed hall for some 250 bright, articulate young women, pioneers of a sort.

During a welcome reception for new personnel, the Provost told me he was sure I would make it at ND if I did two things. He asked if I knew how to change fuses. I didn't. He proceeded to distinguish between circuit breakers and screw-type fuses and then commissioned me to track down all the fuse boxes in Farley as soon as possible. His second directive was short and to the point. "Never miss a meal; you will need all the energy you can muster." As time went on I translated these directives into their deeper meanings: stay practical and use your good common sense. And I passed them on to every staff member I trained.

As I welcomed that first class of some 140 freshmen to Farley Hall, two former hall presidents were at my side in chapel. Not too happy about having to vacate their "Farley College," as they called it, to make room for the first women on the North Quad, these two gentlemen were gracious enough to offer moral support and $150 "to get us started" at carrying on Farley's fame. They also challenged us to keep a variety of their hall traditions alive, most especially the Farley Striders, a running group that had already made a name for itself by sending monogrammed T-shirts to the pope, the emperor of Japan, and Johnny Carson, among other notables.

Of all the topics that I dared to touch upon that night, and on many succeeding arrival nights, two have stood the test of time. I remember strongly stressing that I hoped I wasn't going to have to tell them too terribly often to grow up. It rather seemed the time had come for them to start giving a great dose of thought and effort to growing deep. This got to be known as my "grow up, grow deep" talk which I have been reminded of affectionately in Christmas cards and countless reunion conversations.

I also invited them to consider doing what I had done when I first came down between the maples on Notre Dame Avenue: pray the Our Father with all their hearts so they would have the life they needed to open up to all that Notre Dame was about to offer them and expect from them. How well I remember "hanging" on the words of that precious prayer. It seemed a sure fit for freshmen, too.

Through my first weeks of rectoring, Farley turned into "home" in spite of me and my newness and the growing awareness that ministry was definitely going to be a twenty-four–hour way of life— with all the trimmings. It had been that way for generations of rectors before me, including the Reverend John Francis Farley, C.S.C., the hall's namesake. From all the stories I garnered, he apparently had strong pastoral influence on a long line of Notre Dame men who affectionately called him "Pop" Farley. The best eye-witness accounts were often spun by Father Charles Sheedy, C.S.C., Edward "Moose" Krause, and Professor Paul Fenlon all of whom remembered him as their rector in Sorin Hall where, as Krause recounted, "He was always one jump ahead of the most clever lads he supervised."

Father Farley stood at the heart of student life, living by that crucial rector adage, "Be there." One favorite photo shows him in a horse and buggy surveying local bars in town looking for students who were "off limits." Another depicts him in full Holy Cross habit playing ball, catcher's mitt and all. He was infamous for conducting mail calls in person, handing every letter to "his boys" twice a day. Here and there, I'm told, he would catch a perfume scent on an envelope and make a fitting fuss. The more I heard, the more I realized his hallmark was his pastoral presence. I had a lot to live up to.

I remember my first visit to his grave in the Community cemetery, near the large crucifix. His tombstone indicated his birth in 1876 and death in 1939. Many of the Farley women found their way there too, some with flowers. In the fall of 1975, one of them returned from a grave visit out of breath with the news that Pop Farley's 100th birthday was a few months away. With great fanfare the hall celebrated that year and every year since, with a January "Pop Farley Week." Somehow each year residents discover ingenious ways to keep his memory and influence alive.

Farley's first women blossomed into strong "pioneer" women at ND. The media was always just around the corner with the question, "What does it feel like to be a woman at ND?" Sometimes they made it sound like we had just landed on the moon. Often a woman was one among many men in any given class. I have no doubt that these co-eds managed some difficult, stressful, and humorous situations, with a host of stories to tell their grandchildren. What seemed to frustrate them most was being asked incessantly on a myrid of topics for "the woman's point of view" —as though all women were looking in the same direction.

While male students generally approved the University's move to admit women, those who "lost" their residence halls lagged behind a bit. A small percentage thought it was all a big mistake. From what I heard in friendly campus conversations, it was predominantly the male faculty who felt change the most in their classrooms. They cast a resounding positive vote since the women came with outstanding academic credentials and "weren't just looking for MRS. degrees" as some had suggested would be the situation.

I learned fast that I wasn't rectoring Farley alone. Over the years, my Assistant Rectors and RA's (resident assistants) were a veritable life-line for me. Together we knew every resident in Farley (and more often than not, their families and friends as well) and were able to touch lives in very daily ways. Generally, the Assistant and the RA's were strongly motivated, gifted with an array of talents including innate people skills. They put precious energy into their work, bore the burden of late hours on duty, and served well in difficult situations. When good RAs were least aware of it, they were incredible role models, unconsciously beckoning underclassmen to follow in their footsteps. Year after year, to a person, RAs would agree they learned unexpected lessons that would serve them a lifetime.

Curiously, RAs always seemed destined to carry their title for life. Long after their Farley days, I would hear them affectionately referred to far and wide in a variety of social settings as "my RA." One football weekend a former RA, who is now an obstetrician, stopped to visit at Farley and spun a fanciful tale. She was on intern duty at Northwestern Memorial Hospital in the Chicago area when a call came through that a woman was on her way to the emergency room to deliver her baby. Surgically dressed for intern duties, she rushed to meet the gurney as it rolled along the hallway. In the midst of the urgency and excitement of the moment, the expectant mother looked up at the budding physician and queried, "Aren't you from Farley Hall?" The intern quickly owned up to her heritage, "Well, I am," only to hear a very nervous retort, "You were the RA, and I was a Freshman. Please take good care of me." And the drama carried on.

Farley Hall was never in want for drama. From the moment students settled in each fall with all their "stuff," including all their gifts and talents, stories unfolded. There was so much joy and pain and daily existence to share. Amazingly, the life of the hall produced its own "peer ministry" activity. Farley women found endless ways to care for each other in the face of minor illnesses, upsetting news, difficult relationships, academic stress, and decision making of all sorts. Of course, there were some selfish moments, but in general I watched peer ministry thrive and prayed it would continue year after year. In fact, I came to believe it was the outcome of our prayer together around our Farley altar.

The altar of our residence hall chapel was a place where many students gathered to celebrate the Eucharist, in large groups on weekends and in smaller groups for daily celebrations. And it wasn't unusual for students to meet in advance with Eucharistic celebrants to plan upcoming celebrations. Many music ministers trained with Campus Ministry, played a variety of intruments, and led the hymns. Others baked the Eucharisic bread. Some practiced with those who volunteered to read the Scriptures. One year to my surprise, Farley had a team of sacristans who "wanted to learn how to take care of Church things." At another juncture a young woman came carrying the large Sacramentary from the sacristy with a simple request: "Would you please teach me the parts of the mass? I want to become the Liturgical Commissioner of Farley." And she did. In fact she went on for doctoral studies in theology. Watching the Hall's liturgy commissioners in action put hope in my heart, since I was convinced that much of their experience and energy was destined for the Church-at-large in the years ahead.

Hardly a Sunday night went by without someone standing up at the end of mass informing the women and men assembled about someone or some group that needed help. The request might focus on Logan Center or the Center for the Homeless or someone needing a wheelchair or food. It might be an announcement about a deadline for applying for Holy Cross Associates or for ACE (Alliance for Catholic Education), each of which attracts seniors to a period of committed service after graduation. There was always some student or student group, which was usually associated with the Center for Social Concerns, recognizing a need and asking for assistance in the form of time, money, or other material support.

Helping others gets a strong and consistent press on campus. This Gospel value was, no doubt, alive and well in those who arrived here in covered wagons back in 1842, and it has hung in the air and lots of hearts since then. As rector, you stay close to that inheritance which has its own way of getting into your bones and changing your heart, too.

All in all, rectoring was a terribly purifying experience. Many residents knew all my idiosyncrasies, weaknesses, and strengths. Amazingly, there were also some who sensed when I needed to be ministered to. One young woman hit the mark every time. Somewhere along the line she heard me say that "violins soothed my soul," and she would remind me of it with a supportive question whenever she saw me standing knee high in some stressful situation, "Maybe it's a violin day?" Another resident often returned from the Huddle with an "extra" double-decker ice cream cone. A sophomore once told me I looked as though I could use a long walk around the lake so she stayed and covered the office and phone. One of the most compassionate moments came when an RA who had lost her Mom to cancer met me returning from a weekend visit to my Dad who was dying of the same. I told her I thought I might not see him alive again. We wept together.

My ten-year stride of rectoring Farley Hall came to an abrupt halt with an early Monday morning phone call in February 1983 from the Vice President of Student Affairs. Would I "go to England next year as Rector/Chaplain for the College of Arts and Letters London Program"? I went silent trying to find my path through an explosion of thoughts. It took a meeting or two to get me on that journey.

In August I was walking the streets of Londontown spending English pence and pounds and getting used to hearing that a purchase in the marketplace would cost me a "quick quid." I took public transportation every which way, discovering the best approaches for travel from Sutherland Avenue in Maida Vale where students would eat and sleep, to 7 Albemarle in the Mayfair district, where they would take classes—a stone's throw from the Ritz Hotel. One week later, ministry turned real in British circles when some sixty juniors arrived at Heathrow Airport for their semester abroad. Since the London program was in its infancy, there were few files and no official job descriptions in print for the Rector/Chaplain. I should have known. It would be lived and written out in the aftermath for those who would follow.

Amazingly, we all adjusted quite easily to holding the gift of a London semester in our hands. Students knew I had expectations of them, and vice versa. Residence hall life was a shared experience, so many things fell into place. We celebrated our London beginnings standing around a makeshift altar in the main foyer at 7 Albemarle, underneath a grand winding staircase. For the occasion, we borrowed a heavy linen tablecloth from the historic Brown's Hotel, just down the street, where Teddy Roosevelt spent his honeymoon. It seemed that everything we touched or looked at had historical hinges.

Our century-old Sutherland Avenue residence was so like a London home in a late night movie, complete with a high wrought iron fence and basement apartment. There was no central heating, only gas-heaters in old fireplaces. Showers were "created" in the basement. We managed. Most of all, we shared good times learning so many things so fast and so painlessly. In addition to regular classes, there were first-rate concerts and stage plays which were attended as class assignments. The London Symphony and Derek Jacobi's "Cyrano" led to easy discussions just about anywhere.

We were constantly debriefing each other after travels around the British Isles, the continent, or wherever. All along the way we leaned on each other through minor illnesses and needs of all sorts. Often there were students who came by my room "just to talk" about the deepest things going on inside themselves. During the day, there was always a quaint pub for lunch with a quiet spot for discussing concerns of the moment that touched on faith questions, relationships, poor self-image, and sometimes emotional upsets that students had buried in themselves back on campus.

Quite naturally there were always some discipline issues brewing. Students knew they had to follow travel regulations. The London "bobbies" forbade them to play frisbee down Sutherland Avenue. This was not the North Quad. Kitchens and sleeping rooms had to be kept cleaner. Since they were of legal age for consuming alcohol in England, they were expected to act their age, use good common sense, and drink responsibly, or catch a plane back to the USA. Without too much fuss, Notre Dame expectations filtered into London life.

To my delight, the semesters abroad surprised me with sabbatical trimmings. No teaching, no committee meetings, no endless activities typical of campus life. I simply stayed close to sixty students studying their way through London. However, little did I realize that this English expedition would mark the end of my rector years and bring me to the doorstep of a dozen years of ministry in the Office of Student Affairs.

As Rector of Farley and adjunct instructor in the theology department, I had heard myself say on too many occasions that I would never want to work in "that" office. Over the years I had watched the Office of Student Affairs supervise ten student support departments, including twenty-four–hour security services. All student accidents, serious illnesses, and significant student life disruptions of many sorts were handled by that office. It was also responsible for hiring and training head staffs and RAs for the twenty-four undergraduate and three graduate residences. In addition, serious discipline matters were handled in the Office of Student Affairs. All in all, there was an intensity of life on the third floor of the administration building that did not attract me.

The invitation by a new Vice President of Student Affairs to bring my rector years of experience to a newly created Senior Staff as an Assistant Vice President was against everything I felt drawn to. When I was initially asked, I put my hands up in front of me as though I didn't want the request even to touch me. Then reasons were laid before me that made me give serious positive thought to walking into the very office I so shied away from. Thoughtful encouragement from others who knew me quite well cast still more light on the situation. I prayed hard, letting myself get used to the idea of feeling so unanchored— and agreeing once again to shape a new job description.

The Office of Student Affairs was as intense a place as I

had imagined. Not knowing what would happen next in a world of 10,000 students can shape you into living on the edge a bit. Something was always happening and kept me riding an emotional roller coaster. There were so many uplifting experiences of life; and then so many serious twists and turns followed by such difficult decisions that had to be made.

By far the hardest moments came when facing the death of a student, sometimes in terribly tragic circumstances. I have stood so helpless in hospitals and in cemeteries offering only my presence and prayers. By now I know all too well how the loss of loved ones and attending grief can invade the deepest parts of human beings and cause such inexplicable pain. Over and over I have been so deeply inspired by parents and siblings, relatives and friends of our Notre Dame students who have gone to God before the rest of us. Many of those left behind have become dear Notre Dame friends.

The Office of Student Affairs also stays close to the South Bend hospital scene. It's very familiar territory, especially the emergency room. Students admitted there reach out for all the support you can give them as they await emergency appendectomies, stitches for major cuts, casts for broken bones, medicine for complicated infections, and tests for serious drunkenness. I simply can't imagine my life for this last quarter of a century without a hospital emergency room, its caring staff, and all the medical technology available.

There were a handful of years when I helped to jury some of the most serious student discipline cases that came to the Office of Student Affairs. Far too many times alcohol was a major topic since it was invariably linked with violent behavior, daredevil antics that led to serious injury, and destruction of property. It became clearer than ever to me that exercising good discipline procedures was one of the most important educational things Notre Dame did. I often summon up the words of one of our students who, after his major "alcohol mistake," was suspended for a semester. On his return, he was man enough to come back and say, "The best thing you ever did was to kick me in the butt and get me out of here for awhile. I began to see ugly stuff in my life that I never saw before."

During my first four years in the Office of Student Affairs, we suspended forty-one students and dismissed a handful of others for what we deemed were serious reasons. Those suspended left us for a semester or two, took stock of their lives, and got the help they needed. Forty of them returned to graduate. It became somewhat obvious that what Notre Dame said it "stood for" got tested out in our office on a rather regular basis.

One Holy Cross priest with years of experience at watching people go through some of the agonies of growing up, put it on the line with me: "Don't be afraid to be tough on our students. They're the first ones to send their kids back to us." He saw it happen hundreds of times.

But curiously, parents often found it difficult when we were "tough" and expected the best behavior from their sons and daughters. They made endless telephone calls and inquiries, and wrote long letters. Some parents got angry at us when it seemed they were really angry at their offspring or themselves for whatever reasons. On the other hand, some parents cooperated in the best of ways. I suspect there is a wonderful correlation between the growth of parents and their Domer offspring. Forever I salute the energies that go into "parenting" and the wisdom it takes to do it well.

After twenty-three years I am convinced that to live life "in loco parentis" at Notre Dame is to be at the heart of student ministry. There was a time when I was very suspect of that phrase. Now I would put my life on the line for it in its deepest meaning. Nothing, but nothing, can take the place of one generation taking on the responsibility of standing with and for the next generation coming down the line. I have been so honored to be associated with a host of individuals who continually struggle to expect the best of our students. I can tell by the expectant look in their eyes and the energy in their actions that they simply care. They find engaging ways to congratulate or correct our young scholars—sometimes in the same breath.

Finally, as I continue to lean hard on the "inheritance of ministry" in very daily ways at this university, I realize there are some great forces at the heart of this place that daily feed my soul. One is the campus I walk on that fills itself up with the breathtaking beauty of all four seasons, each lending a change of landscape colors to buildings of all sizes, shapes, and vintage positioned along many paths. One young man visiting campus caught the power of it all when he remarked to another, "Just walking across this campus makes me want to get inside one of these building and study something."

Another great force is the community of people around me. I had heard talk about the Notre Dame family. Gradually, I came to see for myself that I was surrounded in great part by folks who knew how to work together, as well as enjoy each other's company in groups of all sizes, sometimes big enough to fill a stadium. It's a community that strives to care for its own and others. While I never once doubted that there would always be someone nearby to assist me with my ministry, I never realized how many would become my friends. Dear friends, close friends, grace givers.

By far the greatest force is faith life practiced unabashedly. Eucharistic celebrations stay at the heart of some of the largest gatherings we annually host: Freshman Orientation, Junior Parents Weekend, and Graduation Exercises. Chapels across campus draw students and staff regularly for daily and weekly liturgies. Various types of prayer services are held to meet the needs of all kinds of human spiritual yearnings. But what leaves me speechless is to hear one student simply invite another to come to pray. And what really takes my breath away, each time, is to come upon someone simply at prayer.

Sometimes in prayerful moments late at night in my Farley room, names and faces come out of nowhere. My thoughts latch on to particular Farley memories at the blink of an eye. Phone calls from alumni make past events seem like they happened yesterday. At times I think of "the students I have taught" or of "all the women who have lived in Farley," and I pray for them in those phrases, not able to see all their faces or say all their names. On special days I recall my ten Franciscan Sisters from my Joliet community who also joined me in rector ranks over the years. I think of my friends, my best friends. My family. At times I muse about all the conversations that the walls of my room have heard. A chorus of stories hidden in plaster forever.

In the midst of some late night musings, especially when the heat hangs heavy, I think I've heard a knock at the door. I'm always ready for another good run through the sprinklers, in midnight moonlight, with hopes of catching a glimpse of the Dome over my left shoulder. But maybe it only happens once in a lifetime.

Teaching Good and Welfare

BLAKE LEYERLE

Catholics are in the habit of remembering the dead. This is good for a historian. The living quality of the dead is indeed so pervasively transmitted in Catholicism that it tends to be taken for granted. My colleagues look surprised when I mention it: What other perspective is there? But in answer, one need not look very far. As I learned at the somewhat Methodist Duke University and the even less Congregationalist Yale University, Protestants tend to concentrate on the essentially a-historical Word: the Word which became incarnate in Jesus spoke to Luther, Calvin, and Wesley, and speaks to us the same. In this theology, the pursuit of history becomes a redundant, if relatively harmless, pastime.

From a Catholic perspective, however, history is crucial. It is the story of how we became who we are, potentially as fascinating and ultimately determinative as stories about one's own forgotten infancy—if not always so cosy. "Tradition," as one of my colleagues is fond of remarking, "is not just what your grandmother did,"[1] although it, of course, includes her. Our shared past comprises some pretty strange folk and some even more angular opinions. Adopting a selection of these "traditional" postures would strike many today as radical innovation. As we change, so does our history. Or as one wag commented, "History isn't what it used to be." It is endlessly surprising, and that is its joy and challenge.

My own work as a historian of early Christianity focuses on social rather than doctrinal issues. I want to know how ordinary Christians ate their meals, raised their children, spent

Blake Leyerle is Assistant Professor of Theology.

their money, and prayed at holy places, rather than what learned fathers were saying about the Trinity. This interest in community matters, in turn, influences how I teach my classes. Some years back, an undergraduate in my introductory course on scripture and history asked me why I didn't begin my classes with prayer, "like all the other theology professors." My response was to say, "Quiet everyone! Jack wants to lead us in prayer." He was, of course, appalled: "Wait a minute! That's not what I meant!"

If not prayer, I do have a ritual with which I begin my classes. Borrowing directly from one of my teachers,[2] who looked in turn to *Robert's Rules of Order*, I begin by asking whether there is any "Good and Welfare." "Under this heading," General Robert writes, "members who obtain the floor commonly are permitted to offer informal observations regarding the work of the organization, the public reputation of the society or its membership, or the like."[3] For my class, this is an invitation to anyone to make announcements of either general interest (special musical, athletic, or liturgical events) or personal achievement (making a sports team, getting an award, having a birthday). Over the years we have celebrated new brothers, sisters, nieces, and nephews, sung "Happy Birthday" more times than I could count, enjoyed Halloween cards ("Werewolf I'd be without You") from grandmothers who occasionally slipped ten dollars into the envelope, and laughed with one of the stars of the football team when he told us about going backstage after Janet Jackson's performance in Chicago and getting to kiss her: "Best day of my life!" he said grinning. As the class grows accustomed to this ritual time, the news changes: students not only urge us to visit their dorm's "Haunted House," but also tell us that their grandmother is sick in the hospital; we celebrate not only Kyle's haircut, but also the news that Beonca's mother does not have cancer; we are reminded not only of the test dates for Organic Chemistry, but of the men and women from our ROTC program who are going to keep peace in Bosnia.

This time of shared personal and communal announcements provides a way for me to get to know my students: what is going on in their lives and hearts. But it is not without pedagogical value. This informal, conversational beginning accustoms my students to hearing their own voices and those of their peers, making them much more willing to participate in discussion later. In a real sense they are preparing to learn. Hegel commented on how modern Europeans prepare for their daily tasks by first orienting themselves horizontally through reading the newspaper. Their medieval ancestors, in contrast, had oriented themselves vertically through saying their prayers. [4] His point is that a similar sense of negligence, uneasiness—even guilt—haunts us if we have been too rushed to take in the morning news as used to dog our forebears who skipped their morning orisons. The analogy is strengthened when we register how ritualized the reading of the paper is for many people: the paper itself must be folded in a precise manner, the sequence of reading must be the same, the proper accoutrements must be to hand. If any of these features is absent (no milk for the coffee) or violated (the first pages of the front section are missing), the ritual does not "work," i.e., it fails to confirm our sense of being in a right relationship to the world: it becomes a "bad day." Thus while Good and Welfare may strike my students as just an opportunity to delay the beginning of class, it is instead a necessary prelude. On those days when no one has anything to announce, a heavy inertia sets in, from which it often takes the whole period to recover.

Good and Welfare also establishes from the outset that learning is a communal endeavor. Whether an individual class goes well or not depends not simply upon my preparation and energy (and hence upon a complex mesh of life issues), but upon theirs. This fundamentally dynamic quality of education, however, is easily overlooked or obscured. Strengthening the illusion of the instructor's sole responsibility is the pedagogical strategy of pitching the style and content of courses a little out of reach. And by this I mean more than the use of specialized vocabulary, though that is part of it. As one of my own professors once commented, education is "like football: a good quarterback throws the ball to where the receiver isn't."[5] Throwing to where the receiver stands brings any momentum to a halt. This rings especially true for anyone trying to teach theology at Notre Dame. Not because we are fond of football, but because our students often come to us already certain about their belief. If we pitch our classes to where they stand there will be no growth: no real education. Our job is the often unsettling one of presenting familiar topics as "problems" well before they have been perceived as such.

In this task, discernment is crucial: one must not foist one's own concerns on students, ("If this isn't a problem for you, it should be!"), but instead prepare them for issues that are certainly on the horizon. For example, my class, some years back, was discussing the fate of the citizens of Jericho described in the sixth chapter of the book of Joshua; they were outraged at such clear evidence of innocent suffering. "Where," they asked quite rightly, "was God in that slaughter?" I responded by asking them what explanations for "the problem of suffering" they had heard elsewhere. With exemplary facility they repeated the standard justifications. "Do these satisfy you?" I asked. "No," they answered. And as every one of those fifty people looked at me expectantly, I agreed, "It's a problem." "Aren't you going to tell us the answer?" they asked with outrage. "I can't," I admitted, "It's a *real* problem." In the face of their honest frustration, it would have been glib as well as patronizing to say, "Welcome to adult faith." All I could add was my own conviction that whatever else one says, the reality of the suffering of others must never be minimized.

When I told this story some time later to a former student now working as a hospital chaplain, he was amazed that the students had been able to confront this question in a classroom. Most of the people he saw daily on the wards, he said, were wrestling with the problem of suffering for the first time in a situation of crisis. By education, we hope to prepare students for a future which will assuredly have hard times. This preparation entails not so much giving them answers as welcoming them into a process so that when some of these questions do become their own, they will remember, not so much how we dealt with them, but rather that we did deal with them: that there were ways available in the tradition that they could find again.

As a time of enhanced freedom, college challenges students to discover new limits. It is important to honor this growth, although it can be unsettling for teachers. I was happily suggesting to my class that perhaps the most important message of Abraham's near sacrifice of his son Isaac was encoded in the angel's "Stop!" when Kurt intervened like some other forbidding angel: "I don't believe a word of what you've been saying." I was taken aback, not so much by the objection, as by its placement: I would never have anticipated a crisis of faith over the priestly series of covenants. His commitment to what he believed and his courage to protest, however, I admired. "You don't have to believe it," I answered him, "You just have to hear it." He looked angry at what seemed, I suspect, a cheap shot. So I explained that I wanted him—and each member of the class—to know that he had every right to his own religious beliefs and integrity. But since it was a class, he would be asked how he supported his position and must in turn respect how I arrived at mine, even if, in the end, he still wanted to disagree.

Openness to dialogue is one of the best aspects of academic study. There are precious few places where the setting forth of a position and the reasoning behind it constitutes an invitation to dialogue—a serious engagement at the end of which I may say, "You're right, you've convinced me." In theological terms, to honor the divergent contributions of others is to welcome the stranger, to be open to the Christ who comes in unexpected guises. This kind of welcoming is, of course, much more easily said than done, especially in an institutional setting. But it is no use for me to speak peace—to claim that I honor difference—while waging war on everyone who disagrees with me. Honest intellectual give and take can provide a model of some utility not only for our relations with one another, but also for what a living faith might look like.

Students often come to the study of theology with a firmly embedded idea that faithfulness means a posture of respectful distance: as though faith were some dear, fragile, antique ornament that was best served by wrapping it in multiple layers of bubble-wrap and setting it carefully on the highest shelf far from any rude jostling. But a better model for faith would be relational. Like any other good relationship built on trust over time, faith should be able to withstand a certain amount of friction. An excessive caution about what can be said or thought suggests a lack of confidence in the tradition, a suspicion that faith might in fact be essentially indefensible and easily crushed. It is a stance of faith to insist on the durability of our tradition: that having been forged in response to the most pressing human problems, it can sustain our most searching questions.

Teaching is finally far more about creating a space in which education can happen than about throwing information to students like fodder. This sounds very therapeutic, but I actually learned it from Aristotle, who commented that while "beginning students can reel off the words they have heard," for real education to occur "that subject must grow to be part of them, and that takes time."[6] For knowledge to be real it must be lived, incorporated into the stuff of one's life. Almost everyone who has gone into education has experienced the excitement of finding some aspect of daily life transformed by what one has read or discussed. In religious terms, this is an echo of the word becoming flesh: the mystery of the Incarnation. The power of this experience is such that it makes missionaries: one wants to share it.

When I arrived at Notre Dame, fresh from my own graduate education in the history of Christianity, my colleagues often asked me, "When will you start doing theology?" This question perplexed me. I understood theology to be a subfield within the wider field of religious studies, one primarily indebted to philosophy and concerned almost exclusively with the history of ideas. As someone interested in issues of daily life in early Christianity, I suspected strongly that I would never "start doing theology" if this meant writing a learned article on the doctrine of the Atonement. On the other hand, I wondered whether I was already doing something quasi-theological by virtue simply of my position within the Department of Theology. As the semesters passed, however, I began to appreciate more pointedly how my work in social history enriched the context in which my students learned their theology. I started suggesting that knowledge about ordinary life might provide some crucial human framework for the development of theoretical structures. Lately, I have become more radical. I now understand my research into social issues within early Christianity as giving due weight to the process by which communities of people work out their lives, asking, as we all must do, "What truly matters?" And how they answer that question, in turn, shapes their food, clothing, and interpersonal practices. These ordinary life issues therefore inevitably mediate beliefs about the Incarnation: the way in which God is found among us. This is theology. It is these pressing human problems that drive the theological engine.

With this realization, I can now revisit Jack's question about why I do not begin class with prayer. Only the slightest shift in perspective reveals "Good and Welfare" as a space set apart for communal thanksgiving and petition: the place where all prayer—as well as all education—begins.

NOTES

1. With thanks to David Burrell, C.S.C.

2. With thanks to Kalman Bland.

3. Henry M. Robert, *Robert's Rules of Order* (Glenview, Ill.: Scott, Foresman, 1990), 357.

4. Quoted without citation in Benedict Anderson, *Imagined Communities: Reflections on the Origin and Spread of Nationalism* (London and New York: Verso, 1991), 35.

5. With thanks to Jaroslav Pelikan.

6. *Nicomachean Ethics* 7.1147a, in *Nichomachean Ethics*, trans. Martin Ostwald (Indianapolis: Bobbs-Merrill), 183.

Our Way

TERENCE H. LINTON, C.S.C.

Final exams are over at last. It's Saturday morning and as I watch out my window I see small groups of twos and threes standing around, suitcases bulging and handy, waiting for taxis to take them to the airport. Those who are driving home have gone already, wanting to be on the road before the holiday traffic gets too thick. Or, at least, that is how they explained it last night when many of them dropped by to say "Merry Christmas" and inquire after my plans for the holidays. Some are still waiting for parents who are making the trek from nearby towns and neighboring states to pick them up.

It's very quiet in my room. There is no sound from the weight room directly below me—usually very loud rock music accompanies the clank and thud of iron weights being dropped on the concrete floor. The phone is strangely silent and there are no knocks on my door. In the preceding months, I have often looked forward to this moment, but its arrival takes me by surprise. It's an abrupt transition from a place alive with people to empty rooms and deserted corridors. Grace Hall normally houses 520 people (although this year we are closer to 540)—mostly young men ranging in age from eighteen to twenty–three. I am the exception, being (I am shocked to realize) older than many of their parents.

For the next month, I can step out of my usual dorm role and become, for a while at least, a normal human being. Not that being a rector disqualifies one for normalcy, but sometimes it seems so. When I talk to old friends and they ask what I am doing

Father Terry Linton, C.S.C., was rector of Grace Hall and Concurrent Instructor in the Freshman Writing Program from 1992–1996.

now, I find it frustrating to tell them: "I am the rector of Grace Hall at Notre Dame," as though that explanation could sum it up neatly. Of course, we have a job description listing responsibilities and expectations, but that hardly captures it either—proving woefully understated at such times as sitting at the hospital bed of an ailing or injured student at four in the morning, or when bailing some wayward lad out of the county jail.

That's not to say that everything a rector has to do involves tragedy or misfortune. But as any parent knows, being responsible for young men (or women) as they go about the business of becoming adults is rarely a smooth process. Probably there are other ways to do it than the way we operate at Notre Dame, but ours is an important part of our heritage. We are heirs of the French boarding school tradition which Father Sorin and his companions naturally continued when they began this enterprise over 150 years ago. They lived with their students, sharing their lives with them. And we continue to do the same.

Of course, this is not the only tradition which we continue in our residence halls at Notre Dame. We are a Catholic university and that fact informs and motivates our ministry here. Most of our students are Catholic but even they are sometimes surprised by our allegiance to the Church and its teachings. When I asked my freshman writing class recently to think about the reality of their university life in comparison to what they had expected, one told me that she hadn't realized the place would be "so Catholic." When I asked her to explain what she meant by that she said that everywhere she goes she is surrounded by visible signs of religion: crucifixes in the classrooms, Sacred Heart Basilica, the never-deserted Grotto, religious statues, hall chapels, and so on. She was not displeased by this, only a bit in wonderment.

In the residence hall, our faith life centers around our Sunday mass. Ironically, for a hall its size, Grace has a very tiny chapel, adequate for weekday masses, but not for Sunday. So each Sunday night (our mass is at 10 p.m. and is, by no means, the latest on campus) we have to transform our social area into a worship space. Out come the altar and candle sticks, the credence table and the ambo. The "Grace Tabernacle Choir" tunes up and the readers practice. Gradually, men filter down from the upper floors and friends come from other dorms. As mass begins, there is little floor space uncovered and when the time comes, the communion ministers have to thread their way carefully to their stations. Someone looking at this from the outside might see confusion, but everyone involved seems quite content. As the rector and one who celebrates this mass often (I share this privilege with two other Holy Cross priests who live "in residence") this is one of my favorite times of the week. People come to this mass because they want to be here, not because parents or anyone else forces them. A friend reports in this regard that he was recently walking on the quad behind several freshmen. One was overheard to ask another: "Are you going to mass tonight?" The other replied: "Of course—I can't believe the peer pressure around here to go to mass."

Worshipping with our students, whether on Sunday or at weeknight masses is a very important part of our hall ministry. Our purpose is not just to fulfill obligation, but to help our residents to find their place in the wider worshipping Church. I am very conscious of the fact that these young people will not always have the supportive community of peers and sense of friendship that they do at Grace Hall, but they are developing their own sense of what it means to be an adult Christian, and that part of that responsibility is community worship.

Certainly mass is the center of our religious life at Grace, but it is not the only thing we do. I have noticed in the last few years that more and more people seek me out for the Sacrament of Reconciliation. I'm not sure how to interpret that—one thing may be that the longer I am here the better I am known. At any rate, these are graced moments that usually begin with a tentative knock on my door and end with a stronger sense of the presence of God for both penitent and confessor.

Before I started in hall ministry at Notre Dame, I taught for a number of years in a large Catholic high school. I went into that work relatively unprepared for it, but found that I had a kind of aptitude for teaching and stayed far longer than I had intended. As in many of our experiences, I learned as much about myself during those years as I was able to teach others. And it is on that learning that I most often draw in my present ministry. In fact, I think that had I not had the experience of working with people of high school age I would be seriously handicapped in what I do now.

Perhaps one of the most important lessons I have learned is that not everything needs to be treated at the same level of intensity. For example, two roommates who annoy one another doesn't have the same weight as the young man who is dealing with a serious illness or death in his family. In the first case, the two people would like nothing better than for me to take it in hand and make a decree. Joe would like me to find John to blame for all the trouble they have been having—the late night noise, the dirty laundry strewn around the room—and give him an ultimatum: shape up or ship out. John, of course, would like Joe to be the object of the rector's wrath—it seems that Joe's friends visit at inopportune times, and he insists on leaving the window open even on the coldest nights. It comes as something of a shock to them both when I say: "I am not going to move either of you—you are adults, you work it out." Rarely does the problem go any further. When they realize that they are indeed now adults and are expected to supply the solutions to their own difficulties, they do so.

The young man with the weightier problem is another story. He is finding that life, at times, can be very painful and lonely. Coming to adulthood, for him, means coming to grips with some of life's mysteries and that there is no longer anyone there to "kiss it and make it better." Facing the death of a loved one, or any of the other pains of life, can be agonizing, but it can also be an invitation to greater strength and faith. We can only befriend him and support him as God draws him into grace.

I have in my living room what has come to be known as "the couch of shame," or so I refer to it when talking with friends. It is a rather handsome piece of furniture actually, hardly distinguishable as a sinister object, but it is here that I have the young men sit who are visiting me because of a disciplinary problem. It tends to be most busy on Monday nights which is the time I reserve for dealing with any mishaps the previous weekend might have seen. Those mishaps are many and various, ranging from "accidental" restructuring of the building, to violations of parietals (the university policy requiring the opposite sex to be off the residence floors by a particular time—usually 2 a.m. on weekend nights.) Sometimes, a problem will be serious enough to warrant its being sent to the Office of Residence Life—an overnight parietals violation, for example, or a serious question of harassment. These things are rare, however, and mostly I can deal with whatever happens. As one might imagine, the "couch of shame" sessions can be anxious moments. But another thing I learned when teaching in high school was always to treat the person with respect and to try as much as possible to separate the person from the particular behavior. It is my intention in these sessions to have the student take responsibility for his actions, and in doing so, to help him realize that all actions have consequences. The particular consequence might be a monetary fine, hall service hours, an apology to anyone offended or hurt, or a combination of these things. When Pete comes to see me (at my invitation) because he got angry at his roommate and in frustration put his fist through a bathroom partition, he may leave my room with a lightened wallet (he would have to pay for the repair,) and a sore fist, but he should in no way leave as a diminished person. I am happy to say that Pete has never had to visit me for the same thing twice.

Of course, alcohol presents a special problem. Most of the disciplinary problems I deal with involve alcohol at some level. Our students drink and often feel they have a right to do so even though it is illegal for anyone under twenty-one. For the most part, they see it as something that college students do and are quite puzzled when I, or another member of the staff, point out to them that they are in the wrong. But this, too, can be an opportunity for growth. Sometimes I think that I must keep our Office of Alcohol and Drug Education in business for when a student comes to me more than once because of an alcohol-related incident, I send him for an assessment. I always explain that the easiest thing for me to do would be to turn a blind eye, but that in all conscience I can't. If he has a problem, or even the beginning of one, it is important to find

that out quickly so that he can make adjustments in his behavior before something occurs which is outside our control.
The student goes reluctantly and usually the assessment results
in nothing more than a few mandated alcohol education
sessions. But it has made him think, and it has made him take
stock of potentially harmful behavior patterns. I have even had
some thank me for my intervention, but as in the Gospel, that
is usually only one out of ten.

I think that residence hall life at Notre Dame is unique. Of
course, I don't have much experience of other colleges, but I
know that here it is a very important part of our mission. We
are less reluctant to intervene in the lives of our students if we
think it is necessary than might be the case at other schools.
We are convinced that a great deal of education takes place
outside the classroom as well as within it. Learning to live
with others, to take responsibility for one's own life (accomplishments and mistakes) accepting faith and its obligations
as an adult, acknowledging the part we play in the lives and
needs of others—these things are worthy objects of reflection
at a Catholic university. Our students come to us wanting to
receive a first-rate education. We are bold enough to want to
send them away closer to God.

Our success is partly born out by the number of our
graduates who want to be of service when they leave the University. A significant number enter formal service programs
for a year or so, perhaps teaching or working among the disadvantaged. Others choose to be of service where they work
and live. Whatever they do, I am convinced that they all know
that to be a Christian means to take responsibility not only for
themselves, but also for those who cannot help themselves. It
is a lesson that they learned, not in small part, because of their
residence hall experience.

Alumni who return to campus in great number each year
immediately visit their old dorms to ask after the rector and
staff. Perhaps another indication of the extent to which we in
hall staff ministry become a part of the lives of those we serve
can be seen in the weddings and baptisms I am asked to

celebrate. And nothing gives me more joy than to receive a call from a former resident who just wants to keep in touch, or maybe ask for a letter of reference, or perhaps to ask me to pray for him or someone he loves.

A few days ago I was in conversation with one of the residents of the hall—I don't remember the reason for the meeting—it was probably just a chance encounter or he might have seen my door open and dropped in as many often do. The subject came round to how people were looking forward to our moving to a new hall next year (the residents of Grace are moving to two new halls which are being constructed on the south side of campus.) He asked if I would be going to one of the new halls and I answered that I would. "I'm glad," he said, "I like the way you run things. You expect us to be responsible people, and you call us to account when we aren't. You treat us like adults." I couldn't have received a better compliment.

It's still quiet here. The phone has rung a few times, but now they are long distance calls. Jay has forgotten his knee brace and can't really move around much without it—could I send it to him? Tom bought some Christmas presents for his family but left them under some laundry on his couch. Could I . . . ? And Andy thinks he might have left his door unlocked. Could I check it for him, please? They might be gone, but they're not forgotten. I wouldn't have it any other way.

Notre Dame's Invitation to Ministry, a Life-time Commitment

I am pleased to have been invited to contribute personal perspectives as an alumna about mission and ministry, specifically, how Notre Dame's Catholic identity and character are realized in my day-to-day ministries. As with many invitations I've received from Notre Dame and the Holy Cross Congregation, this one, calling for reflection, was just what I needed at the time. My recent pregnancy was troublesome, but gratefully God blessed us with another healthy daughter, our fourth. While still basking in that joy, my father, who has been a significant creative force in my personal sense of mission and ministry, became seriously ill. These were typical life experiences but their close proximity to one another and the invitation to focus on Notre Dame's impact on mission and ministry in my own life inspired much reflection. Not knowing how to aptly articulate the overwhelming impact Notre Dame has had on my life, I share my personal reflections, taking great refuge in the Lord's assurance that we need not be anxious about what to say because the Holy Spirit will supply the message.

What has transpired since the undergraduate Notre Dame experience?

For reference, I include a chronology since graduation from Notre Dame in 1981, as a government major. I first served as a

Irene P. Loftus, ND '81 and J.D. '90, is an attorney. She and her husband Jamie (ND '81 and M.B.A. '90) serve on the Advisory Council of the Institute for Church Life.

Holy Cross Associate, volunteering in this Holy Cross post-graduate program. In 1985, I received my Masters Degree in Public Policy from the University of Chicago, began a position I held for two years as policy and budget analyst for the Office of Management and Budget (O.M.B.), and married Jamie Loftus, another Notre Dame graduate and former Holy Cross Associate.

While I was earning my masters degree, Jamie explored the possibility of the priesthood through the candidate year at Notre Dame's Moreau Seminary. Deciding that this was not his ministry, we were married eighteen months later at Sacred Heart with a nuptial mass celebrated with two of our Holy Cross friends, Fathers Tim Scully and John Jenkins. Jamie then worked for the Refugee Policy Group and later the U.S. Catholic Conference analyzing refugee issues while we were in Washington, D.C. We returned to Notre Dame in 1987, Jamie in the MBA program and me in law school. Our first two daughters, Bridget and Kathleen, now eight and six years old, were born during our graduate studies and baptized in the log chapel by our Holy Cross friends, Fathers Don McNeill and Bill Lewers, respectively. We then relocated to my hometown, Davenport, Iowa, where Jamie is an administrator at St. Ambrose University. I work part-time in a law firm, predominately practicing health care and education law, and teach a little at St. Ambrose University. Our two other daughters, Molly, now three years old, and Claire, were born in Iowa. Molly was baptized by another C.S.C., Father Bob Loughery, who was a candidate with Jamie at Moreau. I have recently decreased my law practice and focused more on family, community, and church activities.

We continue a strong relationship with Notre Dame. Jamie and I serve together on Notre Dame's Advisory Council for the Institute for Church Life. We return often to Notre Dame to visit friends, some of whom also act as mentors, inviting and challenging us to constantly evaluate the effectiveness of our ministries and pursue other opportunities. We also maintain a strong bond with those with whom we graduated, although we aren't in contact as often as we'd like.

What is mission and ministry?

Recent events, namely Claire's birth and my father's illness, helped me clarify my layperson's definitions of these theological terms, mission and ministry. My father most recently had had a minor stroke, but the cumulative effects of his health history were taking their toll. In 1994, he had fallen and subsequently underwent brain surgery to remove a blood clot. This procedure had left him in a severely weakened state. After this subsequent slight stroke, it appeared as though my father's body might be "shutting down." Our family was now asked to decide whether to resuscitate him if his heart or breathing would stop.

Personally, our decision was not made easier for me by the fact that I am a health care attorney with purported expertise in how these decisions are made. I give speeches to community groups, advise individual and hospital clients and even helped draft the document used statewide to educate the public on related issues. Confronting these issues for my own father illuminated the essence of our true earthly mission. We were momentarily resolved to the fact that Dad may be ready for that to which we all strive, the kingdom of heaven. When given fifteen minutes to make our decision, I caught myself quickly responding aloud what I believe we were all thinking, "His mission may be over." Momentarily no one spoke but the shared glances through our tear-filled eyes acknowledged this and how beautifully he ministered to us in fulfilling his earthly mission. Fortunately, his mission is not over. Today, even though on a feeding tube, he continues to enjoy our visits, especially with his grandchildren, and teaches us much about strength and endurance.

I know my quick response was founded in the brochure I give Catholic clients in helping them, after moral contemplation, draft durable powers of attorney for health care. My family's recent focus on life and death decisions became the starting point for my reflections on mission and ministry. What was my father's mission and how had he accomplished it?

What is my mission as wife, mother, daughter, sister, community member, parishioner and attorney? Having just baptized Claire, what do we, as parents, emphasize in building a faithful foundation for all our daughters? I realize that though we may hope to keep our loved ones alive with us as long as possible and we also may fear our own death, we are all actually striving to live our lives, from baptism forward, preparing for that very day. It is only then that we may achieve our goal to finally join the Lord in the glory of everlasting life. With minds focused on this goal, the Kingdom, our mission is to fully use the individual gifts God has given us to make the earthly kingdom more akin to the heavenly one. This is our mission. The ways we achieve it through our various roles in serving others in this earthly kingdom comprise our ministries.

How do we develop our sense of mission from which we derive guidance on living out our ministries? Our mission is developed and internalized by accepting daily invitations to minister to others. My sense of mission and choice of ministries has been defined by my family's influence, educational opportunities, and personal relationships and experiences. Notre Dame constitutes more than just one of those educational opportunities.

Familial influences on mission and ministry

I had concluded that my father successfully completed his earthly mission. He had served his country, been a loyal son to his Irish immigrant parents, been a faithful husband, and a strong Christian and Catholic influence to his six children. He showed us that it doesn't matter what you have. What matters is who you are and what impact you make on the world. He knew the daily grind necessary to put food on the table for six children and how burdensome and consuming that ministry could be. Knowing this, he lightened that burden for others, telling us how little it cost to brighten someone's day. He also taught us to stand up and speak out against injustice. In hindsight, as his children, we've come to realize that late night debates about politics and religion were not just orchestrated to instill in us Church teachings and our parents' basic values but to provide us the confidence and skills necessary to speak out in support of those values. We were taught, as Christ stated, that we cannot hide a light under a bushel basket but must let it shine for all to see. This light is Christ working through us and we must do all we can to assist in its illuminating power.

My mother added another element in helping us realize our missions and preparing us for our ministries. She nurtured us with gentleness, attentiveness, and religious devotion. She was always comforting and encouraging. If the Church's role as an institution is to be comforting yet challenging, so too, must our parents and other instruments of the Church be comforting and challenging to prepare us for the mission of the Church. My parents' support and the challenges they presented helped us develop our own senses of mission and define what ministries might best utilize our God-given talents in service to others. This has forged a bond amongst all of us.

Jamie's upbringing was similar in this respect and best illustrated by his father's repeated paraphrasing of former Notre Dame President, Father Cavanaugh, defining success as the ability to know one's God-given talents and use them to their fullest. When marrying Jamie I knew not only that I loved him deeply but that he and his family would enable me and challenge me to be a more faith-filled Christian. The two families provide a great sense of strength for our children as well.

Education as a source of defining mission and ministry

My grade school and high school Catholic education established a foundation for defining mission. However, my Notre Dame education and the post-graduate opportunities it and the Holy Cross Congregation provided were powerful in personalizing that sense of mission and exploring what constitutes genuine ministry to others. Having realized the significant impact Notre Dame and Holy Cross have had on my life, I am amazed that at the naive age of seventeen we make the major decision of choosing a college. Oftentimes, as in my case, families try not to influence the student's choice. I sought influence and despite my family's silence sensed that Notre Dame was the family favorite even though it presented quite a financial obstacle that other choices did not. It was the Catholic nature of Notre Dame that attracted me and my family.

My freshman year was quite exciting with the 1977 National Football Championship, the January blizzard filled with snow football, basketball, and parties, some academic success, and a lively social life. I was impressed that moral issues and Judeo-Christian perspectives were presented in almost every class, including, for example, Spanish. The intellectual and divine were thus studied more completely. The rich liturgical opportunities, from casual dorm masses to the elaborate services at Sacred Heart, could not be paralleled. However, the Catholic nature of Notre Dame and its influence on my formation reached a pinnacle when I met Father Don McNeill, Director of the Center for Experiential Learning, the precursor to the Center for Social Concerns. At the Center, theology came to life and students experienced the link between the Word and action. Students learned firsthand about ministry through personal experiences with those in various ministries dedicated to the mission shared by the individual, the Church, and our Catholic university. These experiences became a foundation upon which to focus a study of theology, economics, or government. Courses in various disciplines invited students to analyze the social ills of this earthly kingdom and their relation to academic disciplines.

As with many courses, fifteen years after graduation I cannot recall the specifics of the theological interpretations or economic theories studied. What is vivid, however, are lessons learned in how to minister. These lessons continue to influence my ministries as lawyer, friend, community member, spouse, parent, and daughter.

In one course, entitled Theology and Community Service, each student regularly visited two nursing home residents and kept a journal of how these visits related to our academic readings. One resident I visited, John, was an elderly gentleman blinded by diabetes. He had little family or other visitors and I was bound and determined to find something he could do or experience to enrich his life. While still searching for that enriching element for John's life, I entered his room one afternoon to find the bed made and no sign of him. I stopped a nurse in the hallway. She matter-of-factly told me that he had died yesterday. Seeing the shock on my face, she asked if I were family and realized her message was delivered somewhat abruptly. After composing myself and reflecting on our visits, I realized two basic lessons about ministry. First, when trying to serve others we must not force upon them our opinions of what they need. We must take time to learn from them what, if anything, they need. Second, I had firsthand evidence that whenever you try to serve others the return to you is tenfold. I greatly enjoyed our visits, and came to miss them. Perhaps unknown to him, John's last days were enriching to me as he expanded my understanding of history through his personal perspectives, not paralleled on the page of any textbook.

Other popular courses were associated with a two-day inner city experience over Christmas break, the "Urban Plunge" and "Unseen City" for undergraduates and "Galilee" for law students. After readings and other preparation, students were immersed into the daily plight of those combating social ills such as poverty, hunger, illiteracy, homelessness, violence, and substance abuse. After students submitted written reflections, faculty from various disciplines led them in group discussions in their homes. This interdisciplinary endeavor exemplified the unified effort needed to carry out the work of the Church. The various parts of the body of Christ, comprised of individual Christians, must each understand the mission of the whole and use individual talents and expertise to that same end.

The more extensive course, "Unseen City," broadened the focus to study economic and political aspects of these problems, elicit theological perspectives, and challenge our responsibilities to create short-term and systemic solutions. The perspectives presented in these economic class discussions can be contrasted to my economics courses years later at the University of Chicago. While the latter education was excellent and prepared me well for my later work at the President's Office of Management and Budget, only a small minority of students took issue with the absence of social justice in the fundamental assumptions underlying the premises of the rational man and pareto optimality. (These premises assume that everyone's choices are self-serving.) At Notre Dame, social justice implications would have been directly addressed and not as a tangent professors and students might avoid.

Because these courses touched my heart as well as my head, I remember them more strikingly and maybe incorporate their lessons more readily. As a health care attorney analyzing reform proposals, I distinctly recall peering into the tear-filled eyes of a homeless man with new-found self-esteem. He had been defeated at one time by unaffordable health problems, but attributes his new beginning to the South Bend Center for the Homeless. Its director is a Notre Dame graduate, Lou Nanni, and the University a sustaining force. This one moment from the Galilee program beautifully illustrates aspects of Notre Dame's mission. Its programs not only challenge the mind and inspire critical thinking, but they ignite the spirit. Its endeavors reach beyond campus parameters into the South Bend community, the United States, and the world.

The college years are often purported to be the best of one's life. I'm not sure to what this refers, but fifteen years after my college years at Notre Dame, I believe they were amongst the most formative—spiritually, intellectually, and socially. My Spanish professor often stated that a university education, by definition, requires its students to expand their horizons to the entire world. I propose that a Catholic university requires its students to expand those horizons to include understanding the Church's mission, the student's individual strengths, and how those can best serve the Church, and thus the world. In essence, a Catholic university's mission should include influencing each student's development of mission and ministry, whatever his or her degree. Notre Dame profoundly influenced my personal mission and ministries through its invitation to directly meet victims of injustice, look into their eyes, and listen to their words. I hope that every Notre Dame student shares in similar experiences and that a Notre Dame graduate is perceived as not merely one who graduated from its academic rigors, but one challenged by its ethos to combat injustice and make a difference in the world.

As with any university, the full experience is much more than the classroom. The students, alumni, faculty, and administrators who have befriended us have also reinforced our senses of mission, ministering with us and to us. With many of these friends we reconnect after long periods of time and converse meaningfully, often directly discussing our values and ministry.

My undergraduate graduation ceremony itself illustrates the distinction the Notre Dame degree provides. President Reagan spoke at our commencement exercises, his first appearance after the assassination attempt on his life. Security was understandably heightened. Amidst the hype of the president's visit, the speaker stealing the show in her humble and unobtrusive fashion was valedictorian, Nancy Haegel. This twenty-one-year–old's eloquent challenge to her peers mesmerized listeners of all ages. Her speech embodied the University's ethos as it urged us to utilize our education to vigorously embark on our search for social justice. It is no wonder that she has been reappointed to the University's Board of Trustees.

The role of other personal experiences and relationships in mission and ministry

Since Notre Dame, the experiences and relationships I've pursued are somehow linked back to it or lessons learned from it. Although overwhelmed with debt, I spent a year after graduation in the Holy Cross Associate Program. This "hayseed from Iowa" shared a small three-bedroom house with four other recent graduates in the San Francisco Bay area. The program espoused community, simple living, and service. We pooled our meager stipends from social service placements into the community coffer, spending it in light of our promise to live simply. A local Holy Cross priest acted as our director. He arranged our placements, introduced us to the local Holy Cross community, celebrated mass, filled our social calendars, and provided guidance and friendship.

As a woman interested in government and social service, my placement was ideal. I worked as an administrative assistant for Gail Steele, Director of Eden Youth Center and city councilwoman. She was the force behind transforming a vacant school building into a youth center, complete with child care, health care, recreational activities, and job training. In addition to my administrative duties, which included program development, I taught job search skills to youth including CETA participants, young men only a few years younger than I. My age and gender made the situation uncomfortable at first.

I traded interpretations of the Bible verse referencing "an eye for an eye" with one participant, the leader of the local Chicano gang. He told me how he stabbed someone and fled, never knowing what became of his victim. He became a father and was ready to change his life. Eventually, we overcame his criminal record and encouraged a local employer to give him a chance. Briefly, he left the gang and was drug free. Years after I left California, however, I learned that he returned to his earlier ways and was now imprisoned for shooting his neighbor.

I knew my Notre Dame and Associate experiences would impact all dimensions of my future, from how I'd vote to the jobs and friendships I would seek. I planned to serve others by helping empower them. I pledged not to impose upon them my view of their needs, but listen, understand, and respect their outlooks. These outlooks proved beneficial in later situations. For example, I saw firsthand in California how access to affordable transportation was a substantial obstacle to obtaining and maintaining employment. This memory resurfaced when working on President Reagan's transit proposal years later. Additionally, one CETA participant told me that in helping him complete job applications I enabled him to understand other documents like hospital forms used to admit his baby. With this in mind, I'm more sensitive when drafting such forms today.

Other dimensions of the Associate program have also affected my marriage and family life. The program confirmed my parents' teaching that mission and ministry may require confronting and challenging others in a community. Our ideas concerning the laity's role in the Church have also been enriched by the relationships fostered with the Holy Cross Community through the Associate year and hence. Discussions with members of the Holy Cross about parish or university issues, the role of women in the Church, or approaches to problems faced at work established a collaborative relationship in this shared mission. The priests at St. Clement's parish and the "Berkeley House," together with the Brothers at the Moreau High School and the local Holy Cross Sisters, invited us to join in their community. This daily acceptance as friends and co-workers in the mission outside the university setting also highlighted the breadth of Notre Dame's mission beyond the university.

Obviously, the mission of Holy Cross expands beyond its educational institutions. However, the easy flow of the Holy Cross priest from a university position, to the Chilean barrio, to a parish exhibits some insight about mission and ministry and the collaboration that should occur amongst a university, its alumni, and other partners working outside the campus confines. A great Catholic university should not only be a beacon of light intellectually, but spiritually. It should serve the Church as a whole. Jamie and I think of this now as we sit on the Advisory Council for the Notre Dame's Institute for Church Life. Its four centers inspire, support, and rejuvenate all segments of the Church in their varied ministries. Its programs reach not only the Notre Dame student, but the religious and laity nationally, if not globally. Its mission gives great distinction to Notre Dame's Catholic character.

After the Associate program, I set out to better equip myself to address systemic problems. A fellow Notre Dame graduate inspired me to obtain my Masters Degree in Public Policy from the University of Chicago. That intellectually stimulating program challenged me to appreciate other viewpoints and confidently express my own. It also led to an exciting analyst position with O.M.B. where I further developed my analytical skills and began to appreciate the political process. After working on some major legislation, we returned to Notre Dame where I pursued my law degree and Jamie, his M.B.A. We hoped these degrees would afford us more opportunities to affect change. We chose

Notre Dame not solely on the basis of its academic merits but the fullness of opportunities it offers intellectually, spiritually, and emotionally.

While back at Notre Dame we rekindled old friendships and made new ones while our family blossomed. We began the struggle to balance our roles. I completed my degree over seven semesters instead of the usual six. I've always been driven and initially this "slowing down" was against my nature. However, I knew it would be better for the family as a whole. Dean Link, then Assistant Dean Carol Mooney, and the entire faculty were most accommodating.

While in graduate school, we both served on the Holy Cross Associate's Board of Directors. I worked part time for Jim Roemer in the Community Relations office, making my small contribution to the University's extension of itself into the South Bend community and well beyond. Occasionally, I would speak to undergraduate classes for Don McNeill, C.S.C., or help promote service opportunities for Mary Ann Roemer and Kathleen Weigert at the Center for Social Concerns. As I finished my law school career, I received an honor I will forever cherish, the John Gardner award. While undeserving of its accolades, the inscription reads, "A graduating student who exemplifies the ideals of the University through outstanding volunteer service beyond the University community." Because of the Catholic nature and mission of this institution, I was deeply flattered. The existence of such an award reveals the essence of the University's commitment to fostering mission and ministry.

As mother of two already, I struggled with what to do after graduation. I had clerked in a large Chicago firm after my second year, while pregnant with our second daughter. One young attorney there noticed my condition and assumed I was a new partner. He told me that because of the demands on associates, most women waited till they made partner to begin their families. Nearing the end of my summer, I asked one female partner if the firm would entertain the idea of an attorney working part-time. She quickly replied that the practice of law required time and devotion. I suppressed the thought to tell her that so did parenthood. While the firm offered a commendable pro-bono program and attractive salary, we turned down its offer.

Since my oldest was born I've struggled with the dilemma of whether to work outside the home. Should I translate my academic successes and subsequent opportunities into a calling in the workforce? Many encouraged me to do so. I contemplated non-traditional positions allowing for service while affording me time to be the mother I wanted. A knowledgeable friend advised me that a law firm would afford me the experience needed to become a skilled attorney. Then I could pursue whatever avenue I thought would most effectively benefit others.

Heeding this advice, I became a clerk and then part-time associate at one of the largest, most established law firms in Iowa, Lane and Waterman. I predominately work in health care and education law. These areas incorporate my public policy and law degrees and involve issues affecting the health and vitality of individuals and communities. My individuality will more likely make a difference in this practice.

My practice, however, has always been part-time so that I might best live out my ministries as lawyer and mother. With that part-time status comes sacrificing the partnership track. This can be difficult when this profession measures and rewards such achievements. When considering the goals defined by our mission, we chose this personal sacrifice which enables me to better minister as a mother.

Jamie and I have always been partners in parenting but all along I've wanted to increase my time with the girls. After six years, I'm devoting less time to practicing law so that I may do that. We continue to take stock of whether our endeavors are truly serving others. I became an attorney, not for financial security, but to help empower others underrepresented in our society. To that end, I've recently received invitations to consider other ministries for future endeavors that I previously may not have believed achievable, such as teaching law or public service. At thirty-seven, I feel as though I've been preparing all my life to obtain the necessary education and experience to make a significant difference. While making some contributions along the way, I now feel equipped to discern how these potential ministries might best use my skills, better serve others, and interrelate with my other ministries, predominately as a mother of young children.

In no way is my pursuit of education, training, and experience meant to imply that only the highly educated or professional are able to make a meaningful difference. I do believe these tools may allow me to most adequately use my particular God-given talents. Paraphrasing John F. Kennedy, "One person can make a difference and every person should try."

I further acknowledge that while obtaining my education, skills and experience, I have been living out various ministries as daughter, sister, student, Associate, friend, spouse, mother, and attorney. No matter what our role at each moment of our lives we must consider it a calling to ministry, to assert our faith and mission into daily life. We must also accept the fact that our ministries change throughout our life and we should be open to God's new callings for us.

Today, I am called most predominately to my ministry as mother. I want to be a role model for my girls and show them that women can use their God-given talents to make significant contributions. Nurturing children at home serves the community in and of itself. They also see me continue to be active in the community while involved in bar association activities, our parish's board of education, girl scouting, school activities and a community assessment of health and well-being. I want them to see that ministries change with various stages of life and incorporate many, sometimes competing, responsibilities. My focus has turned to providing the same strong foundation for our children that our parents provided us.

Conclusion

Notre Dame has impacted us profoundly. It has influenced the further education and career choices we have made and continue to make with prayerful discernment. It has provided friends who support and challenge us. It has brought Jamie and me together not simply by providing a location, but by its creative force in shaping the people we have become, intellectually and spiritually. Those associated with Notre Dame have ministered to us well. Through their ministries, touching students, alumni, and the Church, Notre Dame fulfills its own mission as a Catholic university by inviting all to seek lives committed to ministry. Through our ministries, Notre Dame will further touch our children and others we are called to serve.

"Their Blood Is in the Bricks"

EDWARD A. MALLOY, C.S.C.

In retrospect, and with the advantage of over thirty-five years of a relationship to the same institution, I feel that I am still in the process of giving back what I previously received from others. There is an old and well-established image here that describes what I feel—"Their blood is in the bricks." It evokes a sense of deep loyalty and commitment to the institution and of selfless service to countless generations of Notre Dame students, friends, and visitors. This is the Notre Dame that I have been fortunate, as a student, faculty member, and administrator, to know and to participate in.

My own personal story is not all that exceptional. I first made Notre Dame my home in the fall of 1959 after I had accepted a basketball scholarship to attend the University. I was happy from the first moment I arrived. I say this despite the fact that I had severe academic problems in pursuing the first-year engineering curriculum and even though my basketball career was less than stellar. The main reason that I overcame these difficulties is that I always had people there for me like Professors Bill Burke and Ed Cronin and Coach Jim Gibbons. I also came to know various Holy Cross priests and brothers during my four undergraduate years. I remember well—Father Ted Hesburgh, still relatively young in his presidency, Father Joe Barry, warm counselor and gentle confessor, Father Joe Garvin, hard-working medieval scholar and my rector for two years in Badin Hall, Brother Boniface, sacristan of Sacred Heart, Brother Conan Moran, affectionately

Father "Monk" Malloy, C.S.C., is President of the University.

known as Brother Bookstore, and Father John Dunne, inspiring teacher who first turned me on to theology.

The most providential choice that I made during those undergraduate years was to risk joining a summer service project in Mexico under the direction of Father Larry Murphy, a Maryknoll graduate student, and Father Ernie Bartell, C.S.C. While I was in Mexico, I had a kind of mountain-top experience at a place called Cristo Rey (Christ the King), a pilgrimage site which afforded a sweeping view of the heart of middle Mexico. My experience did not take the form of a vision or voices from the heavens. Rather, I knew a kind of certitude about my calling to become a priest. Upon graduation I pursued this vocation in a formal way and joined the Indiana Province of the Congregation of Holy Cross. After seven years of formation I was ordained a priest in Sacred Heart Church on campus on April 4, 1970.

Except for my years of graduate study and one year of sabbatical for research and writing, I have lived and worked at Notre Dame for my whole ministry. I believe deeply in the unique apostolate of Catholic higher education. Especially in the American context, Catholic higher education is an extraordinary achievement. There are presently around 230 Catholic colleges and universities in this country, each with its own history, traditions, and present-day challenges.

With regard to Notre Dame I consider its Catholic character to be its greatest attribute and strength. But the realization of this character comes at a price, for it raises questions that can be divisive and controversial. That is why in our recent long-range planning document called *The Colloquy for the Year 2000* I attempted to articulate from my vantage point some of the essential elements that constitute our Catholic character. It includes: a commitment to excellence at all levels of education; the provision of improved resources so that research, scholarship, and artistic creativity might be sustained at a high level; the determination of academic configurations such as centers and institutes that have particular relevance to service of society and the church; the maintenance of a strong tradition of residentiality and the accompanying support provided by Student Affairs and Campus Ministry; and the visible role that the institution plays through celebration of its common life and the continuation of a vibrant relationship to its graduates and friends.

The Catholic character of Notre Dame, and the special role that Holy Cross plays within that, is the context within which my ministry has played out through the years. I am one minister among many dedicated ministers, ordained and non-ordained, female and male, students and those entrusted with their care. With this in mind I will focus on five dimensions of my personal ministry at Notre Dame.

Let me begin with some reflections on my activities in *teaching*. I came out of graduate school convinced, as many newly credentialed faculty tend to be, that the students I would encounter would be brilliant, well-prepared, and indefatigable. As a result, during my first year of teaching I had enough material in hand to overwhelm and impress whoever ended up in my classes. It did not take me long to realize that there was a difference between raw ability and prolonged interest. It was up to me to touch my students' own level of experience, to pique their curiosity, and to expose them to the riches of the Christian theological heritage.

In my undergraduate sections I always tried to promote in-class discussions, particularly by examining concrete cases. As a moral theologian, we analyzed human sexuality, war and peace, social justice, bio-medical ethics, and other contemporary issues. In their research papers I encouraged my students to choose topics that had already, or would in the future, touch their lives and responsibilities. Inevitably, some of my students would come to me with problems from home, or dilemmas at school, or concerns about relationships or career plans. There was never a sharp boundary between the role of classroom instructor and ministerial counselor or guide.

At the advanced level of seminary or graduate teaching I tried to prepare my students for their professional obligations after graduation. That is one reason that all my exams were orals because it forced the students to integrate and articulate that which they were learning. My own research and scholarly writing flowed naturally from this type of engagement.

Never in my ministry as a teacher/scholar have I felt distant from my priestly vocation. I ended up teaching and writing about matters that were of concern to me as a believer. I continue to teach a freshman seminar course as president because I did not want to give up this rewarding side of my life.

In addition to teaching, I am also engaged on a regular basis in *liturgical leadership*. It is a privilege as a priest to lead the community of faith in prayer. At Notre Dame this has taken many forms for me. I regularly celebrate mass in the student dormitories. During the course of the academic year, especially since I have become an administrator, I make an effort to get into each of our twenty-six dormitories at least once on a Sunday or other special occasion. It provides the students a different sense of me and I receive a more balanced exposure to the student body as a whole. I also lead the liturgy in Sacred Heart Basilica and the parish crypt church.

My most poignant memories have been at the high holidays like Christmas and Easter and at funeral masses for students, faculty, and staff. When the women's swim team was in a bus accident several years ago on a snowy Indiana Toll Road, the Notre Dame family filled the Basilica to overflowing for the memorial mass for the two women who died and the many who were hurt. It was as though the whole campus turned toward each other before God in their sense of loss. On a more upbeat note, I enjoy participating in Notre Dame–related weddings and baptisms both on and off campus. It always becomes a gathering of the clan, as though all of us have Notre Dame emblazoned on our foreheads.

Notre Dame prayer encompasses everything from the formality of the baccalaureate and Junior Parent Weekend masses to quiet visits to the Grotto of Our Lady of Lourdes to the youthful energy of student encounter weekends. I am continually uplifted by the student choirs who celebrate Christ's presence in song. Whatever style or mode of worship one prefers is available here on campus. Two summers ago we hosted representatives from Catholic higher education from around the world. At the completion of the conference they reported that their favorite part of the week was the beauty of the worship, particularly the faith-filled contribution of the Liturgical and Folk Choirs.

Perhaps the most challenging but rewarding form of liturgical leadership for me is preaching. To attempt to interpret the Word of God in language and imagery befitting the talent and experience of an academic community is the standard we are called to. And every time I become discouraged or complacent about my preaching ministry, someone will pull me aside or drop me a note thanking me for something I said in a homily that touched a need in them.

Another dimension of my involvement in Notre Dame life comes through my residing in a *student dormitory*. I am now in my sixteenth year in Sorin Hall. For the first five I was assistant rector. Since then, I have been in residence. During the first segment I was heavily involved in every aspect of residence life even though I was a full-time faculty member. More recently, I have distanced myself from administrative and disciplinary functions in the hall and have concentrated on a ministry of presence. It is a characteristic part of the Holy Cross heritage at Notre Dame to live with the students and thereby to share their college years in a familiar and comfortable fashion. When I was elected president, some trustees and faculty were laying bets that I would move out the first year. Now it is about a decade later and I still feel Sorin is where I belong.

In the context of dorm existence I have come to know students at their best and at their worst. Most of my jarring and uncomfortable experiences have been connected to the abuse of alcohol. On some occasions I have worried that an inebriated student (our own or a visitor) might even die. But far outweighing these moments that required active corrective intervention has been the exhilaration and satisfaction that have come from watching young people mature and come into their own. Our students are innately generous, usually reflecting their family upbringing, and they respond quickly to overtures to assist the poor, the young, the elderly, and others in need.

In a dorm I never know what a knock on the door might bring. I have heard confessions, unraveled roommate problems, consoled the grieving at the loss of a parent or friend, checked out potential spouses, clarified career choices, and discussed arguments for the existence of God. Perhaps the most difficult counseling encounters have been those involving students suffering from depression and/or tendencies toward suicide.

Our students study hard, but student life is as much fun and hijinks and friendship formation as anything else. As my own contribution to dorm relaxation, I have for over twenty years been playing basketball with students twice a week. For me it is a healthy form of exercise and an informal way to get to know the students in the hall. I also have the practice of taking students out to dinner in groups of five as my schedule allows. I have great admiration for the head staff in our dorms and for all those under the Office of Student Affairs who assist them. As a priest in residence, I have a small role to play but I plan to continue as long as I am able.

My most obvious role at Notre Dame is in *administration*. The pastor of a parish, the director of a retreat house, and the head of a household are all managers or administrators in some sense of the term. They need to tend to personnel issues, to physical plant, and to operating budgets and some even need to engage in fund-raising. The president of a university carries out similar tasks and many more besides. What is different is the scale and complexity.

Like most priests-administrators, I did not get ordained with this particular role in mind. For this task there were no schools to attend or specific degree qualifications to satisfy. Instead, my present administrative responsibility at Notre Dame has flowed rather naturally for me from the prior ministries that I have exercised here. For reasons of religious heritage and historical continuity the presidency of Notre Dame is restricted to a priest of the Indiana Province of the Congregation of Holy Cross. When the Board of Trustees sought a successor to Father Theodore Hesburgh after his thirty-five years of exemplary leadership, I was one of those in the final pool. I sought advice, prayed over my options, and when I was finally elected, I agreed to serve with real enthusiasm and gratefulness.

Counting my five years as vice-president and associate provost, I have been involved in the central administration of Notre Dame for fifteen years. I have learned a lot about my personal strengths and weaknesses. I have been both credited and blamed for matters over which I had little control. But I have grown accustomed over time to the symbolic and representative function that I fulfill as chief executive officer of the institution.

In my judgment, the three most important tasks of the president of a Catholic university are vision, coordination, and communication. The vision dimension begins with the engagement of various members of the University community in the process of analysis, speculation, and consensus formation. My own public conveyance of the vision encompasses everything from formal planning documents to the annual address to the faculty to periodic updates to trustees, advisory council members, and gatherings of benefactors and alumni. The student newspaper, the alumni magazine, and the local and national press and broadcast media are other vehicles for articulating and specifying what Notre Dame hopes to become.

For some, the purgatory of modern institutional life is the time spent in committee meetings. Yet I have come to appreciate how crucial dialogue, conversation, and interaction are for the health and well-being of the common life. As president, I must pay attention to the structures of coordination across the various strata of administration. Concretely, this means for me gatherings of the trustees three times a year; a summer retreat for the officers followed by monthly meetings; weekly staff meetings; daily interaction with particular officers, administrators, and representatives of campus constituencies; and an endless round of council, committee, and search process meetings. There is no substitute, as far as I can see, for such activity. The important thing is that it be well planned and well executed.

By communication I mean less the process involved in arriving at a common vision of the institution's future and more a consistent flow of appropriate information about concrete decisions that have been made and the reasons that underlie them. Since poor communication is the most frequent complaint about the administration in any large institution, there is a constant need for reappraisal. But good communication is more difficult than it seems. Some personnel decisions must remain confidential to protect the reputation of those involved. Some information is proprietary by its very nature, i.e., reserved to established bodies or individuals within the institution. But most other matters of communication involve the exercise of prudential judgment and the proper utilization of the available forms of presentation.

Vision, coordination, and communication are but three of the components of the ministry of administration. Much of the rest of what I do concretizes these qualities according to the annual rhythm of the institution. When I spend the weekend with the juniors and their families at Junior Parent Weekend, when I go out to visit local alumni clubs around the country and world, when I discuss issues of common concern with community leaders in the South Bend area, and when I meet with individual faculty members or students, I am simply living out the notion that Notre Dame is always a family or community in the making with mutual expectations and obligations.

My fifth and last form of ministry at Notre Dame is through *service of the broader society and church.* Flowing from my present responsibilities at the University, I also have the opportunity to provide service off the campus by volunteering with various civic, educational, and religious groups.

In my national civic service I have focused on two areas— combating substance abuse and promoting social service. For many years I was a member of President George Bush's Drug Advisory Council. This then led to participation in the establishment of a new anti-drug organization. More recently, I have chaired two national studies of substance abuse patterns among young people. In the second area of interest I have joined several boards which promote volunteerism in American life, including the Points of Light Foundation, Campus Compact, and President Clinton's initiative called AmeriCorps.

In the education area I have chaired the umbrella organization for American higher education called the American Council on Education and served on the boards of the Association of Governing Boards, the NCAA Foundation, the International Federation of Catholic Universities, the Business–Higher Education Forum, and the Board of Regents at the University of Portland.

My explicit church involvements have included: the

Bishops-Presidents Committee of the U.S. Catholic Conference and the Ex Corde Ecclesiae Committee to discuss the implementation in the American context of the papal document on Catholic higher education. I also readily accept invitations to assist Catholic charitable, medical, and educational activities around the country.

None of these involvements is unusual for a university president. I am expected to have a presence and a leadership role off campus. What I have learned is that such national and international experience helps to maintain a sense of balance and perspective about on-campus debates and dilemmas. I have met with national leaders and the pope. I have visited forty countries. Yet it is often the ordinary folk I have encountered who stand out in my memory. I recall a priest in Jamaica who established a thriving cooperative for the poor and mentally disabled, an African American man in Kansas City who freed his neighborhood from crack houses, a woman in Chicago who proved that inner city kids could perform at the highest academic standards, and groups of Notre Dame students making a major difference in soup kitchens, homeless shelters, and Catholic schools from coast to coast. My ministry to the broader society and church has enriched and inspired me. I have, literally, received more than I have given.

My years of ministry at Notre Dame have passed quickly. I have always relished the next year, the new challenge, the unforeseen opportunity. I am pleased that as president I have been able to develop a working balance among the various roles that I play—as teacher, as liturgical leader, as dorm resident, and as administrator. For me Notre Dame has been a stimulating and rewarding context for ministry. I give thanks to God for my brothers and sisters in Holy Cross and for the thousands of others who continue to share this mission of Catholic higher education. Perhaps someday our successors will pay us the highest compliment and proclaim, "Their blood, too, is in the bricks."

Pastoral Service in a University Setting: The Institute for Church Life

PAUL PHILIBERT, O.P.

How does a highly visible Catholic University that is one of the great symbols of Catholic life in our country relate itself to the mission and needs of the national Church? How do the most pressing problems and opportunities of the local churches become part of the concerns of the University? How can the University try to respond to the challenges of the different local churches in so vast a country? This set of questions is not among the most immediately apparent concerns of a university. Indeed, universities tend to be imagined as places of refuge where contemplative scholars escape from the problems and concerns that can limit, if not overwhelm, the energies of ordinary people. We tend to think about universities as places for books, classrooms, research, publication, and conferences. What does a university have to do with pastoral concerns?

In 1993, when I had completed my term as Prior Provincial of the Southern Dominican friars, I was fortunate enough to be invited to come to Notre Dame as Director of the Institute for Church Life. It was gratifying to be invited to return to a post within a university, since all my previous professional positions had been within colleges, seminaries, or universities. I had been trained in theology with a specialization in fundamental ethics focused on moral and religious development. I had taught at Catholic University, St. Mary's Seminary in Baltimore, and

Father Paul Philibert, O.P., is Director of the Institute for Church Life.

at the Dominican School of Philosophy and Theology in Berkeley. Both at Catholic University and in Berkeley, I had held administrative posts—in Washington as director of an inter-disciplinary center for the study of human development and in Berkeley as president of the Dominican School. Both of these assignments had provided me with a deep interest in interdisciplinary projects and with a concern for the way in which institutions of higher education relate to the needs of society. But never previously had I had the opportunity to work with a university division whose purpose is pastoral service for the Church. It seemed like both the right challenge for me and a rich opportunity to continue my life's work. How did there happen to be such a place as Notre Dame's Institute for Church Life? The development of this department for pastoral service is a fascinating story.

Founding Dreams

In the 1970s, the Catholic Church in the United States was marked by two particular, very powerful experiences that needed attention. One of these was the clear problem of urban unrest. The other was the volatile quality of liturgical renewal, then still in its infancy. By a series of circumstances that I now consider divine providence, Father Theodore Hesburgh, President of the University of Notre Dame, invited Monsignor John Egan to come to Notre Dame for a while to see how the resources of this Catholic university could be placed in the service of the Church in transition. Out of the powerful synergy of these two imaginative priests arose the beginnings of what is now called the Institute for Church Life.[1]

The Civil Rights movement had its decisive decade between 1960 and 1970. Those were days for new beginnings, not for the successful resolution of problems. Yet a climate came to be in which it seemed not only possible to do something about responsible social action, but incumbent upon us to respond. The chaos that followed the assassination of Martin Luther King in 1968 led to a recognition of the decaying infrastructure of many of America's largest urban centers. Monsignor Egan decided to begin at the University of Notre Dame the Center for the Church in Urban Ministry (CCUM) with the goal of networking with urban leaders in all areas of the Church throughout the country and bringing to bear sociological, political, and theological insight upon the problems of each area in their distinctiveness. This was an important development in Notre Dame's outreach from its campus to the dioceses of the country.

At the same time, the Catholic Church in the U.S. was growing in its appreciation of the need for exemplary work in liturgical experimentation and formation. In 1970, the Bishops' Conference decided to invite applicants for centers for liturgical experimentation. Notre Dame, already with a rich tradition of graduate theology in liturgy and ritual studies, applied for and received recognition as a national liturgical center. This Center, now known as the Center for Pastoral Liturgy, came under the umbrella of the Institute for Church Life as the 1970s rolled along.

From those early days as a Center, the staff of the Center for Pastoral Liturgy has kept its eyes on the needs of dioceses and parishes for theological resources, materials for liturgical catechesis, training for new ministers, and pastoral research. Once again, the University began to experience its role as a swinging door—one that let in the problems and questions of the local churches and that likewise swung outward with resources, services, and ideas that could take root in the diverse environments of the U.S. Church.[2]

In this same volatile period of the 1970s, it became increasingly evident that those who were the principal agents of church administration in the local scene—priests—would need first-rate opportunities for theological and pastoral updating. Father Robert Pelton, C.S.C., founded a Center for Clergy Education, now known as the Center for Continuing Formation in Ministry, with the goal of providing to priests a catch-up program on developments in theology and pastoral concerns as well as opportunities to rest and restore themselves in an environment of friendship, solidarity with other ministers, and a critical scholarly environment.

In the mid-1970s as well, Father Tom Gedeon, S.J., brought

to Notre Dame the administrative and educational arm of the retreat movement in the U.S. and Canada, called Retreats International. Beginning in 1977, Retreats International has offered a Summer Institute (originally intended for the staff of retreat centers) that has become the largest and the most popular summer continuing education program in pastoral studies anywhere in the world. In the course of the four weeks of July, Retreats International welcomes a thousand people to the Notre Dame campus for courses in scripture, theology, morality, pastoral service, and spirituality. Toward the end of the 1970s all these efforts came under one umbrella when Father Hesburgh established the Institute for Pastoral and Social Ministry.

This Institute (now called the Institute for Church Life) came into existence piecemeal. Each one of the Centers was the product of a dynamic fusion of graced opportunities. In each case, there was an evident need of the American Church for pastoral service and the initiative of an apostolically dedicated and pastorally gifted founding director. Together these Notre Dame Centers came to represent the most comprehensive example of pastoral outreach by a Catholic university in this country to the problems, interests, and needs of bishops, priests, and other pastoral workers.

At the beginning of the 1980s Monsignor Egan collaborated with others in the Institute to initiate the Notre Dame Parish Study. Father Philip Murnion, director of the National Pastoral Life Center, was in residence at Notre Dame as the parish study was being conceived; he became a dialogue partner in the design proposal. David Leege, a sociologist in the Department of Government at Notre Dame, became the director of research for this landmark project. Mark Searle, Associate Director of the Center for Pastoral Liturgy and a professor in the Department of Theology, played a vital role in shaping the research on worship and reporting out significant findings. The Parish Study was an attempt, carried out throughout the 1980s, to develop a reliable social science survey of the profile of parishes in the dioceses of the United States. The key question was: "How is the renewal taking shape?" This included a number of sub-questions: "Is renewal happening? Is it happening in different ways in different places? What can we do to make renewal as authentic and successful as possible?" The Notre Dame Parish Study remains to this day the most ambitious attempt to understand the dynamics of Catholic parish life ever undertaken. The Institute for Church Life remains responsible for the on-going study and dissemination of reliable research information about Catholic parish life. This dimension is the responsibility of the director of the Institute.

Flexible Structures

The Institute for Church Life is a cluster of pastoral centers with the common goal of serving the national Church in its dioceses and parishes through resources based on the university campus. Each Center, however, has its distinctive projects, independent staffing, particular goals, and distinctive spirit. The Institute currently houses the Center for Continuing Formation in Ministry as a sabbatical program for pastoral ministers, the Center for Pastoral Liturgy as a national research and service center for Catholic worship, the Center for Social Concerns as a training center and initiator of projects for volunteer service, and Retreats International as an administrative and educational resource for the nearly 600 retreat centers in North America. Reverend Don McNeill, C.S.C., is founder and director of the Center for Social Concerns and coordinates activities of experiential learning for students within programs that offer pastoral assistance in many regions of North and Latin America. In part, through the influence of this Center, some 200 graduating seniors go from Notre Dame each May into some years of volunteer service, carrying the University's values and Catholic vision into various programs of education, social organization, and action for justice.

These four Centers, along with the central office of the Institute, constitute a sort of "pastoral council" for the University, among whose responsibilities is the on-going discussion of pastoral needs in the U.S. Church. Every few weeks, the directors and the associate directors of the Centers meet with the director of the Institute to review their projects, plan new initiatives, imagine ways of dealing with emerging needs, and respond to appeals from pastors and bishops. In the process of these meetings, the Centers frequently discover ways in which they can be of benefit to one another. Though each Center is distinctive in its focus and may not have all that much in common with the other centers, all the entities of the Institute for Church Life are united in their focus upon pastoral service. As a result, the spirit of dialogue and mutual support among the Centers is strong and the benefits of collaboration in conversation and mutual assistance are frequently high.

The Institute for Church Life is assisted by an Advisory Council, a group of some twenty-five lay couples invited to assist Notre Dame by supporting the Institute and its Centers in various ways. The Advisory Council for the Institute has much of the feeling of an extended family. Meeting twice a year, the Council receives detailed reports on the projects of the Institute and its Centers. The meetings allow the members of the Council to respond critically to new proposals, long-term planning, and on-going initiatives on the basis of their professional experience in their various fields as well as of their particular experience of the Church in their own areas. In addition, the Advisory Council provides opportunities for frequently valuable networking to allow the Institute's staff to benefit from professional or ecclesiastical expertise. In addition, the Institute occasionally calls upon members of the Council for *pro bono* service when that can be of mutual interest.

The structure of the Institute for Church Life is therefore flexible and effective. Each Center has something to give and something to gain by being part of this umbrella organization. Colleagues outside the University of Notre Dame, including some bishop friends, have called the Institute for Church Life one of Notre Dame's best-kept secrets.

Ministry in a Changing Church

The Catholic Church in the United States is once again in a highly volatile position. A number of superficially contradictory factors seem to be in force all at once. Demographers tell us that we can count on an on-going growth in Catholic population over the next twenty years. At the same time, however, we look for a significant drop in the number of vocations to priesthood and religious life. The ratio between church-goers and ordained priests is rising, but the number of lay people in church ministries is also rising (at a phenomenal rate). While Vatican officials frequently reiterate prohibitions against the ordination of women, the proportion of women as active ministers in service, education, administration, and even pastoral life is growing— to the point that roughly 80 percent of all those engaged in ministry in the Church today are laity and 80 percent of those are women. This is the formula for a lively Church. In the face of these challenges, the Institute for Church Life aims to make a life-giving contribution.

In support of the ordained, the Center for Continuing Formation of Ministers continues to offer a superior program for education, spirituality, and pastoral refreshment. (This program, originally conceived for priests alone, is now open as well to the non-ordained.) The Institute further has proposed to the National Conference of Catholic Bishops a workshop to assist newly appointed bishops to reflect upon their responsibilities and learn from experienced older bishops (and some other experts) about their role and job expectations.

A key responsibility for the Church is the forming and empowering of the laity as ministers. The Center for Pastoral Liturgy does this through its many programs and publications. Retreats International contributes to this effort through its Summer Institute with a newly identified focus upon giving foundational competence to lay people in ministry. Through Retreats International's Summer Institute, Notre Dame is able to offer to pastors and lay leaders in parishes at low cost the possibility of coming together for some weeks of pastoral training on the campus. This has proven in the past to be a breakthrough moment in both pastoral and human communication for those who have taken advantage of this possibility.

Through the Center for Social Concerns, the Institute continues to take strategic initiatives for systemic social change. Most of the work of the Center for Social Concerns is directed toward University students. However, in many of its programs, the Center for Social Concerns places students, with professional supervision and alumni support, in regions of the U.S. Church where they can become experienced in the conditions of economic poverty, social unrest, scarcity of social and pastoral resources, and the particular needs of ethnic churches. As part of its mentoring process, the Center likewise engages faculty in helping students who return from such experiences to reflect upon their learning, debriefing them of their stories, and assisting them to recognize the social ideals of their classroom study in living, critical situations of the local church.

All of these are ways in which the Institute for Church Life today is trying to place Notre Dame's resources at the service of those most in need of support, direction, and networking. In most cases, our programs are the effect of a pastoral dialogue on a two-way street that brings to us problems and hopes from the grass roots and allows us to enter into cooperation with gifted leaders across the country by means of research, education, and service.

Role of the Director

After describing this rich array of resources positioned under the umbrella of the Institute for Church Life, it may seem as though what is needed by way of administrative skills is an ability to juggle more than a capacity to plan. For a bit, let me reflect on what it means to try to be the administrator of such a rich institutional resource.

The director of the Institute is responsible in a particularly privileged way to stay in touch with those needs of the Church and society to which the University may be able to respond positively. As a result, I need to stay in dialogue with colleagues in the theological community, administrators at the Bishops' Conference and in Catholic dioceses around the country, and with colleagues in other Catholic and social centers based both at universities and independently. It is frequently the case that we are able to do something positive for a diocese or for the Church precisely because we are able to work with others.

This will be, I think, more and more the case. In the future it will be a consortium of efforts at different levels from different localities that will make decisive initiatives to assist the Church in its mission of evangelization and compassion.

As director I am also responsible to keep the Centers related to one another. This is one of the great pleasures of the job, in that each one of the Centers of the Institute is doing strategically valuable, high-quality, and enthusiastically engaged work for the Church. Often when we come together for our meetings of directors, one of the great joys is the telling of the stories—often success stories—of the operations and projects undertaken by each of the Centers. The role of the director here is largely that of a facilitator. With highly self-actualized and competent directors, very little sparking is needed to bring about creative thinking. What is needed is the ability to follow through on nascent projects as they come to be imagined in mutual dialogue.

The director is responsible as well for the institutional relation of the Institute to the administration, the faculty, and the Office of Development of the University. In some ways, the director functions as a "dean" for the Centers, responsible for planning, evaluation, budget control, development, public relations, and staff development. The structure of the Institute is such that the University administration counts on being able to deal with the Centers through the director of the Institute most of the time. Additionally the director of the Institute has the responsibility to make the case before the faculty—especially in occasional visits to faculty meetings—of what the Institute is up to, where faculty collaboration might be invited, and how this can be imagined to be a benefit to the University. With the Development Office there is the need to constantly keep one channel of one's mind focused on promotional ideas. Notre Dame is legendarily blessed with support from its benefactors. Our development people, however, need to know what our projects are, why they are important, who needs to know about them, what their significance is, and similar dimensions of practical communication.

The great challenge for the director of an enterprise like this is the constant call to refine the following qualities: vision, communication, implementation, and compassion. It is an unusual and privileged role. With the colleagues in the Institute, I am at one time an administrator and a fellow. I must accept a responsibility for keeping projects within the budget (or finding moneys to make things happen) as well as encouraging new ideas, supporting new initiatives, and finding personal and material resources for emerging dreams. With faculty colleagues in the University, I am challenged to be an entrepreneur: to share the dreams of my Institute colleagues, to spell out (often in proposals) the viability of collaborative projects, and to stay in touch with people most likely to become partners in the execution of our operations. With respect to bishops and pastors and other church leaders, I am challenged to stay in regular contact with an ever growing network of people who are attempting to shape the Church of the new millennium. It is important to speak responsibly about the resources of the University and its desire to be of service, and to listen carefully to the articulated needs of the local churches and respond realistically (within the available limits of our resources and our committed areas of focus).

At any given moment, demands and opportunities may arise from several different directions. I may be asked to monitor planning or evaluation processes in individual centers, to participate in meetings of their own advisory councils, or to assist them with proposals seeking outside funding for new projects. I may find myself in dialogue with other national or university centers to facilitate collaboration on projects of mutual interest. I may be invited to travel to various dioceses to report on research and programs within the Institute that can be of benefit elsewhere. I may find myself the link between diocesan offices or other universities with the programs and resources of Notre Dame. A surprising number of calls come to my office out of the blue to ask, "Can the University of Notre Dame assist with professional training, networking of programs, or pastoral advice?"

Usually we are able to assist. I spend a lot of time each day on the telephone. Much of that time is devoted to listening and trying to understand well the problems that people have. Often, when the Institute is not directly in a position to do something concrete for a caller, I can refer them to others who can respond to their needs. Occasionally the Institute is able to respond directly, as we did recently with a neighboring diocese that had never established a program to train its deacons to preach or as we are now doing with another diocese that is seeking help in bringing together a cluster of parishes in a changing neighborhood for sharing resources.

The Institute staff rarely enters into conducting programs (apart from workshops or symposiums) in off-campus settings. Most often, when we get involved in the local church, it is to assist people in the area to put together new initiatives for mutual empowerment. But it is a privilege on these occasions to enter into contact with leaders in social service and pastoral leadership. As we bring Notre Dame to the Church, the Church opens our eyes to the signs of the times.

The payoff of all of this is complex. The role is extremely enjoyable. The dream that emerged in the 1970s has in large part come to be a reality. The Institute with its four Centers is alive and well, busily engaged in projects too numerous to be sketched here. The Advisory Council and the administration of the University are most encouraging, offering support for yet more dreaming and yet newer initiatives. It is the kind of reality that would make any administrator happy.

Along with this, however, goes the realization that so much more could be done at every level. The term "generative" comes to mind as I think of the challenge that lies before the director of the Institute and all of the staff here. We are being given a rare opportunity, which so many persons in our society would love to share, to devote the primal energies of our lives to the assistance and well-being of others in need. This often brings us into contact with the most creative and erudite members of our own University community—to say nothing of equally gifted persons within the national Church—to forge alliances for pastoral service. I have to remind myself from time to time how lucky I am to have such a mandate.

The Institute for Church Life represents an achievement— the dream of Father Hesburgh and Monsignor Egan and their colleagues of the 1970s. It does place the resources of this exceptional University in service to the wider Church. But that remains a challenge as well. The challenge is to keep asking the question: How does this Catholic University, one of the most visible symbols of the Church in this country, relate itself to the people of God in this volatile moment of renewal and promise? We keep asking the question. Our programs, research, and new projects are our vital response.

NOTES

1. In the previous months, Father John Gallen, S.J., director of the Murphy Center for Liturgy, Father Robert Pelton, C.S.C., founding director of the Center for Clergy Education, and Father Vincent Dwyer, O.C.S.O., director of the Genesis II Program, had raised with Father Hesburgh the question of forming an institute for pastoral research and service at Notre Dame. Monsignor Egan's entry into Notre Dame came at a time when circumstances favored the substantive development of a new initiative for a pastoral institute based at the University.

2. In the academic year 1995–96, the Center for Pastoral Liturgy is celebrating its twenty-fifth anniversary by focusing on the renewal of the liturgical apostolate for a new generation of adult Catholic leaders. Sister Eleanor Bernstein, C.S.J., the director of the Center, has stressed that the Center for Pastoral Liturgy has the role today of providing exemplary experiences of worship and catechesis in liturgical theology to ministers and people with the aim of achieving the goal of full participation of all the baptized in the rites of the Church that celebrate the mystery of Christ in the lives of the faithful.

The Fullness of Faith: Preparing Ministers for the Future Church

MARK L. POORMAN, C.S.C.

A few years ago, I was asked to go to Israel to explore the possibilities of using Tantur, the University's ecumenical institute outside Jerusalem, as an educational site for ministry students in the theology department. After a series of discussions about the prospects, I took a day to tour the Old City, spending time in each of the quarters—Jewish, Moslem, Christian, and Armenian. As I waited in the Jewish quarter near the Dung Gate to catch a bus back to Tantur, I was approached by a young orthodox rabbi who asked me in obviously "American" English if I would help him with his huge load of groceries in exchange for a few shekels. I said I'd be pleased to help as a favor. He explained that he had parked as closely as he could to the labyrinth of narrow streets that led to his house, and his quick nonchalant gesture made it look as though the house were a mere fifty feet away.

It was not. And we had an ample opportunity to talk. He had emigrated from New York and now was teaching at a local yeshiva. "And what do you do?" he asked with a New Yorker's curiosity-tinged-with-directness. "I'm a Catholic priest," I told him. Without missing a beat, he faced me squarely and inquired, "You're all celibate, right?" I stammered a bit, momentarily flustered that my vocation had been reduced to this. Unaffected

Father Mark Poorman, C.S.C., is Executive Assistant to the Executive Vice President, Associate Professor of Theology, and Director of the Master of Divinity Program.

by my reticence, he began a discourse on the advisability of the charism. Suffice it to say that he had a few doubts about it, and our relatively short acquaintance seemed to him no reason to hold them back. So by the time we reached his house, I was relieved, not just for the sake of my arms' burden, but also to be released from his rather expansive thesis on what he took to be the practical challenges of not being married. He announced our arrival with a hearty "Shalom!" at the entrance to his kitchen and then introduced me to his wife and four children, one by one, as they came running to greet him. I began to take leave, and he asked me if I would be returning to my parish soon. I told him that I was on the faculty at a Catholic university. A flood of exuberant joy washed over his face as he said, "Oh, that's wonderful! Anyone who does not have children should have students. They will keep you full of faith!"

Although to my mind it was not necessarily related to celibacy, he spoke a profound truth that I have already known in my heart and in my work, but have not posed quite so succinctly. Throughout my time at Notre Dame—in residence hall ministry, in campus ministry, and on the theology faculty— I've known the "fullness" of faith prompted by service to students. That faith was and is grounded in their serious questions about God and what is really important, their unbounded enthusiasm and generosity, the hopeful way they look at opportunities and problems, and the cumulative effect in my own life of sharing in the particulars of their day-to-day lives.

Many of my present faculty responsibilities continue to find me grateful for the rabbi's prescription. I teach Christian ethics and pastoral theology, and I direct the Master of Divinity program, the University's graduate program for those preparing for ministry in the Church. The teaching and the administration are complementary works for many reasons, not the least of which is that they afford me the chance to help students to discern what might be God's call for them. True, that mission may take disparate forms on any given day. The under-graduates, often remarkably uncatechized in the Christian tradition but nonetheless receptive to moral reflection, are anxious to find out what the Christian tradition has to say to the issues of the day. Indeed, for these talented and good young people, Jesus' simple and straightforward call to discipleship seems to compete on a level playing field with seductive calls by the culture to other rewards than building the reign of God. The Master of Divinity students, on the other hand, are often quite articulate about the Christian message, but their calls to lives of ordained or lay ministry need to be further clarified and strengthened in the course of their studies. Along with other colleagues, I am charged with the academic and pastoral component of their discernment and preparation for service to the Church, and it is that responsibility to which I'd like to turn my attention in these reflections.

When I consider the many blessings that flow from situating a ministry preparation program within the setting of a Catholic university, I often think of Pierre Teilhard de Chardin's apt injunction that "faith has need of the whole truth." That is certainly the spirit of John Paul II's eloquent and repeated calls in *Ex Corde Ecclesiae* for the Catholic university to seek the Truth of revelation and to find it enriched by conversation among academic disciplines.

Long before that encyclical, though, the Congregation of Holy Cross, with education as one of its principal works, could see the wisdom of training and forming its own religious and future priests in the context of the university's world of ideas. In 1968, it transferred its primary location for seminary training from Rome and Washington, D.C., to the theology department at Notre Dame. With that move the present-day Master of Divinity program at the University was born, and Holy Cross seminarians have prepared for ordination here since. From its inception, the program also included a small number of lay people who pursued the three-year professional degree, even though the clerical design of the curriculum, as well as the unusual case of laity studying theology and acquiring pastoral skills at that early time, presented a challenge to those lay pioneers seeking a credential of sorts to offer their gifts and collaborate in the ministry of the Church.

With the enormous flux since Vatican II in the forms of ministry, theological education has evolved to meet the needs of a renewed Church. During the past three decades, various official ecclesial efforts to articulate a revitalized priestly formation have had counterparts calling for the recognition and expansion of lay ministry and the appropriate training for lay leadership. At Notre Dame, we have relied on the common thematic strains of these documents to build a fully accredited ministry program that is firmly grounded in the tradition but is open to the "reading of the signs of the times" that Paul VI characterized as an essential hallmark of the Church in the modern world. The cornerstone of those efforts has been the continuous direction from both Church and educational leaders that contemporary theological training for ministry should attend to four areas of development for aspiring ministers: academic, pastoral, personal, and spiritual dimensions of the student. To that rather ambitious end, those of us who direct the program attempt to provide opportunities for students that would see them grow in all of these ways, so that eventually they can serve as priests and lay ministers in roles such as pastoral associates in parishes, campus ministers, liturgical coordinators, hospital chaplains, teachers, community organizers, advocates for the poor, and numerous other positions.

The academic component of the program is roughly divided into the sub-disciplines of Catholic theology. Students study scripture, systematic theology, ethics, the history of Christianity, liturgy, and sacramental theology, with a view toward gaining a generalist's understanding of the methods and content of each area of theology. The idea is that as aspiring ministers, they should have an appreciation of how academic theology informs and transforms the ministry they do: for example, preaching should be informed by a critical understanding of scripture and biblical theology; liturgical leadership should be enriched by a good understanding of the history of liturgy and the role of the sacraments in the life of the Church; counseling done in a pastoral setting may well benefit from an appropriation of the moral teaching of Church.

While students almost always acknowledge in principle the importance of a sound academic base for their training, the immediate pastoral value of any given academic topic occasionally may be a reach for both student and teacher. Making the specific pastoral translation of some arcane point in theological method remains a challenge for both faculty and student. Sometimes world-class faculty immersed in the intricacies of life in the early Christian community of Qumran or textual nuances of the Dead Sea Scrolls may not immediately warm to the question, "How should you preach about this passage?" and sometimes students who are full of good will and pastoral zeal for helping God's people do not take an intense interest in the finer points of scholarly discussion about some medieval liturgical practice. But I am convinced that the occasional stretch is good for both students and faculty and is one of the distinct advantages of divinity studies in a research university environment.

Pastoral and professional training is provided by the program in several ways. Through the pastoral skills curriculum, we offer a number of courses which stress the practical features of different types of ministry—Hispanic ministry, health care ministry, religious education, youth ministry, campus ministry, preaching, liturgical leadership, spirituality and ministry to families, reconciliation ministry, marriage preparation, pastoral administration, and pastoral counseling. It is hoped that in the short, intensive exposure to studies and practica in these ministries, at least the student can come to know what is involved in the type of service and can even gain initial competence in it. We offer the pastoral skills curriculum on a three-year cycle so that students may have opportunities to get as much exposure as possible, and so that we can constantly revise the curriculum to stay abreast of current pastoral trends in the Church. Some offerings are fixed: preaching and liturgical leadership, for example, are high priorities for all students. (One of the many financial benefits of a university home for a ministry program is evident in the endowed Marten Program for preaching and liturgy directed by John Melloh, S.M.)

Another important way in which we provide professional and pastoral training is through supervised ministry placements for all the students. Under the direction and guidance of Regina Coll, C.S.J., students choose placements that suit their interests and promise some pastoral development on which they want to focus. The "Field Education" program allows students to take advantage of the pastorally rich area of Notre Dame and South Bend, including placements at parishes, medical centers, a hospice, an AIDS care center, a diocesan marriage tribunal, a center for the homeless, youth ministry, campus ministry at both St. Mary's and Notre Dame, a retreat house, and an advocacy center for the poor, and N.D.'s Center for Social Concerns, to mention a few. Students receive regular supervision for their placement, and they augment the supervision with a weekly seminar in which they generate pastoral cases for discussion among their classmates.

In tending to the personal and spiritual development of ministry students, we often refer to a student's "formation." The word implies that a student should be formed (and transformed) by God's grace and the many experiences he or she has in the course of their preparation. Because one cannot give what one does not have, it is incumbent on us to make certain that the ministers who leave the University after graduation will have the personal resources to be of genuine service to the Church. "Formation" is the umbrella term under which a whole genre of personal areas of growth are included— emotional maturity, spiritual depth and understanding, psychosexual development, and advancement in the personal traits, habits and virtues that make for effective ministry.

The seminarians in the Master of Divinity program receive their priesthood formation, which is the responsibility of the Congregation of Holy Cross, at Moreau Seminary on the campus. Formation for the lay ministry students is under the auspices of the M.Div. program itself. Because formation in the past principally has been the province of training for religious life and priesthood, it has not been seen as an integral part of the preparation of professional Catholic lay ministers. During the past three years, with the leadership of Kathryn Schneider, we have attempted to envision, design, and execute a formation program for the personal and spiritual development of the lay ministry students. It is yet a work-in-progress, but we have made good strides in establishing a program that builds a sense of community among the lay students and encourages their spiritual and personal well-being. In day-to-day informal gatherings and at formal monthly meetings, the program provides opportunities for personal and communal prayer and spiritual direction, as well as a regular format for covering subjects of particular interest to prospective lay ministers: lay leadership in parishes, forming supportive structures in lay ministry, and spirituality for lay ministers.

As director of the program, I have the chance to oversee the daily operations of recruitment, admissions, curriculum, and various other administrative components, thanking God daily for Carole Coffin, who is the program secretary and the heart of the whole thing. I also have the privilege and duty of looking at the big picture for an undertaking like ours which must regularly monitor the pulse of both the Church and the academy. Even for the short period of time I have been director, I can think of dozens of changes we have made, challenges we have faced and rewards we have enjoyed in the program. They are interesting, at least to the extent that they may be bellwethers for the life of the American Church. Allow me to mention only three of them.

First, we have seen a change in the constituency of students in the program. In just the past four years, the proportion of seminarians to lay students has shifted from half seminarians and half lay students in 1992 to approximately 25 percent seminarians and 75 percent lay students for the coming academic year. This statistic, of course, is indicative of a much broader trend in the American Church of a decreasing number of men preparing for priesthood and a sizable increase of lay people who seek to do full-time ministry requiring the credential of an academic and professional degree. In 1992, we had 71 inquiries about admission to the lay ministry program; in 1995 we had 246. This explosion of interest in lay ministry studies here has been enhanced by the University's financial commitment to provide full-tuition scholarships to all Master of Divinity students as a practical way of supporting vocations and the pastoral life of the Church. The Graduate School seems to have bought my line that if we build it, they will come. Beyond sheer numbers, though, the relationship between the two constituencies is changing, as both become more accustomed to the shape of the future Church.

In the early stages of lay ministry training and education, it was common for prospective lay ministers to define themselves most often in terms of what they were not going to be—priests. In an effort to galvanize their identity, they at times devalued the traditional clerical calling in the Church. Seminarians, increasingly seeing themselves as an endangered species, often developed a siege mentality and became defensive about pursuing a vocation to the priesthood. Moreover, the whole nexus of issues surrounding married and female ordination in the Roman Church added fuel to the fire. Tensions along these lines are still perennial, but they have lately decreased in both force and frequency. As time passes, the lay students are more assured that the Church can and will welcome their contributions. They are more confident of the "legitimacy" of their vocation as they witness larger numbers of others pursuing it. Consequently, these days they are less inclined to displace frustrations about their relative lack of authority or capped opportunities on the nearest and most personal target—their seminarian classmates. Likewise, in the course of the clerical numbers crisis, the seminarians, somewhat humbled by the mystery and grace of their pursuing a vocation which is not as popular or esteemed as it once was, have become better equipped to articulate its core meaning to themselves and others without defensiveness. Both constituencies are insightful about the value of preparing for collaborative ministry in a setting which ultimately may be a rehearsal for things to come.

Second, we have witnessed changing perspectives and approaches of women to studying and training for ministry. When women first came to the Master of Divinity program, many openly spoke about seeking a credential identical to the priest's, should the Church make the opportunity for women's ordination available. While we still welcome women with those aspirations to the program, fewer women presently hold ordination as their proximate goal, and more join together with their male lay counterparts in envisioning a lay ministry with its unique gifts and authority. Beyond the ordination question, though, my colleagues and I have noticed through the years a difference in the response of women to the perceived under-valuing of their gender, contributions, and roles in the life of the Church. An earlier day saw pronounced anger as the rule. Some of it was the righteous anger of a prophetic kind, and some of it was the free-floating anger of frustration resulting from slow institutional change and other origins which were hard to pinpoint. Presently there is a guarded optimism and hope that there is indeed room for committed, competent female ministers in the Church. In some cases, though, the anger has turned inward, creating for women students a dull pain and periodic bouts with defeatism. Openly expressed anger does not seem to hold the place it once did in the life of ministerial studies for women.

Let me conclude by describing a personal reward that my colleagues and I am privileged to enjoy every year. In the M.Div. program, rather than a comprehensive examination or thesis, the capstone exercise for the degree is a semester-long "Synthesis Seminar" in which each third-year student partici-pates in a seminar during the final semester and is responsible for pursuing a project of personal interest which demonstrates theological and pastoral capability. Every year, I am gratified by the quality of the presentations that emerge from the process, or more to the point, I am grateful for the people who are ready to graduate. Sometimes I find myself completely distracted in these engaging presentations which range in focus from resymbolizing Mary in the Catholic tradition, to the theological meaning of permanent vows, to a model of discernment for families facing end-of-life decisions.

My consistent distractions are my original memories of the presenting students—one who first came to the program for pre-requisite studies as a Holy Cross Candidate with little more than a baccalaureate degree in science and a lot of good will, another who told me her painful life story which culminated in a graced desire to pursue a vocation to lay ministry, another of a man who literally sold everything to come to the program and see what God wanted of him. Knowing that whole progression from inquirer to minister, accompanying these students on their journey, discovering with them what God is doing here and now through Jesus Christ, are privileges that hark back to the rabbi's promise that students will keep one full of faith. For a Catholic university such as Notre Dame, a graduate program in ministry promises to benefit and yield students who will engender and renew the fullness of faith in the living God for both the Church and the academy.

It's All about Jesus Christ

JOSEPH ROSS, C.S.C.

It's all about Jesus Christ. It's all about trying to live like him, and trying to help others live like him. And it's all about doing that for and with college students. The mission and ministry of a Catholic university comes down to this: living the life of Jesus Christ in this place, with these students.

This place is a university. It's a place given to learning. It's also an expensive place. We can't ignore that. Students come here and pay a great deal of money for the education they will receive. They come here from all over the country and that is important. America is home to a success-oriented culture and thus, many of our students would say they come here to prepare for the workplace, to get a good job. While this chafes painfully against the traditional notion of a university, it nonetheless is the attitude many of our students bring. So, in the midst of the affluent American culture, with students who, by and large want to succeed in that culture, we seek to help them live the life of Jesus Christ. Needless to say, this is not easy.

The students at Notre Dame are good people. Of course they have heard of Jesus Christ long before they ventured onto our lush campus on a hot, humid, August day. Many have been raised in loving Catholic homes. Some have been raised in loving homes of other traditions. Most have been raised in homes that hold a mix of love and humanity. In fact, I don't really know any other kind of home. More and more, it seems that our students, like the American culture from which they come, arrive here with many experiences of brokenness. They

Father Joe Ross, C.S.C., is Rector of Morrissey Hall and Concurrent Instructor in the Freshman Writing Program.

know separation and divorce and are still trying to understand how their parents' lives unraveled. Our students know alcohol and substance abuse. Many of them know destructive relationships, their own from high school, or from family members they've seen suffer. Many students have been pressed hard, sometimes unconsciously, to succeed at Notre Dame so they can get a high-paying job. In fact, for most of our students, this is a given. It's in the water they've been drinking all their lives. Success will mean a good graduate school, a well-paid position in the business world, or a secure job in a part of the country they like. All this is good. It is typically American, but not necessarily Christian. And forming educated Christians is what a Catholic university is all about. I don't mind sounding like a Southern preacher, so I'll say it again: it's all about Jesus Christ.

Many of our students come to Notre Dame precisely because they want to live more like Jesus Christ. While they might not phrase it quite that way when asked, I think it's true. A good number of our students say they want to learn more about their faith. Of course they phrase it in academic language (learn more) because their approach thus far is largely mental. But many students choose Notre Dame partly because they know, or hope, that the atmosphere is one in which faith is prized, not mocked. And it's in this atmosphere they want to learn and live and grow. This means that some of our students come very open and ready to experience their faith in new ways. This is a blessing given richly to us at Notre Dame. Our students often want to talk about their faith, question it, probe it.

Many of our students also come to us pretty well set in their ways. They may know they want to be lawyers. They may be positive they want to be physicians. Many are convinced they want to be in business. Some are willing to come admitting they have no idea what they want to be. And these are brave ones. Brave enough to be uncertain: a key element in the adventure of living like Jesus.

My work at Notre Dame basically falls into three areas, although really it's just one. At least there is a great deal of overlap. I am a preacher, a teacher, and a rector. Simply put, I preach a lot. In the residence hall chapels, in the Basilica of the

Sacred Heart, in the Church of Loretto over at Saint Mary's College, as a Holy Cross priest, I find myself often gripping the sides of a pulpit, trying to make some sense out of the Gospel. As a teacher, I serve in the Freshman Seminar. This is a course in which the teacher can select the topic and run a seminar however he or she might choose, as long as there are thirty pages of writing done by the students each semester. My seminar has evolved over the last eight years into a course called "Living a Christian Life in the World." As a rector, I try to pastor Morrissey Hall, a residence hall of 320 undergraduate men. In this role I preach, teach, discipline, form a staff, organize activities, counsel, marry, bury, play, and live with the men of The Manor, as Morrissey Hall calls itself. These are my roles, but again, it's all about Jesus Christ. I try to help students experience the fact that life is joyful and vigorous only if lived in the spirit of Christ. I try to help them see that anything else will be boring and deadening, even while it may look like success. Whether the students are packed into the Morrissey Hall Chapel for Sunday night mass, assigned to my seminar class in DeBartolo Hall, or living above me in Morrissey Hall, it's all about Jesus Christ.

As a Preacher

I am well aware that preaching is a privilege. I am also aware that Saint Francis of Assisi is rumored to have said: "Preach constantly and occasionally use words." While preaching needs to be done ultimately with one's life, I am speaking here of preaching in a liturgical setting, using words to encourage, inspire, move, and form. Preaching is speaking words that ought to take us someplace we currently are not. In particular, for Christians, preaching ought to encourage us to live more like Jesus. Preaching is not illuminating a congregation with new insights. People ought not walk away from preaching saying: "I never thought of it that way before." Preaching need not give anyone a new thought or idea. Preaching is not teaching. It ought to move us to change. The question each preacher should ask before she or he begins is: How will I ask my hearers to change? Change. That's the task of preaching. Change in the direction of Jesus Christ.

In the Catholic tradition, preaching comes from a text. When we preach, we are to preach the Gospel. That is, preaching needs to spring from the text of scripture that has just been read. And in preaching, there are various texts at play. First and most important is the text of scripture. If the Gospel passage that day is the story of Jesus meeting the rich, young man, then that's the text. One has to preach what one hears that story saying. How does that encounter call us to change? Another text involved is the text of the hearers' lives. Who is the congregation? Who is listening? Where are they? Is it one day before finals begin? Is it the first mass of the school year? Has a student in that residence hall recently died? What is the living text who is listening to the scriptural text? So, who's listening? What are they going through? Add that to what the scriptural text is asking us to do, and we have preaching.

I find our students open to a lot of challenge. Our students are not stupid. They know when preaching is fluffy, not asking anything of them. Our students know, too, that when Jesus preached he didn't just congratulate people. They know that he said hard, challenging things. As we all hunger for Jesus, I think our students hunger for substantial preaching. But it is not easy.

It is difficult to preach that Jesus calls us to base our lives solely on the reign of God. When many of our students are building lives around money and success and lifestyle, it is a hard message, maybe even contrary to what they have been told by their parents, to suggest that Jesus calls us to build our lives around the least of our brothers and sisters. To say to those who are working for a degree, a job, a nice house, a nice car, a nice life, that Jesus calls us in another direction, is not easy. Some students argue with me. Some might stop coming to mass. Some use labels I don't like or deserve. But some, many I suspect, will hear that those words are not coming from me. And students know, too, that those words coming from Jesus need not be met in exactly the same way by every person. There are a variety of ways we hear the words of Jesus. But for the preacher to not say the words or for the preacher to suggest that Jesus didn't really mean one is called to leave all things for his sake is to dilute the words of Jesus. And students can recognize that foolishness very quickly.

There are two very challenging preaching moments for me. One often comes at the beginning of an academic year. When the text of the people is the new year, hope, possibilities, and the scriptural text can be almost anything. It seems right to encourage reflection on how one's major will lead to building the reign of God. This is always tough for me. To ask students "How might we study history in such a way as to become more sensitive to suffering? Or to ask "How might we study business so as to build a more just society for the poor?" Or to ask "How might we study engineering in ways that will bring life to people who otherwise would live with hardship?" I see these as essential, beginning-of-the-year questions. But they can be pretty threatening to some students, threatening because some never imagine that the way various disciplines or jobs unfold might not be Christian. Some students assume that the world, as it is, is fair and Christian. Recognizing some of the darkness around us is a crucial part of becoming adult Christians. Those hard questions can also be liberating, because examining one's major can lead to a more deliberately chosen life. And a more deliberately chosen life will likely be more Christian. At least that's the hope.

Another difficult preaching experience I have faced is when scripture shows Jesus treating women so compassionately. In our culture, where there is so much objectification of women, and where, for men, the opinion of their peers is so crucial, this is a tough preaching assignment. To tell students that Jesus saw the way women were treated in his culture and that he didn't like it is to say to them:"examine how you treat the women in your life." This is a crucial Christian message to preach, but it can bother those not ready for it and make people angry.

Both of these examples are simple enough. They are moments when we are asked by the Gospel to change. And change in the abstract is easy. But concrete change is something most of us resist. To preach that we must think about the ways we treat women is one thing. It's a bit abstract, not so tough to hear. However, to invite students to take down posters of partially clad women in their dorm rooms causes a stir. To call students to heal the way they talk about gay students also causes a stir. To encourage students to share with each other how they see their course of study furthering God's reign, this causes a stir as well. My hope is that it's a good stir. I hope that it's God doing the stirring. I think it is.

A couple of years ago I was struck by how many men had posters in their rooms of women draped over larger-than-life beer bottles. These women were often nearly faceless, but the details of the rest of their bodies were quite clear. I raised this in a sermon once and got quite a few interesting reactions. One junior told me that religion had nothing to do with the posters he had in his room. Another accused me of male-bashing. I did notice afterward that the already high number of women present at mass in Morrissey Hall was going up.

For me, it has been important to always have a student critique my preaching. Each year I have asked a student, who attends mass regularly and who I think has the nerve to be honest with me, to give me some feedback whenever I preach in the Morrissey Chapel. This has been a great blessing for me. I have been fortunate to find several generous, honest students. They tell me when an example didn't work, a story was too long, a line was too repetitive. They tell me too what others are saying, and I am grateful to know what they're hearing. It's only with information like this that one can adjust and improve. To assume that I automatically know how best to preach to any one group is probably crazy.

One great blessing about preaching in our residence halls is that one is preaching to people with whom one lives. This is an awesome responsibility because you tend to know the congregation so well, too well sometimes. In living with students you come to know their blessings, their struggles, their sins. And in preaching, that is all in your heart. You know what you think they want to hear, what they might need to hear, and what they might not want to hear. I have come to know that it's important to love the people to whom you're preaching. So preaching in the place you live is a profound opportunity. I think it's true that people can only change to the extent they are loved. To love them and to preach to them is the blessing of my vocation.

Another blessing about preaching to the community in which one lives is a sort of forced humility. As a preacher, I realize I am calling the congregation to many of the same changes that I myself need to make. And what's most challenging, is that they, the students, know this too. In the Morrissey Chapel on any given Sunday night there will be students whose feelings I have hurt, students to whom I should have given more time. There will be students who know that I also fall short of the things about which I am preaching. This need not cause the preacher to be timid, only to remember that we are all on the road. We're all trying to live closer to the way of Jesus. It's all about Jesus Christ.

As a Teacher

My experience as a teacher in the Freshman Seminar has been a delight. I have often looked around that DeBartolo Hall classroom as one student was speaking and thought I was going to see tongues of fire above some of their heads. It has often been a place where God has definitely done some stirring.

I find our students in desperate need of a place to talk about the things that matter most. Many of our students have never spoken about their faith in an adult setting. They have many questions, frustrations, and insights to share. I find too that they often want to talk about their relationships: their loves, their friends. In the normal course of life, they often don't have a forum in which they can share some of their concerns about the ways men and women relate, about the ways black and white people relate, about the ways they have each related to the Church. The seminar has been a place where a lot of this has transpired.

One day this past semester, we were talking about experiences of conversion, times during which we changed. One young man described a spring break trip to Mexico he made with his church youth group. He talked about not wanting to go, preferring to stay at home with friends to lounge around. But he said that when he arrived he met a young Mexican man named Guillermo who was very poor, but quite willing to talk with him about life in Mexico. They hit it off well and really taught each other a great deal. He realized after meeting Guillermo that his desires to stay at home were selfish and that perhaps God had wanted him to go on this trip so he could meet this young man. He described his heart as being broken by the poverty of this young man's life. But he also saw his heart as joyful at the peace and faith present in Guillermo's life. He told us that he was actually afraid of what would have happened to him had he not gone on this trip. As we listened to him I realized the class was entirely focused on him and his story. Thankfully, the moment has been replayed many times in my eight years of teaching Freshman Seminar.

One day when I had planned a lofty discussion of institutional sin, intending to explore how racism was a sin rooted in various institutions of our culture, one woman, out of the blue asked why the church taught that sex outside of marriage was a sin. The teacher's natural dilemma is—do you put that question off so you can get to the material, or do you deal with what is on her mind? Because I had the hunch from looking at their faces that for all of them this was an important question, we dealt with it. It led to an enlightening conversation about the beauty of sexuality, the holiness of relationships, and the challenging joy of commitments. They were also surprised when I used orgasm as an example of sexuality being a great gift from God

It's amazing what happens when we give students a place to talk. I refer to the seminar as a forum of charity. It's a place where, hopefully in love and freedom, students can talk about how they've experienced God and what challenges and joys that has brought. One day, while discussing images of God, I asked one African-American woman to let the seminar interview her as though she were God. She agreed and responded to her classmates' questions with a real authority and presence. We realized, and she did too, that she was unearthing her own image of God as she answered questions from the Divine perspective. The moment became very interesting when one student asked, rather boldly: "God, what color is your skin?" She became very quiet, did not want to answer, and then tearfully said: "White." She sobbed. Three students and I went up and embraced her. She never knew, until that moment, that she, an African-American woman, had stuck in her head that God was white.

One day in seminar this last semester, the day after a particularly tense conversation about the just war theory and Christian pacifism, I came into class and quietly asked two students if they would take a risk with me. Then, instead of starting class in the normal way (asking them for a story), I got down on my hands and knees, took off the shoes of the two students who had agreed to the risk, and washed their feet. Afterward, I got up and we went on with class. I didn't mention what had happened until the end of class when I asked them to respond in their journals to what had been done.

When discussing the Parable of the Good Samaritan one day, we were wondering why people don't stop when they see someone stranded on the side of the road. All the predictable answers were given: You'll get robbed. You can't just stop and help people. You may get killed yourself. Then one woman, who hadn't said much in class to that point said: "I think that we die if we *don't* stop." Her comment generated a lively discussion on the cost of being a Christian, that Christianity isn't just something you put on your resume. It means your life must change in some discernible and costly directions. That day I was looking for the tongues of fire many times.

Providing students with a place to talk, in an organized way, about faith and life is crucial. Our lives can tend toward the trivial if we're not careful. We can discover that all we're talking about with our friends is Notre Dame football or the

Chicago Bulls. While those are fun topics, they really don't live in us deeply. I have found the Freshman Seminar to be a place where students are able to go deeper. It's all about Jesus Christ.

As a Rector

Unless one is familiar with Notre Dame's residence hall system, the average person would never guess what a rector is or does. The role is probably unique in Catholic universities and surely unique among American secular universities. The best way I can describe my life as a rector is to say that it is like being pastor of a parish that lives together in one building. And even that's not a complete description.

As a rector, your work is to help students grow in the direction of Jesus, particularly in the areas of their relationships. At the beginning of the year we welcome the freshmen into Morrissey with a significant program of orientation. There are older students around to help them move in, lead them in discussions about hall life and the living values of charity and accountability.

I work with two assistant rectors, usually law students, and nine resident assistants, all seniors, who help to facilitate community life, growth, and vitality in the residence hall. If students drink too much, we talk with them about their behavior and find ways for them to work toward a more healthy approach to that substance. If students act in some unkind ways toward others, we end up in conversations about those things. Mostly, being a rector is listening and talking with students at all hours of the day and night. My day normally begins around 10 a.m. and ends around 2 a.m.

It's amazing to me how you can talk with a student about his stereo playing too loudly and at the end of the conversation, you're onto his parents' impending divorce and his anger at his father. You can call someone down to talk about the fact that he was a bit intoxicated on the previous weekend and halfway through the discussion, he tells you how scared he is because his brother has just been admitted to a drug treatment facility back home. Everything that can come up, does come up. All the struggles of the human condition that people can face often find their way into these conversations. It's a great privilege and a profound challenge.

I learn that young people in our culture have some very unique problems. And young men in particular have some unique challenges before them. They experience so much pressure to succeed in the world of salaries and prestige. They experience much pressure in just determining who to date, who to have as friends, what kinds of behaviors they will enter into in all of their relationships. It's during the college years, too, that many young people are struggling with questions of sexual identity. These are all holy roads to walk with people. To me, to help someone discover more fully that he is loved for who he is, not what he'll earn, is a challenge and an essential ministry. But again, it's all about Jesus Christ. Not necessarily getting a student to become a more fervent Christian, but to become a conscious, reflective person first. Christ will emerge in his own time. As rector, you get involved in late night conversations about politics, faith, the Church, prayer, and relationships. It seems to me that the late-night discussion ought to be one of the Church's sacraments. It is so fruitful. It so often creates what it signifies.

I must admit that the largest single topic I deal with initially in the residence hall is that of alcohol use. It is such a powerful part of the college culture that it's impossible to escape. Many students have stuck in their heads somewhere that to go to college is to be free to drink. This is particularly a problem at Notre Dame. We talk about it often with students, particularly around how they used alcohol in high school, how alcohol was used in their home, and most instructively, how their friendships are going. Whether a student feels that he or she belongs seems often to determine how he or she will use or abuse alcohol. I surely don't have any magic solutions to this problem, except that I ask students many questions about it and it often leads into various areas of life where they are hurting or in need of growth.

Part of my ministry in Morrissey includes encouraging students to meet the poor in the South Bend area. There are some students who are very eager to do this, while others cannot find the time. It's important for me to be supportive and encouraging of those who can do it. And it's important for me to continue to gently challenge those who can't. In Morrissey Hall, we have been connected to St. Hedwig's Outreach Center for several years now. Morrissey men go there twice a week to tutor youngsters from the west side of South Bend. As they get to know these kids, their situations, their sadnesses, their joys, our students' world gets so much bigger. I see them growing in patience and compassion simply because they see how others suffer. And they see that they are able to touch and soothe some of that suffering.

The residence hall is also a place of great enthusiasm and personal identification. This is very true where I live in Morrissey Hall. Morrissey is a grand, old, gothic building. It is seventy years old and looks it. It's beautiful on the outside, lots of stone carvings and high arches. On the inside it's tight, cramped, and over-heated. The students in Morrissey get involved in hall government, where we have an active hall council and hall officers. They get involved in hall sports. This is a highly competitive, enthusiastic experience. They also get involved in the liturgical life of the hall. We are blessed in Morrissey Hall to have a large and beautiful chapel which the students run. They organize the Sunday night masses, the weeknight masses, scripture reflection meetings once a week, discussion groups to talk about different forms of prayer. I guess I'd say that life in Morrissey, as its rector, is not solely about growth. It's also about enjoying life together. Maybe that is about growth. Growth toward Christ.

In all of this, from preaching to teaching to serving in Morrissey Hall, the hope is that our life together forms all of us more closely into the person of Jesus Christ. To learn to forgive as he did, to serve as he did, to challenge as he did, to enjoy others as he did, to love as he did, all this is the mission and ministry of a Catholic university. It's all about Jesus Christ.

We Drink from Our Own Wells

TIMOTHY R. SCULLY, C.S.C.

Just outside O'Shaughnessy Hall, commencing the south quad, lies a beautiful shaded green. At its center rests a small fountain carved from black marble; dark, cool water springs quietly, almost imperceptibly, but uninterruptedly from the center of the fountain—from somewhere deep down. The fountain is flanked by two dynamic sculpted figures: on the left, a rather unconventional rabbi from Galilee, on the right, a somewhat impetuous woman protecting Samaritan turf.

In a unique and powerful way, Iván Mestrovich's artistic creation recaptures for us a brief but extraordinary exchange in John's Gospel (John 4:1–42). Jesus is tired and thirsting, in the midst of a long journey from Jerusalem back to Galilee. He finds himself in an alien and inhospitable territory. He has sent his fellow travelers to a local merchant to acquire food and drink. Meanwhile, alone and under the heat of the midday sun, Jesus takes refuge beside the ancient Samaritan Well of Jacob, the only source of fresh water anywhere near the desolate place. After some time, a woman carrying a large stone vessel approaches the well of her ancestors to draw water for herself. She purposely circles to the opposite side of the well. Avoiding any contact whatsoever with this stranger, she prepares to draw water from the depths of the well. Jesus unexpectedly breaks the silence, thereby breaking with centuries-old customs and cultural norms. He invites the Samaritan woman, step by step, to reexamine her life, to question the conventions. Jesus engages her as a teacher would.

Father Tim Scully, C.S.C., is Vice President and Senior Associate Provost, Associate Professor of Government, and was founding Director of the Alliance for Catholic Education.

209

If you are on the campus and the opportunity should avail itself, take the time to examine this beautiful Mestrovich scene. Look carefully at Jesus' expression: he is poised and concentrated, communicating urgency and understanding. Though thirsting and tired from the long journey, he reaches out to relieve the sadness and unspoken pain of the other. Jesus seeks for the woman what God seeks: a life free to know and experience complete love, and to love in return.

Examine closely the woman. She is uncertain and perplexed by the encounter, still clutching the heavy stone vessel as if holding on to her painful, but at least certain, past. She is taken by surprise by the provocative and intrusive words of Jesus. Her eyes are cast slightly downward as she ponders the meaning of this surprising encounter. Though impertinent and clearly improper, this strange teacher has been the first in memory to deal with her honestly, and caringly. Though troubled, she senses the love. This Galilean invites her into his life so that she might experience "living water," life itself welling up from deep within. John's story continues, of course, with the woman bursting with newly discovered freedom and joy; she runs off to the village with news of this prophet, leaving her stone vessel behind.

Mestrovich's moving re-creation of the well springing up from beneath the parched Samaritan landscape and of this extraordinary encounter between two strangers provides an image for viewing ministry at Notre Dame. Imagine a place in the midst of contemporary bourgeois America where, year after year, almost magically, fresh and unspoiled young people, some of the best and brightest the Church has to offer, gather to grow together in knowledge, wisdom, and faith. It is a mystery how, generation after generation, this grace is sustained. But, like the waters that continuously spring forth from the inhospitable Samaritan countryside, God draws to Notre Dame a truly exceptional group of young people to live and study in the midst of a vital Christian community. At its most fundamental level, it is this continuous stream of uncommonly graced students that is the wellspring and vouchsafe of life of the Spirit at Notre Dame.

It almost goes without saying that to share in three different dimensions of ministry at Notre Dame as I do—hall life, teaching and scholarship, and administration—is the privilege of a lifetime. To live and celebrate faith daily with our students in the residence halls provides an uninterrupted flow of opportunities to interact intimately, to invite them into our lives, and even to catch an occasional glimpse of the love of God. Not unlike the chance encounter between two strangers at Jacob's well, unlikely and seemingly insignificant interactions with students in the residence halls—from late-night mass to mid-night hockey—provide limitless opportunities for real engagement and even moments of deep grace and genuine transformation. In fact, it is almost invariably in the unplanned and unanticipated events of daily life that we are able to naturally invite our students to come to experience "what was from the beginning, what we have heard, what we have seen with our own eyes, what we have looked upon, and our hands have touched, we speak of the word of Life" (1 John 1:1).

Teaching and studying comparative and Latin American politics, a subject I love, with students and faculty colleagues as bright and talented as any in the world provides the principal setting for engaging students and challenging the life of the mind. In my own field of study, uncovering the institutional roots of democratic stability, and breakdown, and exploring the implications of these processes for building just and free societies provide a privileged context for exploring larger questions of meaning and vocation. Our students often bring to the study of politics a set of normative convictions, grounded in faith and in an understanding of the profound dignity of each human being, thereby catalyzing sharp exchanges about what is good and true and how life is to be lived. As a teacher, there is no thrill comparable to that of participating in some small way in the discovery of the vocation and the truest and best self of my students. I know of no greater pleasure than inviting students into real and substantive exchange about ideas that matter deeply.

Of late, I have been invited to contribute, together with exceptional faculty colleagues, to the task of shaping Notre

Dame's academic mission in the Provost's Office. Here, we are faced with an exciting challenge: to build a great university where faith and the life of the mind are encouraged to come together freely and interact dynamically. There exists no real precedent or model in the contemporary world which has succeeded in becoming a world-class institution of teaching and learning while maintaining its religious commitments. To build such a university is the most exciting and energizing project I can imagine; one certainly worthy of spending a lifetime pursuing.

It is difficult to imagine a more exciting time or place to be a Catholic priest than the present, on the eve of the twenty-first century, in the American Church. And I cannot envision a more privileged place to carry out this ministry than the apostolate of higher education. To my mind, at the very heart of the ministry of the priesthood, and our most urgent obligation, is the task of actively creating substantive opportunities for talented and committed young people to place their gifts meaningfully at the service of the Church and the world. Essential to my understanding of the mission of a priest, especially after the inspiration of the Second Vatican Council, lies the responsibility to both create real opportunities for new forms of ministry in the Church and to help recognize and call forth to service the many leadership gifts abounding in our students.

Our Church and our world are tired and thirsting for new and creative witness to the Gospel. I am utterly convinced that God is not calling fewer or less talented people to discipleship and a life of ministry in the Church today than in an earlier era. Rather it is incumbent upon those of us who currently minister in the Church, and especially those of us who hold leadership positions, to create the structures and opportunities whereby the gifts and talents of our Church's young adults can find creative and responsible expression. As Pope Paul VI so powerfully stated it, "At every new phase of human history, the church, constantly gripped by the desire to evangelize has but one preoccupation: whom to send to proclaim the mystery of Jesus?" (*On Evangelism in the Modern World*). It is critically important that we respond effectively to the challenge of creating new expressions of ministry for our young graduates to serve the Gospel.

Living and working among the students at Notre Dame over the past years has been, indeed, a bit like discovering Jacob's well in the midst of a parched and inhospitable land. It is, as Bernard of Clairvaux reminded us, from "our own wells that we must drink,"[1] and it is from among our own students today that tomorrow's leaders of the Church must come. I have enjoyed the multiple dimensions of my life and ministry at Notre Dame enormously: in the residence halls, the classroom, and in the Provost's Office. But, as exciting as these have been, perhaps none of these involvements have provided more hope and encouragement to me for the future of the Church than helping create new ministerial opportunities for our young graduates and inviting them to experience the joy of service to the Gospel. My life in ministry as a priest has demonstrated to me time and time again that the Spirit continues to call forth new life and vitality for the Church. We have only to be vigilant in recognizing those among whom we teach who themselves are anxious to respond, and to call them by name.

I am the beneficiary of such a call. I recall that, as an undergraduate at Notre Dame in the 1970s, people such as Father Don McNeill, C.S.C., challenged me by both word and example to view life in terms of service to the Gospel. Thanks to him and others, I became quite involved as a Saturday volunteer at Logan Center, an active member of the World Hunger Coalition, and the founder of the bail-bond project for prisoners in the St. Joseph County jail. These experiences of service found an important echo in the classroom, where Roger Skurski, Father John Dunne, and Father Charlie Sheedy made the Gospel come alive, awakening both heart and mind. In retrospect, these experiences, perhaps more than any others, led me to see my life as a gift, a gift to be freely given in return. Ultimately, the joy I experienced in seeing God use me in small ways to touch others led me to want to spend my life in ministry as a priest.

It was also these experiences which led me, as a Holy Cross seminarian, to initiate, with the help of many others, the Holy Cross Associates Programs. The basic idea was simple enough:

we would invite talented young graduates to live in Christian community and join in the apostolic efforts of the Congregation of the Holy Cross, especially where we are present to the poor. We began this small effort in 1978 with five Associates in Portland, Oregon. Today, more than 400 young people have spent at least a year in service and faith, and have experienced the Gospel in this tangible and often life-transforming way. What God has done in and through the lives of these energetic young people, both in the Associate year and, most importantly, in the years beyond, ratifies the importance of providing opportunities for young people to experience the powerful grace of ministry. At the same time, the Church and the world are refreshed and renewed continuously by the enthusiasm and new life springing forth from deep within Her own springs.

More recently, I have witnessed the boundless vitality and potential for creative service to the Church and the world present in our students with my involvement in creating the Alliance for Catholic Education (ACE), an initiative to help bring resources of higher education to fill the critical needs of under-resourced parochial schools. My work with ACE over the past few years has been among the most exciting and promising apostolic endeavors in my life as a priest. Perhaps the story of its creation and brief evolution might be instructive for the promise of creating future ministerial opportunities at Notre Dame and other Catholic colleges and universities.

Like so many initiatives of its kind, ACE was born unintentionally. I had traveled to Washington, D.C., in the fall of 1994 to deliver a paper on Latin American party systems at the annual meeting of the American Political Science Association. I had arranged to have dinner with a great friend, Sister Lourdes Sheehan, R.S.M. At dinner, Sister Lourdes, who at the time was Director of Education for the United States Catholic Conference, was lamenting the fact that the shortage of qualified and committed Catholics to teach in parochial schools, particularly in the south and southeast, was causing real hardship for the teaching mission of these schools. In addition, reflecting upon the diminishing numbers of vocations to religious life, it became clear that the "clock is ticking" for America's 8700 Catholic schools. Who will carry on the great legacy of Catholic education in the United States, providing needed leadership for the future? After discussing the problem, I asked why Sister Lourdes hadn't tried to develop a corps of talented and faith-filled young people to respond to the need. Surely they would respond if asked, and gladly. Sister Lourdes retorted that, while she'd be happy to help, she thought I was in a better position to start such an effort at Notre Dame. If you know Sister Lourdes at all, you know she can help you walk on water, so I promised her I'd give it a try. We contacted a few well-placed friends at the NCEA, and received their blessing and promise of support. We also spent valuable time with Sister Rosemary Collins, S.S.J., the energetic founder and director of the Washington Teacher Corps, who proved to be exceedingly generous and helpful with her advice and experience in shaping our Alliance for Catholic Education.

Returning to Notre Dame, I decided to test the waters. I spoke with Father Monk Malloy, C.S.C., and asked if he would provide a bit of "venture capital" for our initiative. Character-istically, Monk smiled, shrugged his shoulders and said "Sure, why not?" Monk's confidence and trust, as well as his support for Catholic education, was unquestioning from the start. Father Dick Warner, C.S.C, Tom Doyle, C.S.C., and several other friends in Holy Cross formed an informal steering committee. Together, we began to think about recruitment strategies. We placed a colorful ad in the student newspaper, *The Observer*, and announced our first organizational meeting with a challenge to graduating seniors in bold print: "Tired of getting homework? Then give some! Become a teacher!" Though we expected a dozen or so to show up, over 200 seniors packed LaFortune's Notre Dame room! Somewhat unwittingly, we had struck a deep chord with our students, and soon had more interest in teaching than we knew what to do with!

This wonderfully enthusiastic response among the students triggered a bit of anxiety within me. Clearly, there was enough raw talent and commitment in that room to staff a dozen schools. But, in fact, we had no concrete offers of teaching positions yet. We had no housing for the teachers to live in. We had no education department at Notre Dame to provide teacher training. We had no money, no office, no staff. In short, we had no program! Besides this, I am by training a political scientist, and by passion a teacher and a writer. Where in God's name would the energy and time come from to put all this together?

Yet the need for energetic teachers and the talent and commitment to meet those needs were staring us in the face. I was gazing out my office window at the Kellogg Institute for International Studies wondering what in the world I was going to do, when I heard a knock at the door. Sean McGraw, a former student of mine in comparative politics, was just returning from completing his Master's Degree at the London School of Economics. He inquired if he could work with me for a semester or two as a research assistant while he made application to a few select doctoral programs. I responded that while I thought I could give him a few hours a week on a new book project I was beginning, I could not pay him much. Would he be interested, I asked, in helping for a few additional hours a week on a small project to recruit teachers for under-resourced parochial schools?

To my great relief, Sean responded that he would be "happy to do whatever needed to be done." It was only later that I discovered that Sean is always happy to do whatever needs to be done, if he is convinced of the value of the undertaking. Very quickly, Sean became a believer in the project and, with incredible industry and intelligence, became the linchpin of the incipient Alliance for Catholic Education.

I moved a small additional desk into my faculty office at the Hesburgh Center for Sean, and the two of us rolled up our sleeves and got to work creating a viable program. Since I was teaching and writing full time, and Sean was continuing his own work in comparative politics and teaching tennis to stay alive, we worked to develop ACE in our free time, usually early in the day, and then again late at night. We worked at a fairly frantic pace as we raced against deadline after deadline to reach our goal of recruiting, selecting, placing, training, housing, and paying for forty new teachers in eight cities by the following fall.

Sean and I traveled to the annual meetings of Catholic school superintendents in Louisville, Kentucky where Sister Lourdes had arranged to introduce us to a number of interested superintendents from the south and southeastern United States. To our surprise (and relief!), each of them responded to our ideas with enormous enthusiasm. I recall one of the superintendents present, Sister Mary Michaeline, O.P., of Baton Rouge, Louisiana, exclaiming, "This is an answer to my prayers!" We promised to visit each of them, and their schools, during the coming Christmas holidays.

In the meantime, we had our work cut out for us. First, we needed to enlist the help of professionals to provide teacher training for our novice teachers-to-be. We had studied other efforts, such as Teach for America, where teachers had simply been parachuted alone into inhospitable teaching environments and had quickly become targets, and soon casualties, of hostility from both students and suspicious veteran teachers. We turned to our sister school, the University of Portland, for help. Father David Tyson, C.S.C., Portland's president, immediately understood our need and sympathized deeply with the project. He promised the help of his School of Education. And, he delivered. Over the course of the next several months, we scrambled, together with the faculty of the School of Education and several generous faculty colleagues from Notre Dame, to develop and recruit faculty for a teacher-training program. Designed to take place during two summers on the campus of the University of Notre Dame, the Master's Degree Program in Education we developed seeks to train teachers from the bottom up. We began our efforts by asking local teachers and superintendents what they believed to be the essential skills of effective teaching, and worked to design a model that drew directly from the experience of the classroom. With Christ-teacher as the only model worth imitating, ACE provides novice teachers with necessary pedagogical preparation while at the same time reinforcing the faith and service commitment that drew them to teaching in the first place.

While we were designing our teacher-training program with faculty both at Portland and Notre Dame, we needed to concentrate at the same time on selecting the most promising ACE participants from among the many qualified applicants.

We put together a team of over a dozen hall rectors and staff who brought to Notre Dame significant experience in the parochial school system. With no compensation other than the satisfaction of providing new life to needy parochial schools, already taxed hall rectors dedicated hour after hour to interviewing prospective applicants from among the leadership of the graduating class. After listening to hundreds of stories from our graduating seniors reflecting grace upon grace, we emerged from the selection process with an even deeper sense of the depth of talent, generosity, and zeal of our students.

For some mysterious reason, the Holy Spirit has decided to bless our efforts in ACE with extraordinary dynamism and life. All who have become involved in this faith-filled endeavor have been touched in some way by the power of the Spirit. After only two years of operation, ACE had 110 teachers serving in over seventy schools located in twenty cities across the south and southeast, and had become, due to the efforts of the entire community at the University of Notre Dame and Portland, a refreshing and important dimension of our common ministry. Providentially, Sister Lourdes Sheehan, R.S.M., left her work with the Bishop's Conference in Washington, D.C., to live in a residence hall on Notre Dame's campus and lead ACE in its efforts to prepare a new generation of leadership for America's Catholic schools. Sean McGraw left the leadership of ACE to pursue a vocation to the priesthood in the Congregation of Holy Cross. A gentle, visionary, and spirit-filled Catholic school teacher from Philadelphia, Lou delFra, himself a recent Notre Dame graduate, left his classroom at our invitation to join Sister Lourdes on the leadership team. Had we searched the planet far and wide, we would never have found more inspired or grace-filled people to lead our novice teachers by their example and to shape the uncharted future of our ministry to Catholic education.

Whether it be ministry in the residence halls, the classroom, in the Provost's Office, or in newer initiatives like ACE, at Notre Dame we return to our own wells, to draw deeply from the springs which nourish and refresh the Church. We have a graced opportunity, and a special responsibility, to call forth our students to experience the joy of ministry themselves, to come to know their truest and best selves. Listen to the words of Kevin Monahan, a Notre Dame graduate who has been teaching middle school math at Our Lady of Lourdes in Mobile, Alabama as he reflected on his involvement in ACE in a recent letter: "Nothing in my life has brought me such peace, pride, and challenge. I feel that ACE has given my life a direction and has kept me in the Church. I have strengthened my faith to a point where I know I will never leave it behind.... I began this program thinking of teaching, but now I am in this program commited to a life of service. I have a calling to help others and to serve as the Lord sees fit. I have often related these feelings to the call of the prophet: 'Here I am Lord. Is it I Lord?' The only difference is that I know that it is I who have been called. I will try to listen and respond." Kevin completed his two years of service as a teacher in ACE in 1996 and continues to teach and serve as Assistant Principal, at Our Lady of Lourdes School.

As the story of Kevin Monahan and my own experience in ministry at Notre Dame suggest, our students are anxious to discover their passion, to receive a call. Like the Samaritan woman, our Church and our world are thirsting to receive the new life and vitality that wells up from deep within. We drink from our own wells. And like Christ that afternoon at Jacob's well, we at Notre Dame must be untiring in inviting our students into our lives to experience the joy of following the Lord's call. May God make us equal to the task.

NOTE

1. More recently, this phrase was used by Gustavo Gutierrez as the title of his book on spirituality and Liberation Theology, *We Drink from Our Own Wells* (Maryknoll: Orbis Press, 1984).

Surprised by Joy
on Howard Street

THOMAS L. SHAFFER

My colleague Tex Dutile asked me the other day if I liked being a legal-aid lawyer who works with law students. I said I did, but that I have surprised myself (or maybe God surprised me): I didn't think I would, when, five years ago, I asked the Dean to let me work with students in the Notre Dame Legal Aid Clinic instead of teaching law in the classroom. It has been a sort of conversion for me—a conversion to good and unexpected things; I have, in C. S. Lewis's phrase, been surprised by joy.

I date the conversion from 1991, in my fifty-seventh year and in the thirty-first year of my being a full-time classroom law teacher: Jonathan Kozol came to campus to talk about homelessness. He lectured in the law-school courtroom; lots of students were there. I sat next to my old friend and teacher Tom Broden, '49L; we ate our brown-bag lunches as we listened to Kozol's moving description of families on the street or in one of Mayor Koch's New York welfare hotels.

Afterwards, I said that I was moved by Kozol's account, and I hoped the students were. Tom agreed that Kozol was eloquent; but, he said, our students would not learn about poverty from listening to Kozol. He said law students learn about those we are told to prefer—in the Torah and the Gospels and in modern Catholic social teaching—not from speakers, but from being *among* the people we are told to prefer.

Tom spoke there of his own way of being a law teacher. His way has been to go, with his students, again and again,

Tom Shaffer is the Robert and Marion Short Professor of Law.

year after year, into the broken neighborhoods and prisons and dumping grounds of Northern Indiana, and there show his students how to practice law. His programs in law and poverty (under a dozen titles and with a score of precarious funding arrangements) were, for most of three decades, almost the only thing of its kind at Notre Dame. (Tom retired in 1993; he still works with us.)

I hadn't paid much attention to what Tom and his students were doing all that time—nor to similar efforts by our colleagues Frank Booker and Con Kellenberg. I was, in Auden's phrase, trudging on time to a tidy fortune, contributing a little money to the missionary sisters, and occasionally listening to people like Kozol. Listening to people like Kozol was like going to church during the week.

When Tom alluded to his own work, after the Kozol lecture, I thought of what my wife Nancy has done, since our youngest went to kindergarten in 1970, which is what Tom was talking about doing with students in tow: She has been an advocate in legal-services offices in California, Virginia, and Indiana, and in the United Religious Community in South Bend, for twenty-five years. She recently qualified as a Court Appointed Special Advocate for children. She is very good at helping people—calm, purposeful, hardly ever *really* indignant, and never judgmental. And she is not a lawyer.

The central reality in Tom Broden's ministry—and Nancy's, too—is that it runs in two directions: Tom and Nancy have been ministers to people who need help, and who sometimes need advocates, lay and licensed, and do not have them, *and* they have been ministers to students and friends (including me) who otherwise would know nothing about such people beyond what they read in the newspaper or hear from padded chairs in the law-school courtroom.

Very few of our students have much to do with the poor when they are at Notre Dame, and even fewer will end up in a career of being lawyers for low-income people. The typical law graduate leaves us with between $50,000 and $100,000 in debt that has to be paid off from law-practice income, and legal-services lawyers make less than parochial-school teachers do. Even if our law graduates left us debt free, most of them could not find work in our kind of practice; there are few legal-services jobs available for them—fewer all the time.

Like most moments in my life with Jesus, the realization, which came to me slowly, was quiet and obvious and familiar: I went down to the basement of the law building to see if the able young mothers who created our latter-day Legal Aid Clinic, Eileen Doran, '86L, and Barbara Gasperetti, could use my help. And then I talked to my classmate the Dean, Dave Link, '58, '61L. . . .

Since then, thanks to these sisters and brothers in the Lord, I have spent four-fifths of my time as a "supervising attorney" in the largest law office in Northern Indiana. (I use the other fifth to write—but, until this little piece, not much about being a legal-aid lawyer.) Eileen, Barbara, and I have two part-time colleagues—Christine Venter, '94 LL.M., '95 S.J.D., a South African lawyer who has otherwise been at Notre Dame to earn our first research doctorate in law, and Steve Morse, '64L, who retired a year ago from the large law firm I worked for in the 1960s. We work with an average of about fifty students during the academic year, fifteen during the summer, and take on about four hundred cases a year for clients who cannot afford lawyers.

We work in an old, comfortable, three-story building on Howard Street which the University bought from a defunct religious sect, across from Pandora's Books, in the high-crime area between campus and St. Joseph's Hospital that the University is gradually extending its influence over. Some of our clients are also our neighbors. Some of our neighbors, who drop in for talk or a cup of coffee, are not (yet) our clients.

My greatest contribution to the Clinic has been talking Linda Harrington, who has worked for the Law School for fifteen years, into becoming the Clinic's office manager. It is she—not a bunch of lawyers—who holds the place together. We fifty-five practicing lawyers have one able secretary, Becky Carlton, whom we stole from the law library, and a couple of undergraduate students who help us part-time, under the work-study program.

I mention these women, and should mention as well that most of our legal interns are women, not only out of necessary attribution but also because one lasting grace I have from this new work is the amazing experience of working in a *feminine* place, of dealing with legal issues from a feminine perspective, of sharing daily—sometimes as a kind of grandfather—in the remarkable stress Eileen, Barbara, and Christine have in being mothers of young children and at the same time busy, involved lawyers.

Involvement goes with being feminine in a way that would be unusual in most law offices. In one case, Barbara gathered together a crew of law students and painted the inside of a client's apartment. Twice a week she leads a team of students— as many Spanish speakers as she can find, and others—and goes to La Casa di Amistad, the Hispanic community center in South Bend, to lead people there through their complex involvement with the Immigration and Naturalization Service.

Eileen blends her legal work with young-mother persistence, to locate baby-sitters, medical care, and garbage service for her clients; she argues with public-school officials and welfare workers on a range of questions that few male lawyers would think of as part of their job description. Christine is working with editors, English teachers, and publishers on a manuscript for a book that one of our clients wrote.

In a sense that is real (and that we repeat often), and in a sense that is also feminine, we, like any serious set of lawyers, put a top priority on clients: Clients come first. That traditional professional sense of priority is part of the ministry of our students, who are as much a part of our ministry as the clients are. What I am calling the feminine part of the priority is that it does not stop at what I once thought of as what a lawyer does.

Our office is the only law office I know about that observes birthdays, arrivals, departures, returns, engagements, and pregnancies. About once a week our busy professional activity has to stop for a brief party in the waiting room. Everyone within earshot is invited to the party—students, older lawyers, clients, and whichever neighbors happen to be around.

Another discovery I have made in this work, after years of writing books on the virtue of friendship as an aspect of legal ethics, is that our students learn from us, and as often teach us, how to go about making friends of our clients. People in our law office *hug* one another, rather more often, I think, than people in law offices downtown. Our student lawyers make house calls. I think, as I notice what I learn from students, and from my partners through students, of Rabbi Judah ha-Nasi, who said, "I learned much from my teachers, more from my colleagues, and most of all from my pupils."

As law offices go, all of these ways of being feminine make us a bit unusual, both in comparison with other offices and in comparison with what we five supervising attorneys experienced when we were in other law offices. All five of us entered law practice as "associates" (that is, hired hands) in law firms where the young lawyers help the older lawyers serve the clients of the older lawyers. In our clinical law firm, the older lawyers help the younger lawyers serve the clients of the younger lawyers. In a small way, as Notre Dame on Howard Street, our students turn things around, as Jesus and the other Prophets did. What started out as an educational agenda has come to be training (for us and for our students) in the virtue of *benevolence*—friendliness, to put a modern tag to the idea.

I am not as good at this as Eileen and Barbara and Christine are. This is not precisely a male-female distinction; it is, though, as C. G. Jung noticed, a masculine-feminine thing: The masculine shows up in my female students' ability to be tough-minded and, on occasion, remarkably aggressive. The feminine shows up, a little more than it used to, in my being able to celebrate the faith, the stubborn courage, and warm compassion—Faulkner called it "endurance"—of my clients.

In my law practice—more, I think, than in Eileen's, Barbara's, and Christine's—it is the students who really get to know the clients, who often form friendships with them, sometimes deep friendships. The students, with varying amounts of nudging, decide on goals and tactics, identify risks, predict results. And it is the students who advise, warn, and console our clients, and who go downtown to the courthouse for them. (The root meaning of "attorney" is someone who goes to town for you.)

There is nothing uniquely lawyerly in the practice of friendship in the practice of law. The grace that allows me to see it in the Clinic, and to change a little myself, is familiar among Notre Dame students. I see it every day among my law students, but I also see it in the eyes and nods and smiles of the undergraduates who help us out or who come to visit from Father Don McNeill's Center for Social Concerns.

There is no clear difference between these moments of surprise by joy and the mundane business of being lawyers. Our law students, who are permitted by the Indiana Supreme Court to practice law under supervision, interview the people who come for our help. A student lawyer is on duty for this purpose during every office hour of the week. Those who have done the interviewing meet in teams and decide which cases to take. (We have to turn down more than we can accept.) Then one of us signs on to be, as we have come to call ourselves, guru for each of the cases our students decide to take.

This is standard, Wednesday-afternoon stuff for a law office, but it is also an enlightening and puzzling business in a social order which resolutely puts our clients at the bottom of the economic and social pecking order. It turns out to be, in its ordinariness, training, for us and for our students, in what the thinkers at Notre Dame would call social justice: The people we serve (and I guess at this from what has happened to me during five years of this work) provide ample material for our students to form opinions on jurisprudence and social order (those being elements of what legal education says it aims for).

More than this, and still in its ordinariness, this is what Tom Broden was talking about, and what Nancy's life with her clients and with our children illustrates—our clients *form* people in ways that are something like the ordinary way our students were formed in friendship and affection in their families and neighborhoods. Our clients *influence* our students in that ordinary way.

It is ordinary, but it is also puzzling, a mysterious human process. I suppose it is a matter, as the Letter to the Hebrews put it, of stirring one another up to love and good works. If I am right about the way grace works on Howard Street (one of many ways), it is grace that was in our students' lives before they came to us, as well as grace that comes to them from their clients.

I don't pretend to know how it works. But there is plenty

of evidence that something is working: Our students typically—
typically—work more hours for their clients than our academic
standards require of them. Many of them volunteer to continue
working in the Clinic after they have exhausted the possibility
of academic credit for what they do. Our students, and Father
McNeill's, show me a human possibility that is under and over
and all around us. Our law students show me, when I think of
myself, more narrowly, as a lawyer, that justice is not so much
something you get in a law office or from the government as it
is something people give to one another.

If, following Tom Broden, we put a priority on service, we
are also an educational venture, and, being teachers as well as
lawyers, we worry a little—as our colleagues on campus regularly
remind us we should—about letting go of classroom focus
and clarity of concept. And so we try to get the classroom into
the Clinic.

We have orientation and training sessions for our students,
those being rather like the "continuing legal education"
sessions most lawyers attend under court or bar-association
sponsorship. The Keck Foundation, the Retirement Foundation
of Chicago, the Cord Foundation, and the DuPont Foundation
have given us grants for doing more than that, for having
clinical seminars in children's rights, elderlaw, mediation,
immigration law, and ethics.

In the clinical seminars the students read books and
handouts, hear lectures, prepare papers, and talk about ideas.
They talk, more than in regular law classes, about clients. Our
clients—real people. One version of the clinical seminars, for
example, is limited to students who are interns and therefore
"members of the firm," and therefore able to talk together about
confidential client matters. We devote most of our time in those
sessions to moral reflection on what we are doing. They have
proved—even more than we thought they would—to be law-
firm meetings on the morals of our practice.

The clinical seminars spill over into most of what we do—
so that it is routine to have an earnest debate going on in the
hallway or the interns' work area, over something we are doing
or should be doing in a case. The intake meetings, where

student lawyers decide which cases to take, which not to take, which to refer—and to where—have become extensions of the clinical seminars. We could do the necessary lawyers' business of one of those meetings in twenty minutes, but they routinely run more than an hour.

Of course there are still things I puzzle over.

Sometimes our students don't live up to the demands of what they have signed on to do. Law practice anywhere is difficult, complex, and demanding. In the old sexist days when I started as a lawyer, the elder males I worked for (and before that the late Dean Joseph O'Meara, LL.D., '68), used to say that the law is a jealous mistress. Law practice demands the best that a bright, industrious person has to give. Sometimes we and our students fail to give it.

Occasionally students neglect their clients (and I have to be severe about that). More often the problem is not neglect, but the fact that each of these students is with us for so short a time, and the law grinds slowly. At the end of every semester I have twenty or thirty cases that have to be handed on to new student interns, or that I have to take over and continue by myself. Once in a while, I have to go to court alone. Before my Clinic days, I usually went to court alone; now I feel incomplete when I have to do it.

These transitions are unsettling for clients; they tempt me to cool down the relationships the student lawyers have with clients, in favor of clearer dependence on me—lest our practice become a matter of exploiting clients in order to provide education for students. The turnover problem is uncomfortable to work through, but I tell myself that it is inherent in a ministry that goes out in two directions. Maybe it is one of those things, to use philosophical language I learned from my old friend and colleague, Professor Frederick J. Crosson, that is more a mystery than a problem.

Another thing to puzzle over is the number of potential clients we turn away (about five out of every eight who apply). Like any lawyers anywhere (or, for that matter, pastors or physicians anywhere), we have to be concerned that we not give ourselves so much to do that we don't do any of it well.

That requires some discipline; it provokes a painful concern, especially in the sadness of telling a person you do not have time to help her. (An interesting part of our program of "training" is that we give this unpleasant task to the students or to Linda.) This is a crisis made more compelling as the federal government takes another swipe at legal services for the poor, and more clients, turned away from the local federally funded legal-services office, come to us.

Another difficulty is how to go about serving the lawyers who teach in the classroom at Notre Dame and, beyond them, the university community and the corporate institution. Notre Dame operates the Clinic at a financial loss: Our student-faculty ratio is one of the lowest on campus. The individual attention we give to our students costs money, as do our physical facilities and our non-lawyer staff. In this respect, the Clinic is analogous to the South Bend Center for the Homeless, which the University began supporting in the 1980s, and to the Center for Social Concerns.

We have recently become aware of our opportunity to serve private lawyers in the community who could probably do more for people who cannot pay fees: We are trying to figure out how to involve ourselves and our classroom colleagues in a broad campaign, mounted by the Indiana Supreme Court and the Indiana State Bar Association, to encourage "pro bono" service by practicing lawyers and law teachers. Young lawyers in the community who have been student lawyers in the Clinic—typically young women—will, more often than not, take these cases.

And, finally, there is the possibility that the kinds of law we do could be made simpler, less expensive, more available to people at the bottom of the legal pile, and fairer. Indiana's system of small-claims courts, for example, was set up to provide simplified justice to people who do not have lawyers, but it has become an engine of oppression—an agency of government that evicts welfare mothers and garnishes the wages of the working poor. The law's system for granting divorce (or, as Indiana has come to call it, "dissolution") cries out, especially as we meet it in the lives of the children of our clients, for less rancor and complexity. The federal Social Security system operates its application procedure as a way to refuse help, rather than to give it. If there is a bureaucracy more disgusting than the Immigration and Naturalization Service, I haven't heard about it.

I am tempted to hubris. I get angry at the way "the system" steps on our clients; I nod in agreement with the latent Marxism I read in Latin American liberation theology. And then I am tempted to feel superior to the bureaucrats and judges who administer these systems, and to the lawyers downtown who have to live on what their clients can pay them. I suspect the wonderful women I work with would nod at my confession of hubris. Maybe they would add, "It's a *guy* thing."

The Lord has not, so far, dealt with my hubris by giving me grief, boils, and poverty (as He did with Job), or denied me the Promised Land (as He did with Moses). He has let me stay with Nancy, and that helps a lot: I am tempted to tirades about the way the legal systems we work with dump on our clients; Nancy, who also works with people who don't have enough money or time or savvy in the ways of the world, always finds a way to *do* something. She does not like the phrase "poor people."

I guess this is a question of focus. We lawyers cannot ignore the "system," if only because it is lawyers who tend the system and often have the power to change it. But the feminine, the human skills our students bring to us, the commonsense way Nancy turns to what can be done—all of these influences in my life as a clinical law teacher—help me understand what Father John Dunne may have meant when he wrote (in *The House of Wisdom*) that "I can find God in my heart only by turning somehow to life." I have written in my books, and I am learning, slowly, in my work with students in the Clinic, that lawyers' law is more about people than it is about problems.

It is useful, and a shade humbling, to be made to remember (by Nancy and by Steve and the women we get to work with) that the most important thing about our clients is not that the system doesn't give them very much, but that, as one of the earliest American judicial opinions said it, they are the noblest works of God.

The Greatest Notre Dame Tradition

KATHLEEN M. SULLIVAN

Imagine you received an invitation to attend a banquet with the most renowned figures in Notre Dame's history. You discover that the evening's conversation will focus on one question: What is the greatest Notre Dame tradition? What tradition has given generations of alumni profound meaning, hope, and celebration? What tradition has fused the ordinary with the sacred, transforming a dull life into one of constant renewal despite the heartache of ongoing losses?

At the dinner you listen carefully to the many voices of the group. In moments of levity you hear references to "The Fight Song," to the regalia of football Saturday and to the "luck of the Irish." Near the middle of the evening, each table submits its conviction about the greatest Notre Dame tradition. The great hall becomes silent. Then a voice announces what many know in their hearts. "The greatest Notre Dame tradition is a commitment to learning and caring."

Certainly a great university creates a culture where professor and student engage in a cosmos of learning. But a great Catholic university inspires teacher and learner to journey with the compassionate, the caring one—Christ, who asks us to journey for one another. To help our alumni sustain their commitment to learning and caring, the University asked the Alumni Association to develop a program that would reconnect alumni with the University's greatest resource—its faculty. Alumni would also be called upon to share their professional and personal insights with each other and with their communities.

Kathleen Sullivan is Director of Alumni Continuing Education for the Alumni Association.

Since 1982 the Alumni Association has developed numerous programs through its department of Alumni Continuing Education. As we struggled in those early days to define our mission, a physician from Wyoming and a member of the National Alumni Board, Dr. Joe Murphy '45 crystallized our purpose. I recall his rhetorical questions and his spirit-filled reply:

> Why should we offer alumni programs already available in their work places and in their communities? Why should Notre Dame physicians, for example, come to campus for medical updates when their profession provides this service? But what if we offered the alumni doctor a seminar on medical ethics where theology, philosophy, law, business, medicine intertwined to help our physicians struggle with real life issues in an environment that espouses Christ's love as the guiding principle.

That paradigm became the model for our alumni continuing education programs. By combining the unique strengths of the University with the needs of our alumni, we have focused our outreach in the areas of family, church and spirituality, ethics, social concerns, and the liberal arts.

In describing the University, many of us speak of the "Notre Dame Family." What about the Notre Dame family in crisis? What about our alumni or their spouses struggling with the devastating loss of a loved one? Or our graduates grieving a divorce? Certainly our ministry of learning and caring must be present when we are most vulnerable. Initiated nine years ago by Pat Reynolds, who suffered the loss of her husband Bill, class of 1954, the grief workshop has dramatically touched the lives of alumni, their spouses, and children. Reflecting on the connection between the University's Catholic mission and the outreach of this program, Pat eloquently writes:

> A good university can teach the arts and sciences, but only life teaches us living and dying. Beginning at the moment of birth, the journey to another life begins and yet when faced with loss, we are appalled and deeply hurt and often afraid. We say we mourn. This can be done alone or in the company

of fellow journeyers. Notre Dame in developing the grief workshop chose to offer the second route. People come together, share, learn a bit about the process and go home knowing they aren't crazy, aren't alone, and maybe with a deeper faith now that they've passed through Life and Loss 101.

For Paul Pendergast, the father of two Notre Dame graduates, the weekend "acted as a crucible moment" for him. Throughout the workshop Paul reflected on the blessings of his twenty-five–year marriage to Judy. By sharing a story of "such wholesome goodness that Judy lived, I felt energized to inspire others to build a similar new and more wholesome life in spite of a tragic loss." Paul discovered that his life did not end when Judy died, "it merely acted as a new vector in my new life's journey." Paul volunteers his time in leading a support group in his hometown and in facilitating group discussions at the grief workshop.

The participants arrive at the conference filled with unrelenting pain but discover strength and hope as each ministers to the other. Grieving the loss of her husband Bud, Theresa Farber MA '66 felt in a "forsaken temperament" wondering why she came to the program—it would not bring Bud back. Grief consumed her at home for everything she looked at "reminded me of our life when it was alive, vibrant and shared. Now, here I was, traveling alone, thinking alone, living alone and liking none of this." For Theresa the weekend was a transforming experience—"a miraculous revelation that helped me to come back to reality, pick up the pieces of my life and find some meaning to it all again." Cecilia O'Donnell "wasn't quite sure she could survive after Dean's death." Listening to the grief stories, sharing and affirming each other, Cecilia found "strength and awareness, a kind of resurrection so invaluable in the life and death process."

The grief workshop originally began with a focus on loss from death. Intent on making a statement about Notre Dame's love and commitment to all her graduates, we expanded the program to address the loss from divorce. One participant wrote, "It was wonderful to come home again. I feel like I have the strength of coming into my own again." Of great concern to someone coping with divorce is finding a safe place, free of judgment. As our weekend concluded last year, I remember the relief, hope, and appreciation of a woman working through her divorce: "What a wonderful way to grieve and learn at the same time with people who can relate and understand your feelings of loss." By the Alumni Association providing a vehicle for graduates and friends of the University to confront their loss in the company of soulmates who feel each other's pain but search for hope through the compassion of Christ's love, Alumni Continuing Education can give witness to the University's faithfulness to the Notre Dame family.

If the University's sacred tradition of learning and caring is to reach beyond the boundaries of Notre Dame Avenue, our alumni must live this commitment in the workplace. They must find the courage and wisdom to choose justice over cowardice, relationships over things, and service over power. By offering ethics conferences in medicine, law, and business, we ask the participants to examine the integrity of their public and private lives—to measure themselves against the observation of Gandhi: "A person cannot do right in one area of life whilst attempting to do wrong in another. Life is one indivisible whole."

Reflecting on the role of the ethics conferences, Larry Vuillemin '70, observes: "Unless we continue to grow as professionals, as Christians, as human beings, we may stifle the spirit of God and limit the vocation into which we have been called. The University facilitates an interior growth." Recalling a homily from his twentieth reunion, Larry shares a vision of a Catholic university: "All the buildings, all the fellowship, all the degrees we shared at Notre Dame are rendered meaningless if we do not seek to transform and serve the world as an extension of Christ's mission of salvation." He observes that "too many of my colleagues in law are isolated, disconnected from all but a worldly pace which equates busyness with productivity, success with bottom line. Relationships suffer. The ethics conferences allow for connections; I believe, finally, that it is through relationships that we experience the divine." Professor Thomas Shaffer of the Law School shares Larry's perspective.

"If participants were seeking discussions of the rules under which lawyers practice, they could have found what they wanted closer to home. . . . What they wanted was to *be* the church *as* lawyers . . . wanting to talk to other lawyers about following Jesus in the law."

Eleven years ago, Phil Clarke MD '44, renowned Denver physician, governor of the American College of Physicians, and former board director of the Alumni Association, came to the University with a proposal. He offered to help fund a conference that would bring medicine and ethics together, that would invite national leaders in the field who would join faculty from Notre Dame's philosophy, theology, business, and law school. Thanks to his vision, this program has profoundly impacted the lives of countless physicians and their patients. Dr. Richard Flores, a Notre Dame parent, finds inspiration and application from this program. "I had always felt there was a great need for an arena where physicians and scholars could meet and learn from one another. . . . Almost weekly in my practice I rely on the background information gained from the Medical Ethics Conference to handle difficult ethical issues." Nalini Rajamannan MD '81, '85, appreciates the time "we can listen and think and share points of views on issues like where life begins, where and how it ends, things like assisted suicide, abortion, euthanasia." She admits that physicians find it difficult to "set aside the time to really exercise their minds on such issues. That's why the conference is so important, not only to us but to all the people we treat, to the families of our patients, to colleagues with whom we share the benefits of attending the conference."

Father Richard McCormick, the John A. O'Brien Professor of Christian Ethics at Notre Dame, views the conversation between physicians and scholars as a model for Church teaching. He notes that the "physicians themselves run the conference, do much of the speaking, and are spoken at rarely. The conference invites, indeed insists on physician participation in a very active way." Father McCormick asserts that "if the members of the Church had the feeling that they were participating in the educational process, the whole process would be much more successful. This is one of the important pastoral lessons to be learned from the Medical Ethics Conference."

In October we sponsored the University's first CEO Business Values Retreat. Twenty executives and their spouses explored two fundamental questions: How do business leaders lead their lives morally and ethically in such a way that the personal and professional intersect and are not in conflict? What are the classical and universal truths which should dictate human conduct in the business organization? A major focus of the seminar was the attendees' discussion of their greatest personal and professional challenges. Many spoke about "balancing family life given time demands and pressures from business responsibilities." Others expressed concern about "transforming the company to ensure its future competitiveness while restoring the morale and confidence of the people." For John McMeel, President of Universal Press syndicate, the retreat provided a "real jolt on my attitude on living. It made me look at my strengths and weaknesses. I was struck by Stephen Covey's comment that self-interest is not the problem but rather self-centeredness is the hazard." For John the conference heightened his desire "to reach out and become more aware of family, friends, and acquaintances. . . . For by doing so, you focus on people around you—for they are the ones who create humility, courage, integrity and honesty that one would have difficulty in creating and sustaining without them."

For participants to deeply benefit from our conferences, we must foster a climate of trust, respect, and appreciation for the many voices seeking the truth. Commenting on this spirit of Notre Dame hospitality, Father James Bresnahan observes, "I cannot get over the sense of belonging conferred by the University. One feels 'at home.' That frees both mind and heart for the business at hand, for creative exchange, for a new perspective on problems one has pondered." Our Elderhostel program provides a unique opportunity for the University to open her home to anyone fifty-five and older and to study with our most dynamic faculty for a week in the summer. This experience fills the campus with renewal. Professor Paul Rathburn of the English department and a favorite of the Elderhostelers believes that "the richest experiences belong to us, the lucky teachers. The 'gift' that we have to impart to the 'students' is the realization that they are rich enough as human beings, bright and sensitive enough, to make personal contact with the greatest playwrights who have ever written. It is a privilege to give to those who have given to others all their lives."

Richard and Kathleen Quilter believe that the Elderhostel program makes dreams come true. "Many in our generation grew up with a strong attachment to and love for Notre Dame but never had the opportunity to experience it. Elderhostel provides that opportunity in a very meaningful way—to live on campus, to attend interesting classes, meet and discuss with great professors, meet staff and students, and to spend time with people from all over the country." Moved by the commitment and excellence of the Notre Dame faculty and nourished by "the joy of spirituality that is felt in the campus air," the Quilters joined the Sorin Society, "to share in the future growth and influence of Notre Dame as the world's greatest Catholic University."

Leo and Nancy Cantwell, who journey yearly to our Elderhostel program, likewise experience a sacred presence on the campus. Leo recalls a moment at the Grotto that transcended time. Earlier in the day he savored a conversation with Bill Sherman '30, who described his personal experience with Coach Rockne. Leo felt that he "had truly been touched by years of empirical folklore, and it was exciting!" That evening, as was Leo's custom, he walked to the Grotto.

Just as I arrived in the warm glow of Her love and peace, the church steeple leaned over the trees and began to chime . . . "Notre Dame, our Mother, tender, strong, and true. . . ." As the summer campus quiet swelled in my throat, and I stood there looking up into Her face, I realized that as I reached back through the connecting seconds to touch history through the "eyes on" experience of another, I was now reaching forward through each second as it touched each second about to come to God's eternity. I walked back up the steps into the darkness that night with a deeper feeling that God wasn't so far away after all.

Gifted with so many resources, the University must be a lighthouse to the larger community—to her alumni at home and abroad, and as importantly, to the families and communities of our graduates. Notre Dame must empower its alumni to live that tradition of learning and caring in their homes, neighborhoods, and work place. Through the Hesburgh Lecture Series, alumni clubs share the insights and challenges of Notre Dame faculty with their community. The Black Hills club, for example, typically draws 150 people to their lectures as educational and civic organizations co-sponsor this annual event. For Lawrence Cunningham, chairman of the theology department, this outreach program is an "extension of my vocation as teacher/scholar. I also see it as a ministry and part of the service of theology." He further explains, "My primary duty, of course, is to the campus classroom but if we are serious about the often cited ND family, we must see those who have a close connection to the University (like our alumni) as also the focus of our work."

Jack Conroy '59 of the Naples alumni club believes that a Hesburgh Lecture can have a transforming experience on the community. He recalls a lecture given by Father Himes that addressed the importance of "inclusiveness of the Church's mission and the need for sensitivity to cultural differences." Jack reports that these ideas found "their way into our pastor's soul" and the bounty of the Hesburgh Lecture extended well beyond that evening lecture. Jack believes that "this is the way the Spirit works in history; almost unconsciously, quietly in a sharing of thought that modifies behavior. One is never sensitive to the exact 'when', but the dialectic of history goes on, moved by vehicles such as the Hesburgh Lecture Series."

Perhaps the Alumni Continuing Education's most significant effort to touch the lives of alumni, their schools, churches, and social agencies is through the television and video series on the family. Responding to a hunger for ideas on such issues as improving family communication, raising self-reliant children in a self-indulgent world, parenting our parents, the Alumni Association has produced eleven programs and continues to create two new shows a year. Notre Dame alumni clubs invite their parishes, schools, and hospital to gather the day of the show or to purchase the video and schedule the program at everyone's convenience. For both the live show and the video event, the follow-up discussions allow participants to process their questions and garner support and insight from each other. Summarizing the importance of such an outreach, Frances Forde Plude, former communication consultant to the Bishops, acknowledges, "I don't believe any university in America has the systematic educational outreach to its alumni that Notre Dame has. The fact that a significant part of this community-building and service is done through satellite technology provides a rich model of dialogic enrichment for churches and other institutions in America."

The University of Notre Dame will continue to celebrate its greatest tradition—a commitment to learning and caring— by leading through example, by practicing such things as integrity, fairness, and service, and by fortifying our minds and hearts to seek first the Kingdom of God.

Campus Ministry at a Catholic University

RICHARD V. WARNER, C.S.C.

During his brief pontificate, Pope John XXIII called the bishops of the world to Rome for what would become the Second Vatican Council. During the years of its discussion and deliberation, there were significant and successful efforts to reflect prayerfully on the Church, on its role and presence in modern society, on the relationship of faith to many dimensions of contemporary life and on a rich life of prayer and worship to celebrate Word, sign, and sacrament. In the immediate aftermath of the Council, a renewed understanding of Church as People of God helped believers—clerics, religious, and lay people—to come to understand new and different dimensions of institutional service as collaborative ministry. A significant and practical application of the Council's approach to ecclesiology took place at Notre Dame.

On January 26, 1967, a critically important event took place which affected the relationship between the University of Notre Dame and the Indiana Province of the Congregation of Holy Cross. After months of sometimes difficult discussion and deliberation, a provincial chapter met in extraordinary session to decide whether or not the Congregation would legally alienate the University of Notre Dame according to canon and civil law, in the Congregation's 125th anniversary of commitment to the institution. It was clear that any future relationship would have to build carefully on a long-standing and mutually

Father Richard Warner, C.S.C., is Director of Campus Ministry and Counselor to the President.

life-giving relationship that the two institutions always enjoyed. Holy Cross religious were keenly aware of the importance of this distinctive ministry, and people associated with the University, in turn, understood and appreciated the role the members of the Congregation exercised in administration, teaching, ministry, and as rectors in the residence halls. Often the rectors of the halls also served as religion teachers.

The discussions at Notre Dame drew national and international attention as a Catholic institution examined ways in which it could be faithful to its Catholic heritage while adhering to the high canons of academic standards in the United States. To an important extent, the role the Congregation would be willing to assume and carry out in order to preserve and further develop Notre Dame's Catholic character was crucial. The acceptance of an appropriate and determinative role by the founding religious Congregation would sustain the best future hopes of both Holy Cross and Notre Dame, with clergy and lay persons working together in a closely collaborative mode. The discussion prospered, the legal alienation took place, and in the spirit of the Second Vatican Council, religious and lay people agreed to face together the challenges presented to Catholic education in a time of significant change.

The legal document approved by the Holy See created a self-perpetuating Board of Fellows, composed of six members of the Congregation of Holy Cross and six lay persons, who assumed the legal responsibility to avoid diminishment or abrogation of the Catholic nature of Notre Dame by providing for "the continuity of the commitment to the Faith and to the role of (Holy Cross)." The Fellows were also given authority to approve changes "in the rules, ordinances and by-laws," elect trustees, and hold the assets of the University of Notre Dame in trust. The Congregation and the University agreed "to make full use of the unique skills and dedication of the members of the Congregation of Holy Cross" in traditional areas which include "the disciplines of theology and philosophy," the pastoral apostolate within the University as "another central function of the priest in Notre Dame life," and different roles within the administration.

Members of the Congregation of Holy Cross and others established a strong and unique pastoral role in the institution from the University's earliest days. The founder of Notre Dame, Father Edward F. Sorin, C.S.C., willingly assumed pastoral responsibility for people in the area. In so doing, he continued a tradition of missionary service within his religious community which dated back at least to the mid-nineteenth century. His successors followed the same pattern, most notably Cardinal John F. O'Hara, C.S.C. He served as University Chaplain in what he called "the city of the Eucharist" before becoming the fourteenth president of Notre Dame, Auxiliary Bishop in the Military Ordinariate, during World War II, Bishop of Buffalo, and finally Cardinal-Archbishop of Philadelphia.

Father William Craddick, a Notre Dame–educated architect, became famous for a daily mimeographed *Religious Bulletin*, which was slipped under the door of each residence hall room, and which emphasized both practical ways for Notre Dame men to live out their faith with fidelity as well as elements of religious education.

In more recent years, Campus Ministry at Notre Dame has evolved and changed, as each director and team developed effective pastoral methods according to the circumstances they encountered and the students they served. More than 85 percent of the undergraduate students live on campus in residence halls which can be like small faith communities, an important continuation of Cardinal O'Hara's legacy. Because of this special residential character, it is possible to promote the direct linkage between faith and its liturgical expression on the one hand, and service to others as an action which flows from faith, on the other.

In the late 1970s, Father William Toohey, C.S.C., was appointed director of Campus Ministry. This ex-Marine, who was a professor of homiletics, was the right person for the position during the years of the Vietnam War. He urged students to become personally involved in social justice activities which the Second Vatican Council had called a "constitutive element" of the Church, including efforts directed toward seeking peace. He wrote several books which were popular upon publication, each of which urged young people to do everything they could to become and remain fully alive in Jesus Christ. His weekly Sunday liturgy, which was celebrated at Sacred Heart Church at 12:15 p.m., was always crowded with people eager to worship together and to come together to listen to Father Toohey's stirring and well-crafted homilies. His untimely death from encephalitis in the fall of 1980 shocked the Notre Dame community, and as many as six thousand people were present for his funeral and burial.

Within the same year, when the building on campus which served as the studios for the University-owned WNDU-TV, an NBC affiliate, became available after newer facilities were constructed in a different location, Father Theodore Hesburgh decided that the building would be used as a center for volunteer service and experiential learning. There was a long tradition of volunteer service at Notre Dame. Today over 75 percent of the undergraduates participate in some type of service during their years on campus and from 10 percent to 13 percent of the graduating seniors each year dedicate at least the first year of their post-baccalaureate years to volunteer service and teaching. Providing space and a staff for the Center for Social Concerns helped the University institutionalize and develop a commendable tradition. Its development made it necessary for Campus Ministry to refocus some of its efforts, while maintaining collaboration with the Center for Social Concern staff.

I was asked to assume responsibilty for Campus Ministry at Notre Dame in 1989, following three relatively short-term directors who left the position to assume other responsibilities within the Congregation or at Notre Dame. I knew from my own experience both the challenges involved in campus ministry and the importance of dealing with this aspect of a "Notre Dame experience" as effectively and well as possible. I looked forward to the possibilty of being in daily contact with bright, talented, and religiously committed young people, and in developing programs that would help them to deepen and enliven their faith. I knew that Notre Dame undergraduates were willing to appropriate for themselves as they became adult believers the religious values they received from their families. I also wanted to carry out my responsibiltity within the context of the relationship of Notre Dame to the Universal Church. Because of my previous services as a Holy Cross priest serving in Chile, I had lived through very exciting times and challenges for a Church that attempted to respond vigorously and with creativity to the "signs of the time."

A proven pastoral approach on two continents, Latin America and Africa, was an important entry point and method for me as I attempted to bring today's young people into contact with one another as members of God's people and as people called to be especially responsive to the poor and dispossessed. The three recent meetings of the Latin American Episcopal Conferences (Medellín, Puebla, and Santo Domingo) urged Catholics and people of good will in Latin America to pursue an option for the poor and an option for the education of young people as priorities. A friend of mine, Father Thomas Smith, C.S.C., who has worked most of his life in East Africa, suggests that if Catholic education is to serve "the world," it must be incarnational. It must join the Word to the world. "The Church insists that educating the human being to truth is an integral part of its evangelizing mission and that the promotion of justice is its constitutive dimension."

During crucial moments, Christian believers must heed the Gospel's demand that a disciple speak forthrightly and without hesitation, keeping clearly in mind the person of Jesus Christ who has gone before us, our participation in His mission, and the ultimate meaning of our words and actions in the context of his life, death, and resurrection. Most of us have lived our lives as believers in the midst of incredibly significant changes. The rise of secularism in our society and culture brought with it many changes in how we see the Church *and* the world, on how we see the Church *in* the world, and on how we see ourselves in the midst of both realities. The drive toward equality, the recognition of civil and human rights as rights of the individual and obligations of governments, the spread of the democratic ideals and of freedom in every sphere of our lives— political, economic, social, and religious, to name a few—are some positive results of secularization. But so, too, are the development of a popular culture that is largely unexamined, the relegation of "religion" to its most basic civil manifestations or predictable characterizations by a secular and indifferent media, an uncatechized Catholic people and environment, and an originally well-conceived separation of Church and state which has led to a divorce under the most hostile and negative terms imaginable.

A few years after the conclusion of the Council, Pope Paul VI in *Evangelii nuntiandi* urged us to avoid assuming that we could separate personal conversion from social transformation. "Evangelization means bringing the Gospel into all strata of society, and through its influence transforming humanity from within and making it new."

Hence, as I assumed responsibility for Campus Ministry at Notre Dame, I appreciated the fact that there was a clear and essential relationship between campus ministry and social action, whether based explicitly in the social doctrine of the Church or as an uninformed attempt to make the Gospel derived from faith come alive in a student's life.

My first two years in my new position were dedicated to recovering a bit of the zealous dedication of the members of my team to this important ministry as well as to chairing a special task force which would measure the "gap" between what we publicly declared as our goals and accomplishments in the areas of evangelization, ministry, and social values and our actual achievements. This commission was given to me by Father Malloy before my first day "on the job." This task force, comprised of members of the faculty, rectors, campus ministers, staff, and students, interviewed 10 percent of the students, staff, Holy Cross religious, and faculty in a grouping which reflected perfectly the composition of these groups based on age, race, ethnic origin, and college. Father Malloy suspected that many of our *assumptions* about the Catholicity of our institution would not be reflected on an experiential basis. We assume that we know what it means for a university to be Catholic. We assume the Catholic character is a foundation or a solid base rather than a dynamic force in the lives of our colleges and universities.

The survey clearly underscored the lack of integration between our pastoral and social activities and other sources of influence on our students. Those responsible for directing social justice–related efforts admitted that, from a theological perspective, faith and works inspired by social justice must be integrated.

It is clearly to the advantage of people working in both the pastoral and the social areas that neither stands alone. At the same time, however, it often seems easier to issue a clear call to community service and social action to students, an invitation and challenge to bring social concerns into teaching and research for faculty, and a continuing call to carry values into adult life for alumni when only the social dimension is stressed.

Annual surveys of incoming freshmen regarding faith and religious identity and practice indicate that young people at Notre Dame overwhelmingly declare themselves to be Catholic. In the United States, almost 55 percent of adult Catholics attend mass each week. More than 70 percent of first-year students entering Notre Dame attend mass frequently, that is, once every one or two weeks. This percentage increases as students worship and pray each Sunday night in one of our residence hall chapels or in the Basilica of the Sacred Heart.

Many students have had significant experiences of service, sometimes in the context of sacramental preparation, especially Confirmation, others as a requisite for graduation from the Catholic high school they attended. But sometimes little of this service is with reference to the social teaching of the Catholic Church. In a listing of influential persons, institutions, and sources, incoming freshmen invariably list social doctrine of the Church at 15 percent, compared to 85 percent for parents and 82 percent for peers.

Yet is it not our challenge to work for the development of sophisticated young men and women willing to be trained for roles of leadership in the Church of the twenty-first century with a fuller appreciation of the needs so many face in our world today? In many ways, our institutions must be willing to provide an institutional framework of religious formation that is attractive and sophisticated on the one hand, and that integrates the pastoral and social dimension of our faith in methodologies similar to the models developed by Cardinal Cardign, who developed successful programs of Catholic action aimed at young students and workers in the years preceding the Second Vatican Council

The Catholic character of any institution is the more difficult aspect of the binomial "Catholic university" to achieve. The vision and description of a Catholic university must be elaborated within the context of an aggressively secular society and a culture where there are many other factors over which we, as individuals and institutions, have little if any control. The ability of a core group of believers within an institution to develop and hold out a compelling and attractive vision is what, in the last analysis, carries the day. The continual promotion and development of a community of scholars and believers lies at the heart of what a Catholic university must continually aspire to become. The task is a daunting one under favorable circumstances. It is an increasingly important one in our situation, living and working as we do in an expansively secular society and culture.

Each of us spends many hours doing things that are important and personally satisfying, such as teaching, carrying out normal responsibilities of administration, serving as faithful stewards, and working closely with other members of our community, especially students, faculty, alumni, and friends. Yet at this time in history, nothing we do and none of the areas into which we pour so much time and energy are as important as the development of a significant vision of what our future is as a Catholic institution. Then we can give flesh to the vision, each in our own area, and working together with our colleagues.

We cannot and should not do anything to diminish or compromise our reality and our potential as an academic institution. But if we enroll brighter students, attract more eminent scholars, build better facilities, develop and secure more abundant resources, we will only have achieved one half of our self-definition as a Catholic university. Catholic education is education within the framework of faith and hope, and is, because of its relationship to the Gospel, "a series of think tanks, workshops and learning laboratories where faculty and students are encouraged to engage in creative scholarship with imagination and initiative" in the search for truth and in pursuing solutions to the problems we face as world citizens.

So we continue our attempt to develop a vision of what a Catholic university is at a time when securing the presence in our institutions of a predominant number of deeply committed Catholic faculty members is increasingly difficult. We are dealing with the issue of Catholicity at a time when many of the students who come to us are interested in the history, traditions and practices, doctrine and the rich liturgical and sacramental life of Catholicism, but most are ignorant of this, their heritage.

The reason why Catholic colleges and universities must become places of religious formation *par excellence* is because the Church needs us now more than ever. Now it is time for us to take on the challenge which lies at the heart, at the very essence, of our religious heritage and tradition as colleges and universities in the Roman Catholic tradition.

We clearly have the potential to define, evaluate, and carry out effectively this element of Catholicity as we have the area of academic excellence. It is a question of vision, which is not utterly objective. This makes it a bit more difficult but not impossible. I believe we have the strength and the conviction which we need to make our common vision a reality.

Who will give content and context to the vision of a Catholic university if not those who are committed to a comprehensive view which includes an integration of academic and pastoral aspects? Can we give real voice to a vision of Catholicity that is appropriate, challenging, and uncompromising, and that is worthy of what we have become and what we know we have within ourselves to attain?

Yet the signs of the times are clear.

Our society and culture move toward a secularization which is, in fact, taking place, with or without our intending it and in ways which I believe can be irreversible. So we work in an environment which is always deeply secular and at times hostile. We live with the possibility that our academic peers never have and perhaps never will overcome a latent or even a permanent bias against the mere possibility of a Catholic university.

During the past seven years of my service as director of Campus Ministry at Notre Dame, I am deeply grateful to Father Malloy and his administration for understanding and for financial support based on a realization of the important role this ministry plays in a Catholic university. During a time of financial straits in higher education in general and at Catholic institutions, the temptation is to cut back severely on resources dedicated to Campus Ministry. The support I enjoy has enabled me to add four persons to our staff at Notre Dame and to triple our programs in seven years. New programs include a Freshman Retreat to urge first-year students to include spiritual development among the tasks to be achieved during their college years, a program of small faith communities, a systematic religious education program, the preparation of catechists for service to parishes in the South Bend area, attention to the development of a peer ministry model to assist and prepare students to assume responsibilities within and for the Church in the future, sustained work among Hispanic Catholics, a pastoral program which supports Catholic students who are gay or lesbian, a marriage and family enrichment program for recently married graduates, and retreats where students can learn to examine their racial attitudes and responses.

I know that there are very few Catholic colleges or universities with the same resources Notre Dame dedicates to Campus Ministry and to the development of the spiritual life and religious attitudes of undergraduate students. I hope that we will always be willing to share our pastoral resources with others, and to learn new pastoral methods and insights from them.

The Pilgrimage

STEVEN C. WARNER

It is the time of twilight, and you are welcome to join me on my pilgrimage. We are walking next to the priests' residence on campus, Corby Hall. The night is crisp, but the softness of spring is now in the air: the brown earth is beginning to sing, and you can smell her lyrics, especially at the turning points of the day. And as we turn the corner, moving toward the Grotto of Our Lady of Lourdes, a gathering of souls crosses our path, also making an evening journey.

We have come upon an uncommon sight: student pilgrims, hundreds of them, huddled in the darkness, wending their way out of the Grotto. They are being led by a burly bunch of teenagers, carrying an enormous wooden cross. A young woman—one of the regular instrumentalists of Notre Dame's Spanish choir, the *Coro Primavera de Nuestra Señora*—is playing the "Stabat Mater" on the trumpet. The plaintive tones echo across the southern part of the campus, calling others out of their rooms, out into the cold, into the promise of spring, into the season of resurrection. The hundreds of student pilgrims behind her are marching, softly, carrying little votive candles, the color of scarlet. The ruddy color washes their faces, blood-like. It is the week of such a color: Passiontide, when many years before another man's Blood was spent in the name of truth.

This is not a scene from some mythical Christian village, or from some European liturgical drama enacted in medieval streets. This is the campus of the University of Notre Dame, and

Steve Warner is Director of Liturgical Resources for the Office of Campus Ministry.

251

it is a Tuesday night in the first week of April. The year: 1996, on the doorstep of the third millennium of Christianity.

As a campus minister at Notre Dame these past fifteen years, I have been both pilgrim-participant and bystander in this liturgical procession. And not just on a particular Tuesday of Holy Week, but in the broader sense of pilgrimage as well: a pilgrimage of discovery, one involving the whole faith assembly. All communities have their songs and stories, their players, cultural nuances, heroes, and characters. Notre Dame is a Christian community and so, on its most heartfelt level, our stories, songs, people of legend —all of these in some way should point to and be seen through the image of Jesus.

When the Second Vatican Council opened the doors to language and culture in the mid-1960s, the pilgrim story at Notre Dame began anew. We had to make the story our own, to find ways to celebrate our identity as Catholic Christians that were uniquely ours. That is what this small chapter is about—the pilgrimage of our song and story.

My part began in 1979. I had arrived on campus to complete a master's degree in Liturgical Studies, and, having worked in music and liturgy at another Catholic college previous to this, it was natural to seek out involvement in campus ministry here at Notre Dame.

The liturgical life of the campus at that time was an interesting collection of bounty and void. The bounty was to be found at Sacred Heart Church, and within the theology department. At Sacred Heart the Notre Dame Chapel Choir (later renamed the Liturgical Choir) under the direction of Ms. Sue Seid-Martin, was crafting new ritual music, with the current director of the Glee Club and its resident composer, David Clark Isele. Isele's compositions, new psalm settings for Sunday liturgies, and mass parts found an eager publisher with the Gregorian Institute of America (GIA) of Chicago. The 10:30 a.m. Sunday liturgy was a spectacle, a synthesis of fine music and grace-filled ritual expression. By the early 1980s, and at the height of their creative efforts, a medieval musical was presented in the Basilica, a work by Richard Proulx entitled

The Pilgrim. This event brought together a rare collaboration of departmental energy that has yet to be duplicated: theology, music, theatre, and campus ministry all had a part.

In the theology department, some of the best minds since Michael Mathis, C.S.C., were laboring to train a new generation in the task of liturgical renewal. Mark Searle, Robert Taft, S.J., Bill Storey, and many others were setting both a pastoral and academic standard for the discipline, standards that would be emulated by other liturgical centers in the years that followed. The dialogue between Sacred Heart Church and the theology department was strong, lively, creative—and occasionally tumultuous. During the summer session, Morning and Evening Prayer were celebrated daily, with rich, new musical settings. Some of these were edited by John Melloh, S.M., the newly appointed director of the Center for Pastoral Liturgy. And hundreds came over the summer months. The program was in full flower, the market was in great need of trained liturgists, and Notre Dame was ready and willing to provide the assistance.

In other arenas, however, the University was more adrift, and somewhat expressionless, especially when compared to the standards being set at Sacred Heart. These areas of void were mostly felt in the liturgical life of the residence halls. While the Sunday morning 10:30 liturgy was an experience for the heart and senses, it followed a more formal style of liturgical celebration. And for all of its musical labors, it provided no real role model for the kind of liturgy embraced in the dorms. Its counterpart, the 12:15 "folk" liturgy, was immensely popular with students, but still in search of an authentic style of sacred music. In the residence halls, where the majority of the students worshipped, there was still no solid set of liturgical songs upon which to build. Some dorms were making positive steps (such as Breen-Phillips and Morrissey), but these were not campus-wide experiences.

In fact, while there were some twenty-odd residence halls on campus, most of them were just beginning to form any sense of liturgical tradition. This, for several reasons. One was because of the constant, itinerant nature of these communities. Every year more than a quarter of the community disbanded because of graduation or an off-campus move. A rector would leave, a talented musician would graduate, and the community was back near square one. It was (and still is) hard to keep the momentum going with all this turnover. Then too, while daily and Sunday mass were regularly celebrated, the notion of community "ownership" of prayer had not quite settled in. Student collaboration in liturgical planning was informal at best, and later expressions of leadership, like the creation of community service commissioners and liturgical commissioners, were still on the horizon, yet to be enfleshed.

However, the 12:15 Sunday liturgy of 1980 was immensely popular with students, and for a few very good reasons. The undergraduates flocked to Sacred Heart to be inspired by the bold preaching of Campus Ministry's director, Father William Toohey, C.S.C. And while the song was still young and borrowing heavily from the folk and pop idiom, it was well performed under the leadership of Michael Hay. The combination of strong preaching, upbeat contemporary music, and a hit-or-miss landscape of liturgical prayer in the dorms brought the students en masse to Sacred Heart masses. It was the Sunday place to be.

From this community of faith, there began an ensemble which, by the end of the 1980s, would have a significant effect on the faith community at Notre Dame . . . and beyond. Brought to birth in this unique period of liturgical transformation, its focus was—and continues to be—on the prayer of the Church, enfleshed in music. The ensemble can trace its roots to a rather ad hoc choir started nonchalantly in the 1970s, which enjoyed the collaboration of young seminarians such as Pat Gaffney, C.S.C., and Tom Stella, C.S.C. It gathered steam at the dawn of the 1980s, and yet still had no name. Now it is known as the Notre Dame Folk Choir.

The birth of the Folk Choir came from a rather typical womb of the 1970s: a small combo of vocalists, accompanied by guitar, bass, and electric piano, singing the popular folk songs of the time. The guitar was an innovative and radical banner around which they gathered (an identity still plaguing the instrument today); the repertoire was stolen from the folk recording artists who permeated the airwaves of the time. And the Church, which was vaulted into celebrating the Christian mysteries in the English language, was helpless to do anything but embrace this new music. There we were: a new liturgy, a new language —our own—and consequently new ways of understanding God through this gift of the vernacular. At that moment in time, however, we possessed no way to sing about it in ways that were authentically ours to keep. So we took what we had and used it to the best of our ability.

The Folk Choir was subject to the same learning processes as most other parochial ensembles. Accompaniments for guitar or keyboard were rare, usually pilfered or photocopied, and the choir, such as it was, learned their music by ear. Written out instrumental music was in the realm of wishful thinking. Four-part choral singing was rare, if it existed at all, and the part-writing which was available at that time broke most of the rules of good ensemble writing. And in many cases, the repertoire itself was problematic.

The sacred songs which came to be in these early years were written by people like Ray Repp and Joe Wise, and they were most definitely the product of a church embroiled in the social issues of the 1960s. These early attempts at sacred music were found in collections like the *Hymnal for Young Christians*. To this day, there are people who continue to roll their eyes and belt out a verse of "Sons of God," "Here We Are," and "The Spirit Is A-Movin'" (or, as some of my friends deadpanned, "The Spirit Is A-Groovin'.")

What these early composers did, however, was to offer a critical and necessary first step in the establishment of a vernacular repertoire. They created simple songs with melody lines that could be remembered by the majority of the faithful. But as a collection coming out in the 1960s, these songs were plagued by the vision of their day: the vast majority of the songs were based on social justice issues (any surprise in such an era?) or on this new, emerging Christian consciousness called "community." Lyrics which focused on Jesus Christ, the Saints, Scripture, the person of Mary, or the mystery of the liturgical year—all of these themes were in short supply. And song forms that were built upon the reliable structure of traditional hymnody—these too went out the window, along with many other things that spoke of tradition, during this turbulent period of the sixties.

The young musical ensembles at Notre Dame were right in step with the rest of the country. They obligingly strapped on their guitars, created their combos, and marched to the beat of a new kind of music . . . the music of the "Saint Louis Jesuits." The music of the Jesuits brought some advances. Their lyrics were decidedly Scripture-based, a novelty at the time. In both the accompaniments and in the hymnals themselves, one could see the chapters and verses from which these very songs were derived. Moreover, many of the songs had simple, lyrical refrains, many of them memorable. They were easily performed on both guitar and piano.

But there were problems with the Jesuits' repertoire as well. So much of the music was easily learned and easily performed, but sacrificed along with this ease was the depth of integrity. Congregations wanted lyrical music, but the musicians didn't want to be pushed too hard. The Jesuits' music offered a temporary solution to these demands, but the repertoire was like a thin pair of pants, wearing through easily after repeated use.

At Notre Dame, the Office of Campus Ministry, now also a growing presence in students' spiritual life, published its second hymnal in 1985. The music of the St. Louis Jesuits was included in this new anthology, but as a companion to the contemporary music, another section was devoted entirely to hymnody. An entire psalm section was also featured in this second hymnal, with antiphons by Joseph Gelineau, Michael Joncas, and Chrysogonus Waddell. Isele's psalms were included, along with those of the music department chairman, Professor Calvin Bower. Some of my own psalm compositions were also included.

Campus Ministry made other resources available to the residence halls from the very first, and these were closely linked with the gradual development of the student leadership in liturgy that the campus now enjoys. In 1980 Reverend Austin

Fleming started an ad hoc publication of what he affectionately called "the packet." Distributed about five or six times a year, it was filled with ideas about liturgy, music, art, and environment, and preaching hints. Complicated liturgical celebrations like Palm Sunday and the Triduum were carefully and logically explained to those crafting the rites in the residence halls. At first, "the packet" was distributed only to priests in residence and rectors. But the scope of the publication widened shortly after the second year and began to include weekly suggestions for songs, hymns, and responsorial psalms, all of which could be found in the newest campus ministry hymnal. "The Packet" was renamed *Music & Liturgy* in 1982, and over the years its campus circulation has widened, now including hall liturgical commissioners, music directors, and community service commissioners.

In 1983, with the twenty-year anniversary of the promulgation of *Sacrosanctum Concilium*, we had the opportunity to look back at our endeavors, saying yes to some of the efforts, and letting go of some as well. Homily tips and seasonal planning were relinquished in *Music & Liturgy*, and another set of resources, *Sourcebook for Feasts and Seasons* and the *Lector Workbook* began to be furnished to the halls. *Music & Liturgy* continued with its thematic planning, began publishing readings with sensitive treatment of exclusive language in the Scriptures, and crafted weekly intercessions for Prayers of the Faithful. While these were the regular features in the planning pages, seasonal concerns and planning were also highlighted, topics which had been found in the resource from its first issues.

Meanwhile, the labors of the Folk Choir continued, and many new songs were tried, accepted, and modified. Some stood the test of time, and some were rejected. At the core of this process, the criteria for a good piece of music began to be enunciated. Certain elements worked, brought the people to song, to a sense of corporate inspiration. Other things got in the way.

Through the work of the choir, the realization began to grow that although people enjoyed lyrical music, there was also too much of a good thing. Music that was too lyrical sounded pop or saccharine. When embellishing a ritual celebration such as the Eucharist, too-sweet sacred music had the effect of making the service trite as well.

But an equal truth was found at the other end of the spectrum. Music that was too modal, or melodically obscure, seemed to have no life in it. The old church modes could be used, but they needed to be wedded to a sense of lyricism to compel the congregation to join. A good example is the beloved Advent hymn, "O Come, O Come Emmanuel." It has endured the years because it is both modal and lyrical at one and the same time.

Our energies were thrown into expanding and redefining the repertoire of solid congregational song. Part-writing for all instruments, formerly relegated to improvisation (a chancy thing for untrained musicians), became the norm. Little by little, as each liturgical season passed, new hymns were carefully introduced, repeated, and learned.

The treasury of Catholic expression began to open up for the choir, and with this, other insights. Chant began to complement the contemporary repertoire on special feasts like Candlemas, on February 2nd, when the *Liber Usualis* was used. The inclusion of the Folk Choir in the Liturgies of the Triduum, specifically on Holy Thursday, began at about this time. Settings of *Ubi Caritas* and *Pange Lingua* became a traditional part of the repertoire. Ostinato chorales began to take their place in the liturgy, primarily the mantra-like refrains written by Jacques Berthier of Taizé. These repetitive chorales provided the perfect medium to prepare the heart for communal prayer. It also introduced simple four-part harmony to our assemblies and residence hall choirs.

At certain points in the church year, the Folk Choir worked with other musical traditions as well, intergrating them into their sung prayer. The shape-note tradition of the Mennonite hymnal was introduced during this time, with hymns for Lent and Ordinary Time. Time-honored Afro-American spirituals like "Were You There?" and "What Wondrous Love Is This?" were learned and mastered.

As chant began to take its rightful place in our song, more and more hymns also began to complement the repertoire of the Folk Choir, and that of the residence halls. And while this was going on, there was an ever-present push for the most fundamental expressions, the very building blocks of Christian music—strong, vital arrangments of the responsorial psalms. Because the psalms were in a sense so simple, they became the last segment of the repertoire to be given serious consideration by the publishing companies. True, a very strong collection of psalmody had been meticulously crafted by Père Joseph Gelineau in France, and, using the Grail psalter, became the foundation for the *Worship* hymnals of GIA.

But Notre Dame students were by and large unmoved by this music, modal as it was, and usually performed exclusively on the organ. Another approach was needed to complement these already existing labors, an approach which would embrace both metrical and chanted psalm settings, and ones which could be played on both the guitar and the piano—the instruments most at use in the residence halls.

In a way, it was this attention to psalmody that brought the next great influence to the Folk Choir. I was taking a class on psalmody with Professor Bower in the mid 1980s, and by way of a special trip, the class had an opportunity to visit the Abbey of Gethsemani, in Trappist, Kentucky. And when we made that visit, we were introduced to the person of Father Chrysogonus Waddell, O.C.S.O.

Chrysogonus is a rare, wonderful man. His love of music embraces everything from jazz to folk song to chant. His mentoring of students, and nurturing of their own love of church music, knows no limit. When I met him, I knew a friend had been found. And when the Folk Choir visited the Abbey two years later, it was the beginning of an enriching dialogue for monks and students alike.

Through Chrysogonus, we began to study the pointing of the psalms, and how this might be applied to performance on both the organ and the guitar. The Choir had the rare but annual opportunity to make a weekend retreat at the Abbey, where they joined the monks for Evening Prayer and a special concert of sacred music. And through him as well, we began to work toward something which lay at the heart of both his work and mine, even though his song was shaped within the monastic tradition, and ours took place on a college campus. Chrysogonus was in touch with the power of lyricism. And he was deeply in tune with the ancient, modal music of the Church. His feet were firmly rooted in both. And this was something that we were looking for—music which had its own life, an arch, a beginning and an end. Song which modelled itself like Christ, Alpha and Omega, seed which returned to seed. Music which also had a hallowed tradition, be it in the dirty fingernails of folk song or the smoky vaulted ceilings of a monastery church. In many ways, Chrysogonus became the principal mentor for our labors.

It was 1987. I had been in Campus Ministry for seven years, and the church music scene was again on the verge of transition. American liturgical music was populated with another stable of composers, this time from the Twin Cities: Michael Joncas, David Haas, and Marty Haugen. Again on campus, their music began to be learned by the Folk Choir and the residence halls. But this time, a unique process began, one that would usher in the next decade. New music began to be introduced, but *some of the older songs were retained.*

In the 1960s almost all the music that had been created didn't make it beyond its first decade of existence (proof, perhaps, of the continued presence of the Spirit). But by the 1970s, some things were being crafted that would continue to bring life to the Church for years to come. The faithful, almost by instinct, began to collect these better pieces into a permanent repertoire. The collection had no idiomatic boundaries: hymns old and new, contemporary song, psalms from composers all over the world. The pilgrim church tried them, walked with them, sang them, and then cast their vote.

The gift of time proved to be a great ally, especially for those who looked back as shapers of song. This next group of composers and their colleagues also learned from the mistakes of their predecessors. Music octavos, with four-part arrangements and fully transcribed instrumental parts, began to be made available at a frantic pace. Even greater attention was given to the texts of sacred song. Chords and voice leading became more expressive. Chant and metrical styles alike began to be embraced. But again, there were shortcomings. Some of the melody lines were so lyrical, they "belonged on Broadway" as one choir member put it. Some lyrics were so poetic, they bore no resemblance to the original scriptural texts. The vogue was to be constantly new, without embracing the old. At the church music conventions, however, the registers were ringing.

My own journey in church music took me in other directions besides the conventions in big American cities, where the newest musings of the hottest composers were all the rage. Through contacts with Chrysogonus, my road led me to that place where lyricism and ancient music found a happy marriage: to Ireland.

Rarely have professional staff been given "sabbatical" time, but I owe it to the vision of David Tyson, C.S.C., then Vice-President of Student Affairs, to have been allowed a summer of renewal in church music. The Gethsemani contacts, all worked out a year in advance, led me to new colleagues and new composers. Margaret Daly, then director of music at Saint Mary's Abbey, Sean Collins, the director of the Irish Center for Pastoral Liturgy, Father Willie Purcell of the Irish Church Music Association: these and many others became correspondents in the search for new liturgical music. That summer, I embarked upon a mendicant pilgrimage throughout Ireland, visiting Lísmore, Carlow, Dublin, Westport, and up into Northern Ireland, to Portstewart and Coleraine.

Everywhere I went, there were feasts to be had—feasts for the ear and the spirit and the heart. The Irish had many of the answers that I was looking for: a depth of lyrical integrity partly gleaned from their own folk song, and a haunting embrace of their past with the Gregorian-like melodies. It moved hearts and unlocked voices. When my journeys brought me back to Notre Dame four months later, there was a whole new vocabulary in my mind. And an idea began to form. Why not take the Folk Choir, then two dozen strong, over to Ireland, to expose them to the vibrant strains of this sacred music? We could serve as ambassadors—emissaries of prayer and song, carriers of culture in both directions. The idea was brought before two of my colleagues, Father André Léveillé, C.S.C., and Father Bill Beauchamp, C.S.C. Their enthusiastic response set the stage for the Folk Choir's first overseas excursion in 1988.

Every trip to Ireland has had its own memories seared into our hearts. The first trip was no exception. We sang in the poorest parishes, like the high-rise tenements of Ballymon, outside of Dublin. We sang in the richest schools, like Chapelizod on the south side of Dublin. We visited Waterford and swapped ideas with the seminarians. And for an entire weekend, we held up in the Irish Institute of Pastoral Liturgy, learning new hymns, new psalm responses, and the phonetic rules of the Irish language. But most of all, we began to understand God a little differently, through this new, but very old, haunting sacred music.

The Folk Choir has made four excursions to Ireland since 1987. During that time, they have brought back to America the psalm compositions of Fintan O'Carroll and the mass settings of T. C. Kelly. They learned the anthems used to consecrate the Basilica of Knock. They learned music so old that its lyrics were a combination of Irish and Latin. And true to the goal of bringing Irish music back to our own country, in the last five years those very songs that we learned in Carlow have spread all over the United States, from Saint Patrick's Cathedral in New York City to Saint Brigid of Kildare parish in Dublin, Ohio.

And just as important, to an institution such as ours which treasures its Irish roots, they have brought back a viable repertoire which graces the Basilica of the Sacred Heart every March 17th, the Feast of Saint Patrick. That repertoire, first shared with us in County Carlow, is now beginning to be published and distributed to the wider church. The first recording of the Notre Dame Folk Choir, *Mass on the Feast of Saint Patrick,* has many selections which are finding their way into the song of the liturgical year as a whole.

Through their contacts in various parts of the world, Gethsemani Abbey, and the parochial centers and monasteries of Ireland, the Folk Choir has been able to enrich both the faith life of the students in their residence halls and the greater

Catholic Church as well. Their recordings have brought this repertoire to an assembly far wider than we could have originally conceived. Two recordings were the result of collaboration with the Gethsemani monks, recordings which yielded a rich synthesis of chant and folk traditions. One of the projects addressed the feminine images of spirituality as portrayed in song and prayer. In each recording, some of the songs—but not all—went on to enhance the ongoing formation of repertoire in the faith community of Notre Dame, at the Basilica of the Sacred Heart, and in the residence halls as well.

Little by little, the tools and events we needed were being shaped and put to good use. A beginning-of-the-year weekend retreat brought the liturgical and community service commissioners together for the start of the school year. Co-sponsored by Campus Ministry and the Center for Social Concerns, it provided the perfect kick-off for rallying student leadership behind our many programs—and not just the liturgical ones. Special care was taken to maintain the important relationship between community service projects and the spiritual life of the residence halls.

Special liturgies and events throughout the year highlighted the contributions of various nationalities to the campus. Hispanics began to gather at a special liturgy on the Feast of Our Lady of Guadalupe every December 12th. This bilingual celebration featured the labors of both the Folk Choir and the Coro Primavera. The Irish, of course, had the Saint Patrick's Day liturgy on March 17th, and since 1988 the Folk Choir had provided authentic Irish sacred music at the Basilica. African-Americans were the focus of festivities the last week of January, when Campus Ministry and the Office for Multi-Cultural Affairs hosted a week-long celebration of events in keeping with the spirit of Dr. Martin Luther King, Jr. Priscilla Wong, a long-time member of the Campus Ministry staff, was a principal guiding force in King celebrations, as well as for retreat weekends that brought students together to talk about racial issues.

By 1990, Campus Ministry had begun work on its next hymnal, which promised to make great strides in shaping the students' repertoire of sacred music. Over the past decade, psalm settings, hymns, and contemporary song were gathered, typeset, and remembered. The advent of computer technology on campus allowed the ministry staff to provide publishing-quality material to the residence halls, by way of new hymnal resources and accompaniments for the various instruments. A three-year process of consultation with rectors and musicians resulted in the purchase of a hard-bound hymnal for all the residence halls and the Basilica as well, complete with a special supplement containing a rich collection of music by local composers.

Starting in 1992, the efforts of the Folk Choir began to attract the attention of liturgists, church leaders, and musicians outside the campus community. That year, the sesquicentennial year for the University, was also the first time that Notre Dame hosted the National Conference of Catholic Bishops. Both the Folk Choir and the Liturgical Choir joined the bishops throughout the week in their prayer, and as a result of their work, we were asked the following year to be one of a select group of choirs to sing for World Youth Day '93, and His Holiness John Paul II. The years of repertoire building were paying off.

Exploration of song traditions on both sides of the Atlantic have yielded a rich reservoir of material, and the Choir's association with the Abbey of Gethsemani emphasized their advocacy of both new and traditional sources of sacred music. In 1995, World Library Publications of Chicago recognized our contributions by creating a new series of printed church music. The music series *Songs of the Notre Dame Folk Choir* has already begun to spread this special repertoire to the wider church. Songs by Chrysogonus Waddell, and former Notre Dame graduate Ellen Doerrfeld Coman, along with my own offerings, comprised the first year's edition of fourteen octavos. Our fifth recording, *Candled Seasons*, was a joyous collaborative effort with the Gethsemani community, and in a unique way brought together the repertoires of both the Notre Dame college students and the Trappists of Kentucky in a wonderful way. Chrysogonus provided new settings of some of the oldest Christmas plainchant, crafted for the choir in four-part harmony and adapted to the English language. This, combined with new settings for guitar, organ, schola, and choir, resulted in a rare combination of musical styles.

Now, some thirty years after the liturgy was so wisely transformed by the leaders of our church, we are confronting a different set of issues: issues of female and male imagery, issues of collaborative leadership, issues surrounding our ability to bring so many cultural nuances into a collective whole. They are, in fact, very "catholic" issues—having to do with our embrace and formation of a "universal" church. Our repertoire is beginning to take shape, after almost two decades of research, trial, and error. The delights of different cultures have been brought together in sacred celebration, and, much to the edification of all, these very differences have only served to wed us closer together. The residence halls, year by year, continue to own the emerging repertoire of sacred music, and simple musical proficiency is becoming more and more normative.

Now we return to that springtime pilgrimage which was described at the beginning of this chapter. How that pilgrimage increases in meaning, when one considers the vast design of collaboration that has evolved over the years! Liturgical commissioners prepared from the start by prayer and retreat. A ritual drama that is enthusiastically embraced by the student body, even though it is more than a millenium old. A repertoire that celebrates the paschal mystery in a way both new and ancient. After many long years of labor, the vineyard has been prepared, the vineyard of the Lord —the vineyard of our hearts, the house of Israel.

Our songs are a bit different now. During Holy Week we sing the "Stabat Mater" and "Jesus, Remember Me." We sing "Where Charity and Love Prevail" and "I Received the Living God." But on Easter Sunday we break into the joy of the "Afrika Gloria." It is to that dark continent of Africa, with its gift of communal joy and rhythm, that the Folk Choir is now turning its vision, to bring another set of treasures to Notre Dame.

Almost ten years ago, I was waiting to travel to Ireland for the first time, and by design, attended liturgy the day before departure. Here is a portion of the Gospel read that day: "The kingdom of heaven is like treasure hidden in a field which someone has found; he hides it again, goes off happy, sells everything he owns and buys the field."

It occurs to me that for the greater part of my journey in ministry I have been out in that field, looking for musical and ritual treasures in the soil of everyday life. It has been a labor well spent, if in the digging a few more people have been brought closer to the mystery of God. Now, the story and the labors continue. There are other fields to dig.

Towards "A More Just and Humane World": The Center for Social Concerns

KATHLEEN MAAS WEIGERT

One of my most vivid memories of attending St. Luke's Catholic grade school in St. Paul, Minnesota, revolves around an annual collection of our pennies, nickels, and dimes for "pagan babies." It seemed so exotic, so exciting. To think: we were in a school in the northern part of the United States but we were somehow linked—very immediately and very marvelously—with people we would most likely never see. Our actions mattered to them in a way I believed was very real. My pennies could help "save a soul." I was thrilled to know that I was part of a great plan for the salvation of the human race.

I smile now in recounting that memory, knowing that my pagan baby collections, with all their hopes and dreams, may seem strange to the world we now inhabit. But I am convinced that it was experiences like that, nested in the totality of the very Catholic world I grew up in, which have shaped my life and the choices I have made. While it is not a direct, inexorable force that has led me to where I am today, I know that it was seeds sown in that world that have contributed to my desire to work in a Catholic institution of higher learning and, for the past thirteen years, to work in a particular part of one such institution, the Center for Social Concerns at the University of Notre Dame.

Kathleen Weigert is Associate Director, Academic Affairs and Research, for the Center for Social Concerns.

The Center is housed in a not small building, nestled in the shadow of the towering Hesburgh Library, but it houses multiple long-term programs and short-term opportunities for students, faculty, staff, and graduates to deepen their awareness of today's complex social realities. It casts its own shadow of influence near and far. Since its doors opened in January 1983, hundreds of people have participated in and helped develop existing programs or have assisted in creating new offerings for the Center for Social Concerns. It is with the support of these collaborators that the Center seeks to fulfill its mission:

> The Center for Social Concerns provides educational experiences in social concerns inspired by Gospel values and Catholic social teachings. Central to this process is enhancing the spiritual and intellectual awareness of students, faculty, staff, and alumni/ae about today's complex social realities, calling us all to service and action for a more just and humane world.

That mission statement motivates and nourishes me as I go about my work. And it simultaneously contains the crux of one answer to the question, what role does such a Center play in the mission and ministry of a Catholic university? I would like to flesh out that answer based on my years of experience working at the Center. Since I am a very Trinitarian person, I would like to structure this essay into three parts. In the first and second parts, I want to explore two ways in which the Center plays an essential part in making real the Catholic character of Notre Dame. The first: by its very presence on the campus and through its programs, the Center becomes a visible, concrete manifestation of the commitment to the centrality of social concerns in the life and witness of a Catholic university. Through the kinds of service and social awareness opportunities it provides, the Center challenges participants (and non-participants as well) to stretch their minds and hearts not just to examine but also to enter into the real worlds of our most vulnerable sisters and brothers in the local community, throughout the United States, and in other parts of the world. The second: in contrast to most of the teaching/learning at the

University, which takes place in classrooms and laboratories, the Center provides off-campus experiential education opportunities and thus contributes to the expansion of the traditional academic notions of teaching and learning. Its educational programs take participants into the social worlds of those who are most disadvantaged in our society. After discussing those two ideas, I would like to close by raising some of the challenges facing the Center at the dawn of the new millennium in its efforts to contribute to the Catholic character of Notre Dame.

Institutional Witness to Service and Social Action

Since the objective of a Catholic university is to assure in an institutional manner a Christian presence in the university world confronting the great problems of society and culture, every Catholic university, as Catholic, must have the following essential characteristics: ". . . 4. An institutional commitment to the service of the people of God and of the human family in their pilgrimage to the transcendent goal which gives meaning to life."—*Ex Corde Ecclesiae* (para. 12), Pope John Paul II (1990)

When visitors come to campus, one of the places that is pointed out on the standard campus tour is the Center for Social Concerns. Along with such well-known structures as the Dome, the Basilica of the Sacred Heart, the Hesburgh Library, classroom buildings, and the football stadium, the visitors are informed that this university has a Center for Social Concerns and that it is a key strand of the fabric of this Catholic university.

Perhaps what most captures the imagination of the visitors about the Center is the range of service and social action opportunities it offers and the number of students who participate in them. From hunger projects to tutoring occasions, from work with people who have developmental disabilities to assisting those who are new to this country—there is a plethora of opportunities that call for the energies, talents, and time of students. In coordinating so many of these programs and projects, the Center is actually building on a long tradition of such involvement. Twenty-five years ago, James T.

Burtchaell, C.S.C., then Provost of the University, noted in an *Insight: Notre Dame* piece entitled "Notre Dame: How Catholic Is It?" that among his "good signs" of the University's Catholic character was "the noticeable involvement of students in socially constructive service projects." After listing a great number of examples, Burtchaell added, "The simple catalog of projects does not tell the story. What we have is a new desire in students (unmatched in other days) to work for the disadvantaged." That "new" desire has continued with each successive class. Data on graduating seniors over the years demonstrate their involvement. In the Class of 1995, for example, close to 90 percent participated in volunteer service or social action activities at some time during their undergraduate years with almost 50 percent doing so at least once a month or more frequently.

How does the Center facilitate such involvement? In many ways. The Center is the home and resource for some thirty student service and social action groups and their hundreds of members to develop leadership skills, critical understanding of social issues, and outreach expertise. It is a meeting place for students who prepare for and reflect on the social awareness programs coordinated by the Center. It is a hospitality center where luncheons are sponsored to raise funds for and awareness of non-profit groups like Dismas House, El Buen Vecino, and the Catholic Worker House, in whose pivotal work our students share. It is the site of new collaborations like the fall 1995–1996 "Campus Community Introductions" program, a joint social awareness effort of the Center, Student Government, and the Office of the First Year of Studies. While almost one third of the Class of 1999 responded positively to an invitation to participate, resources allowed for just under 200 students to enroll in the program. With the enthusiastic cooperation of eight service agencies in town, the students were hosted at the agencies to learn more about the needs of the local community and how those needs are being addressed. As one of the participants wrote after visiting two of the sites, "Archbishop Roach stated, '. . . all of us are interconnected in one metropolitan family. When one part of our community suffers, we all suffer.' I had never thought about this and now that I've heard it and have seen parts of South Bend, it makes me reconsider some of my views about the inner city."

In initiating, coordinating, and/or supporting these kinds of activity, the Center becomes one concrete embodiment of Notre Dame's commitment to making social concerns a vibrant part of its institutional life. The Center makes a contribution to what the University Mission states is one goal:

> to cultivate in its students not only an appreciation for the great achievements of human beings but also a disciplined sensibility to the poverty, injustice and oppression that burden the lives of so many.

What the visitors on the campus tour may not learn as much about is that the Center serves other constituencies as well: staff, graduates, and faculty. Faculty are the particular focus of my work so I would like to discuss them a bit more. My motivation for and excitement about such work has its roots in that childhood Catholic world as well as in several experiences of the last fifteen years. One of the most important was a two-week educational trip in Mexico that my husband (a sociologist here at the University) and I (then a newly appointed Assistant Dean in the College of Arts and Letters) took with two other faculty couples in the summer of 1979. Don McNeill, C.S.C., now the Director of the Center for Social Concerns, and Claude Pomerleau, C.S.C., now a professor of government at the University of Portland, organized and led our trip. We discussed the social, political, and economic realities facing Mexico with a variety of knowledgeable people who worked for, among other institutions, the Church, the media, and educational centers. We shared the hospitality of squatters in a hillside community in Cuernavaca. We walked the narrow dirt roads of Netzahualcoyotl, a huge poverty-stricken area in Mexico City, and worshipped with a community of poor workers and unemployed in the shadow of the political powers of the country. And at the end of each day, we reflected on what we had heard and seen and felt. All of us were profoundly affected by that comparatively short but intense experience. As a result, once back on campus we formed a community that met weekly for many years.

When Don McNeill asked me to join him as the Center was being formed, it was experiences like that which made me want to work at the Center. We continue to offer similar kinds of trips for our faculty and spouses. What do we hope will happen as a result? It is not that the faculty come back and necessarily teach or research about that experience, although some do so because of their disciplinary expertise. But something else happens: more people on this campus are experientially aware of the social problems and potentials of our global community. Who knows how that awareness might enter into a conversation with other faculty or in an advising session with students who are searching for ways of getting involved? Who knows what the ripple effect of such participation might be? As Professor Steve Batill, Department of Aerospace and Mechanical Engineering, put it,

> If I were to select my top ten 'memorable' or beneficial experiences in the past 18 years on the Notre Dame faculty, I would definitely include the faculty 'plunge' to Santiago, Chile. I have drawn on this experience on numerous occasions both in my personal and my professional life. It made me aware of the spirit, traditions and dreams of another culture . . . it provided a perspective one cannot gather via the 6 o'clock news.

The Center offers faculty other kinds of opportunities as well, from assistance in designing course modules to discussion groups to pedagogical workshops (more on recent efforts below). But faculty are also a resource for us. We could not have the caliber of program we offer students were it not for the contributions of faculty. They serve as speakers, teachers for our experiential seminars, hosts and facilitators for students who participate in the "Urban Plunge" (more on this below). And as a result, the work of social concerns moves beyond the little building that houses all of these programs and becomes integrated into many facets of university life.

As part of an educational institution, the witness of such programs and projects has another layer as well. To read, to question, to talk about alternatives, to analyze structures, to ask "Why are some people poor?" "Why are these people unemployed," "Why are those people hungry?"—the Center must continue to provide the resources and the opportunities through which those questions not only can be but must be asked. And that leads to my second topic.

Experiential Education and Social Concerns

The University prides itself on being an environment of teaching and learning which fosters the development in its students of those disciplined habits of mind, body and spirit which characterize educated, skilled and free human beings.

So states the Mission of the University of Notre Dame. But what is teaching? What is learning? Simple questions to ask; not simple questions to answer! Since its earliest beginnings (as is clear in the name of one of the two organizational units— the "Center for Experiential Learning"—that joined to form the Center) the Center for Social Concerns has been committed to enlarging traditional answers to those questions by offering solid *curricular* experiential learning opportunities to students. Let me explore this by offering an anecdote and then an illustration.

I have a colleague—let's call her Dr. Rose—who is a dear friend. She believes strongly in the importance of the Center for Social Concerns, applauds its efforts to expose students and faculty to the needs of our society, and encourages the Center to entice/cajole participants to do their part in making our world a more decent one. But none of that, she argues, is to be done in the context of the curriculum. Why? Because to do so, she believes, is to undermine "university education." For her, such education takes place in the context of a classroom or a laboratory (extended to libraries, faculty offices, study halls, student rooms, etc.) *on the campus*, through books and related media. Anything else may be good work, but it is not "university education."

I obviously have a different view. Along with others who support experiential education, I believe that "university education" is not confined to its physical borders. That in fact, it wasn't always like this (as the late Ernest Boyer so nicely reminds us in his *Scholarship Reconsidered: Priorities of the Professoriate* [1990])—nor should it be now. That education can take place in many different places, from the traditional classroom to the classrooms of the world. That students learn in a variety of ways and that we who are university educators need to provide them with a range of educational opportunities to enhance their learning. I believe experiential education opportunities are, in short, a *bona fide* part of university education.

But just what is "experiential education"? I have two favorite ways of answering that question. One is to use the simple short-hand phrase, "hands-on learning." A second is to say that it is the kind of learning that builds on the traditional classroom experience by putting people into direct contact with the phenomenon being studied or with the context of that phenomenon. If, for example, the subject is "poverty in inner cities," we offer participants both book learning and *in situ* learning. We provide participants with the key theoretical perspectives and the most recent data on the topic. We then take participants to inner cities where we collaborate with "co-teachers"—those who are experiencing poverty, homelessness, etc., as well as those who are working with them to change the situation. These co-teachers help educate participants about the challenges of living in American cities in the late twentieth century. The necessary book learning is enhanced and challenged by the learning that comes from interacting with real people and places. Let me be more concrete by providing an illustration.

The Center's oldest program, and perhaps one of the best known and most replicated in the country, is what has been colloquially called "Urban Plunge," but which is actually a one-credit theology course entitled "The Church and Social Action."

The course has three major parts. First is an orientation workshop in late fall that provides information about "experiential learning," an overview of the course requirements (both the readings, which always contain some excerpt from Catholic social teachings along with readings on urban life, and the follow-up assignments), and details about the course in its entirety. Second is the forty-eight–hour program in the inner cities around the country in early January through which our co-teachers help the students get a firsthand experience of the problems and possibilities of urban life for poorer citizens. Finally, there is the follow-up which includes a written assignment (incorporating the readings and the inner city program) and an evening of discussion in the homes of faculty and staff, when students return to campus in mid-January, to help them think further about the implications of this course. Upon completion of all parts of the course, students receive one credit. As Professor Barry Keating, Chair of the Department of Finance, commented on his role in the program,

> For 17 years, my wife and I have hosted debriefing sessions for Urban Plunge students. It is an enjoyment to see how each group of students returns with specific awareness of how the Church and others are practicing the spiritual and corporal works of mercy. As social scientists, we personally have benefited in seeing how nonprofit organizations over time modify and adapt their programs to be more effective and above all to do no harm.

We at the Center have worked to extend this kind of opportunity by offering workshops for faculty on experiential learning and social concerns. With the recent national focus on service, we have joined with others around the country to help develop the pedagogy called "service learning" (or "community-based learning" as some of us prefer to call it) and to give more faculty the opportunity to become familiar with this exciting pedagogy. Many of our co-teachers in the local community serve as facilitators in these workshops. The heart of the matter in service learning is the linking of classroom and community in creative ways that meets at least one of the faculty's self-defined course goals, on the one hand, and that fulfills some community-identified need, on the other, through well-structured service work by the students—work that is monitored, integrated into the course, and evaluated accordingly. Holding to the highest standards, all parties benefit: faculty, students, community. And in the process, the University and the community keep developing as good neighbors.

Towards a More Just and Humane World:
Challenges of the Future

> Action on behalf of justice and participation in the transformation of the world fully appear to us as a constitutive dimension of the preaching of the Gospel, or, in other words, of the Church's mission for the redemption of the human race and its liberation from every oppressive situation. —*Justice in the World*, Synods of Bishops (1971)

As the Center continues to seek creative ways of fulfilling its mission, what are some of the challenges it faces? I warned you that I am a Trinitarian person, so as expected, I want to highlight three. First is the pull of the secular world's standards of success and achievement for institutions of higher learning. Second, and related, is the pressure on faculty to pursue more very particularized standards of excellence. And third is the lack of preparation our students have in the rich tradition of Catholic social thought. Let me examine each briefly.

Whether we look at rankings in *U.S. News & World Report* or the more recent list released by the National Research Center, there is a world out there that says, "This is how good we think you are." Now, without dismissing such efforts, I want to add my voice to those who contend that if we let such groups dictate who we are (our identity) and how we are to seek the truth through our teaching, research, and service (our mission), then we will never be the great Catholic university so many of us came here to work for. It is not that secular standards are irrelevant; surely they are relevant. But it is that they are not sufficient in themselves. While we strive to excel in being a "university" in its fullest, best sense, we must also strive to be "Catholic" in its fullest, best sense. And surely, we at the Center would argue, both of those terms call for at least some of university education to be experiential in pedagogy, and in content, the kind that challenges our students to face the growing chasm between rich and poor, the actual worlds of those without education and skills, and the stresses and strains on communities with few economic resources, and to reflect on what they can do, with others, to bring about a better world. As Pope John Paul II stated in *Ex Corde Ecclesiae* (para. 34), "The Christian spirit of service to others for the promotion of social justice is of particular importance for each Catholic university, to be shared by its teachers and developed in its students." That is a standard of excellence beyond what the secular world asks.

Second: because of the reward structures in place in many parts of the world of higher education, including Notre Dame, there are few incentives for faculty to broaden the more particularized definitions of success. While the world cries out for less disciplinary-based knowledge, the structures of the academy militate against this. Interdisciplinary efforts get short shrift. So when the Center offers workshops to expand the pedagogical awareness of faculty, it is working against the tide. As Boyer articulated in his *Scholarship Reconsidered*, we must broaden, not narrow, our understandings of excellence in scholarship. Who will take the lead in doing this?

Third: in spite of the fact that close to 90 percent of the undergraduate body is Catholic, decreasing numbers come with twelve years of Catholic schooling. We now have students who have never heard of Vatican Council II's historic documents, *Lumen Gentium* and *Gaudium et Spes,* or the American Catholic Bishops' 1983 peace pastoral, *The Challenge of Peace*—let alone Pope Leo XIII's encyclical, *Rerum Novarum.* They don't know, in short, about the Catholic social thought tradition. How can we help them learn what a rich resource they have to help them wade through the swirl of sound bytes and countercharges so prevalent in the contemporary public discourse? While much needs to be done, work is already in progress. One recent effort here at Notre Dame is that of a group of faculty from a half dozen departments in the College of Arts and Letters to create a "Concentration" (an academic offering that consists in fifteen credits from courses in two or more departments that focuses on a theme) that would center on the Catholic social tradition.

Three big challenges. But I stand ready—and I know my Center colleagues do, too—to work with our constituencies in meeting those challenges. With enthusiasm and hope, we join together in collective efforts to make real and vital this part of Notre Dame's mission:

> to create a sense of human solidarity and concern for the common good that will bear fruit as learning becomes service to justice.